CONCISE ENCYCLOPEDIA
OF
INTERIOR DESIGN

CONCISE ENCYCLOPEDIA
OF
INTERIOR DESIGN

Second Edition

A. Allen Dizik, fasid

VNR VAN NOSTRAND REINHOLD COMPANY
New York

Copyright © 1988 by Van Nostrand Reinhold Company Inc.
Library of Congress Catalog Card Number 88-5560
ISBN 0-442-22109-6

Printed in the United States of America

Designed by Monika Grejniec

Van Nostrand Reinhold Company Inc.
115 Fifth Avenue
New York, New York 10003

Van Nostrand Reinhold Company Limited
Molly Millars Lane
Wokingham, Berkshire RG11 2PY, England

Van Nostrand Reinhold
480 La Trobe Street
Melbourne, Victoria 3000, Australia

Macmillan of Canada
Division of Canada Publishing Corporation
164 Commander Boulevard
Agincourt, Ontario M1S 3C7, Canada

16 15 14 13 12 11 10 9 8 7 6 5 4 3 2 1

Library of Congress Cataloging in Publication Data

Dizik, A. Allen.
    Concise encyclopedia of interior design.

    1. Decoration and ornament—Dictionaries.
2. Interior decoration—Dictionaries. I. Title.
NK1165.D58   1988   747'.03   88-5560
ISBN 0-442-22109-6

To my wife
Lee

PREFACE TO THE FIRST EDITION

Any number of comprehensive encyclopedias on furniture and home furnishings have been published. None has been specifically aimed at providing a concise, comprehensive, authoritative guide for today's interested homemaker, serious student, or professional interior designer. There is no "open sesame" to understanding the art of interior design, but it is hoped that this factual volume will help you better understand the field of interior design and decoration. It is further hoped that you who read this book will acquire a greater appreciation and understanding of design principles and skills.

All important nomenclature, technical or otherwise, of interior design and related fields is defined. In addition, you will find monographs on the more crucial subjects such as color, furniture arrangement, furniture periods, and carpeting, to add to your knowledge and help you make judgments. Moreover, you will find entries relating to antiques, art, architecture, and building that will stimulate your imagination and help you grasp the meaning of a beautiful, personalized, and satisfying environment.

The entries are arranged alphabetically and are cross-referenced. This encyclopedia truly has a place in every professional interior designer's studio, and in the library of any person contemplating the building, designing, furnishing, or decorating of a home. It will be used by some as a text, by others as a desk reference, and still others will read it for sheer pleasure.

PREFACE TO THE SECOND EDITION

The first edition of this encyclopedia, published in 1976, quickly became a reference widely consulted by professional interior designers, architects, students, and home owners. In the intervening years, much has been happening in the field of interior design, both technically and aesthetically. Less traditional living patterns have become more widespread, so that interior design must accommodate the needs of a wide variety of lifestyles. Houses are smaller; condominiums have sprung up everywhere. Tastes are more educated and sophisticated. Yet despite these changes much of the material from the first edition remains valid. After all, the basic color spectrum has not changed, regardless of what particular tint or shade is in vogue in a particular season.

This edition therefore contains much of the valuable information from the first edition as well as new entries and revised entries that reflect the changes in the field. Considerable attention has been given to discussing the most current terms and developments to assist the designer in keeping pace with technological and educational advances. The fundamental language and principles of interior design are all here, as are articles on such crucial subjects as furniture periods, furniture arrangement, draperies, fabrics, wallpaper, floor coverings, color, and lighting. In addition, answers to many questions related to allied disciplines such as fine art, architecture, antiques, and construction can be found herein. The new material has been culled from a large variety of sources, including books, trade journals, trade sources, and furniture catalogs, as well as from my forty-seven years of experience as a practicing professional interior designer. The books listed in the Bibliography were selected as having been of most assistance to the writer. If any omissions of importance have occurred I beg the readers' indulgence. Nomenclature is solved in favor of conciseness, balanced coverage, and maximum accuracy. The text is arranged alphabetically and cross-referenced.

Home owners, interior designers, students, and teachers will find the book to be an essential reference work.

INTRODUCTION

In this encyclopedia of interior design, decoration, and related arts, the author brings you more than forty years of practical experience. It is an informative book for the professional interior designer and the single most valuable detailed text for the homemaker, design student, semi-professional, or anyone needing guidelines regarding problems and ideas associated with decorating the interior of a house.

Armed with a basic understanding of interior design, the reader will be better equipped to buy, decorate, design, and make intelligent decisions for himself or with his professional interior designer. Furthermore, a study of this book can help prevent irrevocable and costly mistakes that happen all too often to the person gifted with natural taste but lacking the knowledge required for a satisfactory solution to decorating and design problems. In short, this comprehensive encyclopedia covers just about everything you are ever likely to need to know about interior design and decoration.

The sheer joy of understanding how a more aesthetically pleasing environment is created is in itself sufficient compensation for studying the many decorating ideas to be found in this book. You will always have a factual reference library at hand—one that should be invaluable to you for many years to come.

There is no place more delightful than a beautiful home.

Cicero (106–43 B.C.)

Aalto, Alvar (1898–1976): Finnish architect and furniture designer, best known for his innovative use of molded plywood. His best-known designs include the Paimio armchair (1929), the Aalto serving cart (1936), and the fan-leg stool (1954). He designed the Finnish Pavilion at the 1939 World's Fair in New York.

abrasion resistance: The ability of a material to withstand rubbing, scuffing, and ordinary wear.

abstract art: Art characterized by design and forms that are geometric, nonrepresentational, or nonnaturalistic.

abstract expressionism: *See* modern art.

abutment: In architecture, solid masonry placed below an arch to counteract lateral thrust.

A.C.: *See* alternating current.

acacia: Of the many plants comprising the genus *Acacia*, a majority are native to Australia, where they grow as shrubs or trees. Also known as *wattles* or *Australian blackwood*. Acacia varies in color from yellowish-red to reddish-brown and is frequently marked by black streaks. It is a hard, tough wood, similar in appearance to rosewood. Acacia is used for making turned parts of furniture, tool handles, and walking sticks. It finishes well.

acanthus: A carved motif used in decoration and architecture, adapted from the scalloped leaf of the acanthus tree. First used in ancient times, this motif is found on **Corinthian** and **Composite** capitals, as well as on moldings and furniture, especially that of the **Regency** period. It is the most popular design for carved legs.

accent color: A strong or vivid contrasting color introduced in limited amounts to bolster a decorating scheme. (*See also* color.)

accent lighting: Directional lighting focused to emphasize a particular object.

accessories: Personal treasures, heirlooms, and objects of decorative value that give character to a room and express the personality of the person(s) living there. Accessory examples: paintings, drawings, vases, clocks, pewter, pillows, ashtrays, barometers, trophies, miniatures, figurines, antique toys, antique carvings, coins, glassware, masks, screens, porcelains, seashells, paperweights, plates, plants, mirrors, candlesticks, mosaics, collages, needlepoint, bell-pulls, books, candy boxes, wall sconces, pottery, flowers, china, plaques, sculpture, and Oriental scrolls.

The most important thing to remember in using accessories is scale: it is better to have the object oversized than undersized. Accessories need not be limited to the period of the room. Well-chosen antiques are striking in a contemporary room, as are extremely modern accessories in a traditional room.

accordian doors: Doors made from narrow vertical sections of wood, joined so that they will fold against one another into a compact unit.

acetate: A fiber developed from chemically treated cellulose and woven into carpets, upholstery, and drapery fabrics. Acetate materials react well to dyes and drape nicely.

acknowledgment: A notification that states the date of delivery and indicates receipt of an order.

acorn: A motif resembling an acorn used both as a finial and as a pendant.

acoustics: The science of the transmission and control of sound. First used in the design of ancient Greek theaters; also used by medieval architects in designing houses of worship. Among materials that absorb sound in a house are: carpeting, draperies, cork, acoustical ceiling tile, plaster, and upholstered furniture. Sound is measured in decibels. Zero decibels (db) represents no measurable sound. Normal conversation ranges from forty-five to sixty-two decibels. It is estimated that injurious sound begins at one hundred decibels.

acroterium: An ornament or statue placed at the apex of a pediment or on the gable or roof corner of a building. A decorative device of Greek origin, it was commonly found on European case furniture of the eighteenth century.

acrylic: A generic name for a fiber produced by chemical synthesis from natural gas, petroleum, coal, water, and air. Acrylic combines well with wool and resembles wool in looks and texture. It is highly resistant to wrinkling and soiling and cleans easily. (*See also* carpets.)

Adam, Robert (1728–1792): Renowned British **neoclassical style** architect and designer who studied with the French designer J. L. Clerisseau. A firm believer that design, decoration, and architecture were one field, Adam designed everything from buildings to lighting fixtures, carpets, silver, furniture, and lamps. His furniture designs are characterized by elegant simplicity, fine proportions, and classical beauty. He used a great deal of **satinwood,** simple **marquetry,** and meticulously painted delicate decorations. His motifs borrowed generously from the ancient Romans; favorites included drapery swags, festoons of husks, medallions, fans, urns, honeysuckle, lyres, ram's heads, arabesques, rosettes, and wheat sheaves. The **Adam** style in furniture, with its light and graceful lines, was a reaction to the excesses of the **rococo** style, and it revolutionized interior decoration in Great Britain. The style has great charm and livability and is popular to this day.

Adelphi: Trade name used by the brothers **Adam.**

adobe: An unburned, sun-dried brick or block made of earth and straw, used as building material for walls. A nonconductor of heat.

Affleck, Thomas (1740–1795): An outstanding cabinetmaker who worked in the **Chippendale** style in the eighteenth century. Born in Scotland, Affleck settled in Philadelphia in 1763.

African art: A term that refers to the geographic area where traditional tribal art was and is produced. Generally speaking, this area is south of the Sahara Desert, through Angola, incorporating the tropical rain forests and savannahs. African civilizations have flourished since ancient times and produced a superb artistic tradition. African art is often misleadingly labeled as "primitive."

agate ware: Earthenware made with a mixture of clays, which resembles agate in appearance. Agate ware was known in England since Roman times. The process was refined and adopted by **Wedgwood.**

aggregate: A rough-textured concrete composed of sand, slag, pebbles, cement, and water.

air conditioning, central: In addition to cooling, central air conditioning can relieve oppressive humidity, clean and wash the air, and control the temperature. Air can be purified by sterilization; dust and soot can be filtered out by adding an electronic air cleaner. This device will remove more than 90 percent of the dust, smoke, and pollen from the air passing through it. Walls and draperies will stay clean almost indefinitely.

A.L.A.: Academy of Lighting Arts. The aims of this organization are to promote better lighting and lighting design and to keep its members informed and up to date with changing technology. The membership consists of designers, manufacturers, and distributors of lighting fixtures.

alabaster: A comparatively soft, marblelike, whitish stone used for statuary, vases, lamp bases, and ornaments.

Albers, Josef (1888–1977): German painter and stained-glass artist. Director of the **Bauhaus** glass workshop.

alcove: A recessed section of a room. Bed alcoves were common in Europe during the Middle Ages and the eighteenth century.

alder: A **hardwood** that finishes well and will not easily absorb water. Pale brown, aging to a darker golden brown.

Alençon lace: A fine French needlepoint lace made at Alençon, where the craft was established in about 1750.

all-over design: A floral or geometric pattern that covers the entire fabric or wallpaper without any particular feature standing out.

alternating current: An electric conduction current that flows alternately, first in one direction and then in the opposite direction, at regular intervals. Abbreviated A.C.

aluminum: Very lightweight, silvery-white metal found only in combination, chiefly with bauxite. Moisture and corrosion resistant. Since it stays bright, it is used extensively in the manufacture of garden and terrace furniture.

amaranth: A purplish-red **hardwood** used primarily for **marquetry** and other types of **veneering.** Also known as *purpleheart*.

American colonial: This era (1630–1789) encompasses the styles prevalent in the original thirteen states, all of which originated in Great Britain: **Queen Anne, Chippendale, Jacobean,** and **William and Mary.** In the early colonial period, furnishings were of the simplest utilitarian type, with sturdy Jacobean and some **Gothic** characteristics. Pine, oak, birch, walnut, and maple were used extensively. As a rule, furnishings were left unfinished, although sometimes they were stained or waxed. Mahogany was introduced in the first quarter of the eighteenth century, when the Queen Anne style made its appearance. By 1750, despite the fact that English furniture was still being imported, American furniture makers were coming into their own. Chippendale styles were being superbly copied by Philadelphia cabinetmakers. **Georgian** and other styles were executed in Boston and New York.

Other styles related to American colonial include American **Federal** (1789–1830), American **Directoire** (1805–1815), and American **Empire** (1810–1830).

The Federal period began at the conclusion of the Revolutionary War and marked the end of the colonial period. **Sheraton** and **Hepplewhite** styles flourished during this time. Furniture was made of mahogany or rosewood. Most of it was made and improved upon by **Duncan Phyfe** and other American cabinetmakers. Classical motifs were popular in this style—namely, the lyre, lion's mask, acanthus leaf, paw, brass ornaments, saber leg, trumpets, laurel, cornucopia, and drapery swags. The American eagle and other national symbols were especially popular and appeared after the Revolutionary War, as did the stars and stripes. American Directoire is best exemplified by the Grecian and Roman types of sofas and chairs "modernized" and made by Duncan Phyfe.

American Empire style closely followed the French Empire and English **Regency** styles. It was massive, graceless, cumbersome, and heavily ornamented. Rounded wood columns were used in front of chests and sideboards, and carvings were coarse, often gilded. The wood was usually mahogany. The motifs most frequently used were eagles, cornucopias, flowers, fruits, lion's paws, and bear's claws. This period symbolizes the decline of fine furniture design and the beginning of mass-produced, machine-made furniture. Even Duncan Phyfe's work declined and earned the title of "butcher's furniture."

American Institute of Architects: The object of the A.I.A. is for architects to combine efforts so as to promote aesthetic, scientific, and practical efficiency, and to advance the science and art of planning and building; to ensure advancement of living standards for people through their improved environment.

American Renaissance: The period 1876–1917; this term denotes more an attitude or movement than a particular style. A time of grand-scale opulence in furniture and architecture.

American scene painters: *See* modern art.

ampere (Amp): A unit of measure of electric current. Named for the French physicist André Marie Ampere.

amphora: A jar with two handles and a narrow neck, used by the Greeks and Romans.

ancestral portraits: Paintings of older relatives. Chinese ancestral portraits are decorative and charming, but considered out of proportion to their importance as art, because their obvious purpose is not one of art. They do not enjoy any special aesthetic value for the Chinese.

andirons: Two upright brass or wrought-iron standards used in a fireplace, with a log cradle between them, to support wood or coal. Their use dates back to the Roman era. Also known as *firedogs*.

angle iron: An iron or steel bar forming a 90-degree angle, used as a **lintel** support.

angle of incidence: The angle made by a light ray with a line perpendicular to the surface on which the ray falls.

annealing: A process for toughening **flint glass** by raising it to a high temperature and then cooling it gradually.

anthemion motif: *See* honeysuckle ornament.

antimacassar: A small doily or cover used to protect the back and arms of a chair or sofa from soiling.

antiques: This appellation does not apply exclusively to old furniture. According to the U.S. Customs department, an antique is an article made prior to 1830. That date coincides with the beginning of the machine age. Furniture and works of art made in America are considered by many to be antiques if they are at least one hundred years old. Antique furniture is prized not only for its age but for being in the true style of the period. Antiques are also regarded in high esteem for rarity, nostalgic interest, artistic merit, and educational value. Not everyone has a feeling for antiques, but for those who do, antiques add beauty and charm to life. In buying antique furniture it is important to watch for reproductions with counterfeit marks of age. The signs by which genuine antiques are recognized are many: the **patina,** handmade nails, hardware, glue marks, tool marks, and other details. Collecting antiques is a complex undertaking, for the market is one of specialties. For this reason, the consumer should always deal with a reputable dealer.

antiquing: A method of treating furniture to simulate age. The wood is often acid-treated and glazed, edges are worn down, the wood may be beaten, gouged, and wormholes counterfeited—all to convey an impression of the ravages of time. Also known as *distressing*.

applewood: A light-colored, fine-grained wood that takes a light or natural finish. Used primarily for small pieces of furniture (though economically more important for its fruit than for lumber).

appliqué: A decorative motif or ornament that is attached to the surface of a piece of furniture or fabric.

apron: A horizontal band of wood that encircles and connects the legs of a chair, table, or a piece of case furniture, directly under the top (also known as a *skirt*). In architecture, a raised panel below a window sill.

aquatint: A form of etching or print technique capable of producing several tones by varying the etching time of different sections of a copper plate. The resulting print resembles watercolor in sepia. It is a process softer than line engraving and one from which many colored prints are produced.

arabesque: A flat ornamental pattern, painted, inlaid, or carved, used for borders or panels. It is composed of intricately interlaced floral and geometric patterns, scrollwork, branches, leaves, birds, grotesque animals, and humans. Spanish-Islamic in origin, this decorative form first appeared in the Middle Ages and spread throughout Europe in the sixteenth century.

arch: A curved structure in building used to span an opening such as a window or doorway, and capable of supporting weight from above. In masonry, an arch is formed by separate wedge-shaped segments. There are many types of arches: Tudor, Gothic, horseshoe, ogee, trefoil, elliptical, and Roman, or semicircular.

Archipenko, Alexander (1887–1964): Russian-born American abstract sculptor.

architect: One whose profession is designing, drawing plans and specifications for, and supervising the construction of a building. (*See also* American Institute of Architects.)

architectural symbols: *See* pages 8–9.

architrave: In classical architecture, the lowest division of the entablature, resting on top of the **capital** of each supporting **column**. Architraves are also used to decorate case furniture.

arc tube: A glass or ceramic enclosure found on fluorescent, mercury, quartz, or high-pressure sodium lamps, which contains the arc discharge.

area rug: Any rug that is smaller than a room-size carpet.

Arita porcelain: Japanese porcelain made in Arita since the early part of the sixteenth century. It is popularly called *Imari ware* because it was long shipped from the port of Imari, near Arita. This porcelain is characterized by brilliantly colorful designs and overglazes. It was

architectural symbols

PLAN AND SECTION INDICATIONS
EARTH, ETC.

EARTH ROCK STONE FILL

CONCRETE

STRUCTURAL LT-WEIGHT BLOCK
CONCRETE CONCRETE

TERRAZZO

METAL

STEEL, ALUMINUM SHEET METAL
IRON   & ALL METALS
       AT SMALL
       SCALE

STRUCTURAL REINFORCING BRASS,
STEEL   BARS   BRONZE

WOOD

FINISH ROUGH LARGE-SCALE
         PLYWOOD

SMALL-SCALE PLASTIC ON STUD WALL &
PLYWOOD PLYWOOD PARTITION

WOOD FINISH
ON STUD

STONE

CUT STONE RUBBLE CAST STONE
         (CONCRETE)

MARBLE SLATE
     BLUESTONE,
     SOAPSTONE

BRICK

COMMON FACE FIRE BRICK
        ON COMMON

GYPSUM

PLASTER ON BLOCK SOLID PLASTER
MASONRY   PARTITION

METAL STUD & PLASTERBOARD PLANK
PLASTER & PLASTER
PARTITION PARTITION

INSULATION

LOOSE FILL BOARDS OR SOLID, CORK,
OR BATTS QUILTS OR MAGNESIA

STRUCTURAL CLAY TILE

UNGLAZED GLAZED

GLASS

SHEET & PLATE   STRUCTURAL   BLOCK

ARCHITECTURAL TERRA COTTA

VENEER   BLOCK PARTITION

MISCELLANEOUS

WATERPROOFING, FELT, FLASHING, ETC.   RESILIENT TILE   PLASTER, SAND, & CEMENT

ACOUSTIC TILE   CARPET & PAD

ELEVATION INDICATIONS

GLASS   ASHLAR STONE   RUBBLE STONE

SQUARED STONE   RUNNING-BOND MASONRY   STACK-BOND MASONRY

SHEET METAL   CONCRETE PLASTER   SHINGLES SIDING

BRICK   CERAMIC TILE

PLANS OF EXTERIOR WALLS

FACE BRICK   BRICK   CAST STONE

RUBBLE   STRUC. CLAY TILE   BRICK

CUT STONE   CUT STONE   ARCH T C

STRUC. CONCRETE   CONCRETE BLOCK   BRICK

EXTERIOR OF WALL

INTERIOR

SECTIONS OF FLOOR FINISH

TILE ON CONCRETE   MARBLE ON CONCRETE   WOOD

TERRAZZO ON CONCRETE   STONE   BRICK

RESILIENT TILE ON CONCRETE

first exported to Europe in the middle of the seventeenth century. Since 1730 Imari ware has been reproduced in Europe.

arkwright: Denotes late medieval English furniture of simple construction. Also, a maker of "arks" or chests.

armoire: A tall, massive wardrobe or cabinet, originally a repository for arms, but nowadays used for storing clothing and household possessions. It is architectural in design, fitted with two doors and often with elaborate hinges and locks. It is frequently paneled and beautifully carved. The earliest armoires, in medieval times, were painted, the interiors containing shelves that were left unfinished or covered in wallpaper. Armoires lend themselves to conversion into bars, high-fidelity centers, and television cabinets.

armorial china: Services of porcelain decorated with coats-of-arms and crests.

armory show: An exhibition held at the 69th Regiment Armory in New York City in February and March of 1913 that introduced America to the modern developments of European painting, in particular Fauvism and cubism.

Arp, Jean (1887–1966): French abstract sculptor, painter, and graphic artist. A founder of **Dada.**

art déco: A style of decoration popular in the 1920s and 1930s, which took its name from the 1925 *Expositions des Arts Décoratifs et Industriels Modernes* in Paris. Characterized by restrained, stylish ornamentation, simple furniture shapes, and an emphasis on fine craftsmanship and the use of opulent materials. Silver and black was the favorite color scheme.

art nouveau: A style of decoration that flourished at the turn of the century, particularly in France and Belgium. It is characterized by sinuous, stylized depictions of organic forms, plant and floral forms in particular. Though named for a Parisian shop, this movement was not distinctly French. Rather, it was a collective European phenomenon, strongly influenced by the **Arts and Crafts movement** in England. The style is known variously as *Jugendstil* (Germany and Austria); *Niewe Kunst* (Holland); *Stile Liberty* (Italy—after the British firm, Liberty & Co.); and *Moderno* (Spain). Among the chief proponents of this style were the Belgian designer Henri van de Velde, the French designers Emile Gallé and Luis Majorelle, the Spanish architect Antoni Gaudí, and the American designer Louis Comfort Tiffany.

Arts and Crafts movement: A reform style in British decorative arts of the Victorian era. The movement was a revolt against tasteless, ugly, mass-produced furniture; a rebellion against overmechanization. There was a return to fine craftsmanship and hand fabrication.

The chief influence behind this movement was **William Morris,** who dedicated himself to raising the standards of craftsmanship. The movement culminated in the early twentieth century.

ash: A straw-colored hardwood, tough yet flexible, used for furniture, cabinets, and picture frames. The grain resembles that of oak.

Ashcan school: *See* modern art.

A.S.I.D.: American Society of Interior Designers. Formed in 1931, the A.S.I.D. is the largest society of interior designers in the world, with 23,000 members. Members represent the highest degree of professionalism in their discipline and are qualified by education and experience to identify, research, and creatively solve problems relative to the function and quality of housing and office environments. An A.S.I.D. member's areas of competency include: design, color, space-planning, furniture, and the furnishing of all interior spaces. He or she understands construction, design, psychology, and technology. To be accepted as a professional member, an applicant must have fulfilled minimum educational and/or practical experience requirements,

be engaged in professional practice, and have successfully completed the National Council for Interior Design Qualification examinations.

The A.S.I.D. membership consists of the following categories:

Professional member
Fellow Professional member

Associated member
Affiliate member
Education member
Press member
International corresponding member

Umbrella group:
Allied member A.S.I.D.

Professional members and professional fellow members are the only individuals permitted to use the A.S.I.D. or F.A.S.I.D. (if Fellow) appellation after their names. All others are permitted to use the designation "Allied member A.S.I.D."

asphalt tile: *See* flooring.

assemblage: A work of art that is assembled rather than painted, sculpted, drawn, or carved. Assemblages include such materials as driftwood, paper, machine parts, and other objects and fragments not intended as art materials.

astragal: A narrow, convex molding with a semicircular profile.

A.T.M.I. American Textile Manufacturers Institute. The association for fabric manufacturers.

atrium: A garden or inner court in the interior of a house. It may or may not be open to the sky.

Aubusson: A fine handwoven carpet or tapestry with no pile. Aubusson carpets were originally designed by French Court painters.

auction terms *circa:* Latin word meaning "about," used before an approximate date.
　knock-off: slang for a copy of an original.
　reserved action: The lowest price that will be accepted for a certain item. This price has been agreed upon beforehand by the auctioneer and the consignor.
　pool: A group of dealers who choose one person to bid for the entire group. This enables them to buy cheaply and then schedule their own sales after the auction to make an even larger profit.
　buy back: An offer to buy back any merchandise sold at a 10 percent profit.

Audubon, John James (1785–1851): American ornithologist and renowned painter of birds. A brilliant draughtsman and scientific observer. Audubon prints are still very popular and are found in many American homes.

Austrian shades: Shirred, sheer curtains with the effect of many rows of horizontal swags. They can be raised or lowered to any point by the use of cords.

Avery, Milton (1893–1965): American painter whose works show a pronounced **Fauvist** influence.

avodire: A light yellow African wood with a clearly marked grain. Used exclusively as veneer in furniture making.

Axminster: A hand-knotted pile carpet originally made in Axminster, England. These carpets have a thick, long, cut pile and are very like Oriental carpets in color and thickness. The Axminster mills closed down in 1835 when the looms were taken over by Wilton. Axminster carpeting is still available today, but it is now machine made.

B

Baccarat: The most eminent glass works in France. The exceptionally beautiful crystal glass manufactured by this firm was first made in 1818. Today, its stemware, crystal prisms, lustres, paperweights, and objects of art are much sought after.

bachelor's chest: A small, low eighteenth-century English chest of drawers with a hinged leaf underneath the top. This leaf, when opened, doubles the size of the top and provides a writing surface.

backgammon table: A **game table** dating back to the Middle Ages, generally in the French or English styles. In France, the table was exceptionally popular in the eighteenth century and was known as a *tric-trac table*. It was mounted on four legs, had drawers that opened on opposite ends, and was 44 inches square.

back order: All or part of an order that will be shipped at a future date.

back painting: The process of gluing any type of print to the back of a pane of glass, thus rendering it transparent, and then tinting or painting the back of it.

baker's rack: A four-shelf, wrought-iron stand about 6 feet high and 6 feet wide. Developed in France, it was originally used to display breads. Nowadays, its shelves are generally used for the display of art objects and plants.

balance: Equivalence as to value or weight on the right and left sides of a room.

baldaquin, baldachin: A canopy over a bed, projecting from a wall and supported by columns. In architecture, a stone or marble structure in the form of a canopy, usually located over the altar of a church.

ballast: An electrical device that supplies the proper voltage and current to start and operate a discharge lamp such as a fluorescent lamp.

balloon framing: A construction method wherein the studs (wooden uprights) run from the foundation to the eaves, with flooring and ceiling members nailed to them.

Balthus (1908–   ): French painter of Polish descent, whose actual name is Balthasar Klossowsky. Largely self-taught, he does not belong to any school of painting. His works are characterized by muted colors and a strange, even morbid, atmosphere.

baluster: A wood turning or slender column of elliptical shape, used as a support for a stair rail. Also used on chair backs and in **columns** supporting a **cornice** on a cupboard. Half, or *split* balusters are frequently applied to the surface of furniture as a form of ornament. When used in a series, the design is called a *balustrade*.

balustrade: *See* baluster.

bamboo furniture, imitation: Imitation bamboo chairs and chests have been in vogue since the eighteenth century in England. The British made turnings out of beech and finished them to simulate real bamboo. Americans adopted the style in the early part of the nineteenth century.

banding: An inlaid strip of wood in a contrasting color or grain to the surrounding **veneer,** used on furniture for decorative purposes.

banister-back chair: A chair with a tall open back consisting of several **splats** or *banisters*.

banjo clock: A nineteenth-century American pendulum clock in the form of a banjo.

banquette: An upholstered bench or built-in seat.

bar: Appropriate for any entertainment area, such as a den or family room. A bar may be installed in a closet or built into the corner of a room. The bar front, and the wall in back of it, can match the rest of the room, whether it be wallpaper or paneling. Locked cabinets at the rear of the bar should be high enough to accommodate standing liquor bottles and deep enough to allow wine bottles to be laid on their sides so that the corks will be kept moist, thus keeping the wine from spoiling. The bar does not necessarily have to contain alcoholic beverages; it can be a soda fountain. The bar top is useful for serving snacks and buffet suppers. A bar can be concealed behind fold-back, fabric covered doors. Cane and louvered shutters are also effective.

Barbizon school: A group of French landscape painters in the second half of the nineteenth century, who met in the village of Barbizon, in northern France, to paint unpretentious landscapes directly from nature, particularly views of the Forest of Fontainebleau.

Barcelona chair: A chromium steel chair designed by Ludwig Miës van der Rohe for the German Government Pavilion at the Barcelona International Exhibition of 1929. Considered a classic, this chair is still in production and is extremely popular with architects. The back and seat are always upholstered with tufted leather cushions.

barometer: An instrument that records variations in atmospheric pressure. Very popular during the eighteenth century. Handsome cases were often designed for them in mahogany and satinwood.

baroque: The word means a departure from the regular. The baroque style in painting, architecture, and furniture design flourished in the years 1590–1780. This distorted, exaggerated style, which violates every notion of form, scale, line, and proportion, was bizarre, ornate, and ostentatious. Furniture was very theatrical looking, with its fantastically over-decorated look of twisted columns, **broken pediments,** and inlays of bronze, copper, marble, tortoiseshell, ebony, and mosaic tile. This style began at the end of the Renaissance. It was first sponsored by the Catholic church as a counter-Reformation movement using art as propaganda to ennoble and intensify religious zeal.

Barragám, Luis: Architect practicing the Mexican interpretation of the **Interna-tional** style. He used strong colors and monumental forms.

barrel chair: An upholstered chair with a deep, concave, barrellike back. Also known as a *tub chair.*

barrier-free design: Design in which passages, obstacles, steps, or the like are removed so that handicapped persons may freely pass through (for example, the use of a ramp instead of stairs). Specific standards for barrier-free design have been set forth by the American National Standards Institute in their 1971 Document A 117.1. Changes in some basic architectural features that would eliminate a majority of barriers that hinder most handicapped persons are:

- Building entrances at ground level with free passage for wheelchairs, or ramps sloped gradually (at a ratio of 1 to 12 or 8.3 percent)
- 34-inch door-width clearance
- Level thresholds to rooms
- Wide parking spaces close to buildings for the handicapped
- Level walks with no curbs at crossways
- Easy access to elevators
- Restrooms with wide stalls, with grab bars 32 to 34 inches high, and wash basins and towel racks 40 inches high
- Handrails on all stairways, extending 12 inches beyond top and bottom steps
- Slip-resistant floors, and carpeting with tight weave and low pile

- Lower fountains and public telephones for wheelchair users
- Tuxedo-style sofas and chairs (arm height equal to back height), that allow a seated person to use the arms for support when pulling up to a standing position or when transferring to a wheelchair. Sixteen inches is the recommended seat height. Leather upholstery allows the user to slide into and out of sofas and chairs
- A 28-inch-high table makes a good working and eating surface

All fifty states now have laws regarding barrier-free design in addition to local building codes.

basaltes: Hard black earthenware made by Josiah **Wedgwood.** It has been copied by **Spode.**

base-shoe: A quarter-round molding applied at the place where wall and floor meet to conceal the joint and protect the wall from kicks and scratches.

bas-relief: Sculptured carving that projects only slightly from the background. Also known as *low relief.*

bathroom: No longer must a bathroom be strictly utilitarian and sterile looking. It is now possible to design an average-size bathroom in high style. Dramatize it by using vast expanses of mirror to create the illusion of space, and use plants lavishly, for they grow well in a warm, humid atmosphere. Storage and dressing facilities can be used to conceal anything personal or clinical. Your bathroom can be given a fillip by using paneling, glass, or gaily patterned waterproof wallpaper. For a luxurious look, use wall-to-wall carpeting. The carpet should not be fastened down permanently but laid over a thin rubber pad. Consider a square tub to save space, and conceal it with a waterproof curtain. The use of crystal fixtures and artwork adds elegance. Warm-white fluorescent tubes should be used to flatter the complexion and as an excellent visual aid to grooming. A partial or complete luminous ceiling is a worthwhile indulgence. With a large space and a budget to match, the bathroom can also serve as a gym, a place to rest, and, with a skylight, a place to sunbathe. Add a sauna, gold electroplated faucets, twin lavatories, or a small television for a truly luxurious bathroom.

batik: A figured, hand-painted fabric in which wax is used to trace the design. The material is then dyed. The wax repels the dye. By repeating this process several times, intricate patterns can be obtained. The process originated in Java.

batten: A narrow strip of wood or metal that covers the joints between boards or panels.

Battersea enamel: Copper-based articles that are coated with a soft white enamel, then decorated with flowers, birds, portraits, etc. Developed about 1750.

batting: Cotton or wool fiber wadded together and used as a filling for upholstery or for quilting purposes.

Bauhaus: An institute for the study of art, design, and architecture. Founded in Weimar, Germany in 1919, it was the most important experimental school of its kind in the twentieth century. Founded and headed by architect Walter Gropius, its aim was to combine art, industry, technology, and industrial production. Its philosophy was, "function is the basis and aim of all design," and its credo, "form follows function." Artists, architects, interior and industrial designers, and craftsmen worked side by side with those principles as their guiding inspiration. In 1930 Gropius was succeeded by Ludwig Miës van der Rohe. The Nazis closed the Bauhaus in 1933. In America the work was carried on by the Chicago Institute of Design, with Laszlo Moholy-Nagy as its head. Other followers were Le Corbusier and Marcel Breuer. The Bauhaus is perhaps best known for the innovative use of metal, chrome, and tubular steel in furniture design.

Baxter prints: A process of oil-color picture printing patented by George Baxter in 1835. Color was added by successive blocks, one for each color.

bay window: An angular window projection of a wall beyond the house. If curved, it is called a *bow window;* if it is on an upper floor, it is called an *oriel window.*

Baziotes, William (1912–1963): American action-style abstract expressionist painter.

beam: A horizontal member of any structure that supports a load.

Beauvais: A city in France notable for the tapestries manufactured there since 1664. The tapestry works were sponsored by Louis XIV.

Beckmann, Max (1884–1950): German expressionist painter.

bedding: The standard sizes for box springs and mattresses are:

Mattress Sizes	Width (inches)	Length (inches)
Single or Youth	30	75
Twin	39	75
Full (Double)	54	76
Queen	60	75–80
King	76	80–84

Extra-long bedding varies from four to six inches longer than standard.

bedroom, master: This should be the

most personal, restful, relaxing room of a house and should reflect the true personalities of the occupants. If the bedroom is large, this haven may be used as a private sitting room—a room in which to pursue an indoor hobby, a room in which to read or write, or a retreat to get away from it all. A **chaise longue** adds elegance to a bedroom and is useful for reading, napping, or watching television. A small desk is always a practical adjunct. A small table and a pair of side chairs will serve as a breakfast unit and will be especially enjoyable if there is a window with a view. Bookcases or bookwalls and even a small console piano are not out of place in a large bedroom. A sofa, love seat, or pair of lounging chairs are luxuries worth having. With careful planning, space can be made for at least some of these "creature comforts."

A bedroom "set" or "suite" is most uninteresting. Assembling a variety of pieces and diversifying the finishes is much more decorative and exciting.

Using a large cabinet or armoire to conceal a television set is a satisfying solution to the inelegance of an exposed set. The primary purpose of night tables is not decorative. They should be able to house everything from tissues to books and large enough to accommodate lamps so that one can enjoy reading in bed. Overhead lighting is necessary for general illumination. Beds look best when the headboard can be viewed upon first entering the room. The possibilities for types of headboards are unlimited. They can be made of Lucite, chrome, mirror, Oriental screens, wrought iron, grillwork, or leather. Spool type, bookcase type, shuttered, and caned headboards are also available. For an unusual treatment, run the bedspread material up the wall to the ceiling, and it will give the appearance of a headboard. Canopies may be used over single, double, or kingsize beds. It is tricky but elegant to use one canopy or valance over twin beds. The fabric should match the bedspread top or the flounce. Also impressive is the use of one floral fabric for the draperies, bedspread, headboard, and the entire wall against which the beds will be standing. Try pasting the same fabric to the drawer fronts of a chest of drawers. If done with taste, mixing patterns is a good design strategy, as is the use of coordinated fabrics like stripes, plains, and florals. As for colors, monochromatic schemes are generally suggested (*see* color). It is a fallacy to insist on a subdued color scheme, since much depends on the temperament of the occupant. If the dressing area adjoins the room, the colors should be coordinated with or identical to those used in the bedroom.

The control of light is of paramount importance. If morning sunlight is an annoyance, draperies should be lined with blackout lining, or blackout lining should be hung on a separate track.

Here are some additional tips for decorating a master bedroom:

If family photographs or snapshots must be used, this is the room for them.

Install a cut-off switch for the bell on the bedside telephone.

The unstinted use of mirrors will make the room appear larger.

Locate the master light switch and the master heat switch next to the bed.

If the master bedroom is located upstairs and is quite large, install an all-in-one stove and refrigerator unit.

If a couple shares a bedroom, it should not be too feminine, but should be a room capable of putting both occupants at ease. Above all, make the bedroom a place of repose, tranquility, and serenity.

bed-sitting room: A British designation for a one-room living quarter where the occupant sleeps, eats, works, and entertains. Also known as a *garçonnieres*.

bedspread: Custom bedspreads are available in myriad styles, made up as one-piece throws or as two-piece bedspreads with a separate top, called a coverlet. A separate skirt, known as a **flounce** or **dust ruffle,** may be shirred, straight-hanging, or box-pleated. The top may be plain or quilted, made with or without a reverse *sham*. The sham serves to cover the bed pillows. (Bolsters may be used instead of a sham.) The drop sides on the coverlet may be straight, scalloped, or fitted. Fabrics may match the draperies or a chair, or two fabrics may be combined. For example: the flounce could be a print that is used elsewhere in the room and the coverlet a plain fabric that picks up one of the colors in the flounce. Endless combinations are possible, limited only by the imagination.

beech: A light brown **hardwood** that is easily worked. It is very light in weight and absorbs stain readily.

Belleek: Translucent Irish porcelain with a natural ivory color, made by the Belleek factory in the second half of the nineteenth century.

bell-pull: A handle, cord, or embroidered or needlepointed strip of cloth pulled to ring a bell.

Belter, John H. (1804–1863): American cabinetmaker specializing in highly carved rococo and Victorian furniture, generally of rosewood and walnut.

Bennington: A stoneware factory was started at Bennington, Vermont in 1842. Although kaolin, the basic ingredient of porcelain, had been discovered, pottery, not porcelain was manufactured here. (Pottery is heavier than porcelain and has been produced in China since 1368.) The major items made in Bennington were containers of gray salt-glazed stoneware, often decorated with blue floral motifs. Green, yellow, and tortoiseshell finishes were also used. Most of the forms were copies of English ware.

Benton, Thomas Hart (1889–1975): American painter and muralist who specialized in stylized rural subjects.

bentwood furniture: The bentwood process involves the bending of wet wood, usually elm, which is quite malleable. The process was invented in Vienna by **Michael Thonet** in the latter part of the nineteenth century. Bentwood furniture was widely used in Austria; when exported, it was called *Vienna furniture.* Thonet designed the famous bentwood chair, one of the earliest mass-production enterprises.

bergère: An eighteenth-century French upholstered armchair with closed upholstered sides. The sides and back, which are often rounded, are surrounded by a wood frame, which is generally carved. First made in the **Louis XV** style in about 1725, it was later copied in England and America, and interior designers still enjoy using it in combination with many styles of furniture.

Bertoia, Harry (1915–1978): Italian-born American furniture designer, sculptor, and metalsmith. He worked with **Charles Eames** developing plywood molding techniques but is best known for a series of chrome-plated chairs whose seats consist of a welded latticework of steel rods, molded in curves. These include the Diamond chair (1952).

Betty lamp: A seventeenth-century British and American oil lamp. It was usually attached to an iron ratchet hanging from the ceiling. It was also used as a floor lamp when attached to an iron floor standard.

bevel cut: A 45-degree slant cut along the edge of any material, such as glass, mirror, Lucite, or wood.

bias: A line cutting diagonally across the warp of a fabric at a 45-degree angle to the selvage.

bibelot: A small object of decorative value, beauty, or rarity. A trinket.

bibliotheque: The French word for a bookcase cabinet, often with wire inserts in the doors.

bidet: A basinlike bathroom fixture designed to be straddled. Its main purpose is to provide quick, easy bathing of the perineal regions of the body following use of the toilet.

Biedermeier style: A furniture style popular in northern Europe between about 1820 and 1855. A reaction to the opulence of French **Empire** furniture, the Biedermeier style was characterized by simplicity of form, restrained decoration, and a comfortable appearance. The woods used were: ash, birch, walnut, maple, beech, mahogany, and all fruitwoods. The principal center for the production of Biedermeier furniture was Vienna.

bill of lading: A written receipt given by a carrier for goods accepted for shipment to a designated location.

biotechnology: The study of the relationship between human beings and machines. Also known as *ergonomics*.

birch: A close, straight-grained **hardwood** used copiously in inexpensive furniture and paneling. It lacks color and figuring but finishes well and can be made to imitate walnut or mahogany.

birdcage support: A small, cagelike, eighteenth-century mechanism connecting the top of a table to a pedestal base, allowing the top to be tilted to a vertical position when not in use.

bird's-eye maple: A pale brownish-yellow **maple** patterned with dark brown circles. Popular as a decorative **veneer.**

bisque: Ceramics that have been fired but not glazed. Also known as *biscuit*.

blackamoor: An English candlestand or carved figure of a dark-skinned person, used as a table base in the eighteenth and nineteenth centuries, especially in Italy.

Blanc de Chine: An eighteenth-century French term designating a translucent white or ivory porcelain first manufactured during the Ming Dynasty.

blind stitching: The sewing of a fabric or piping in such a manner that the stitches are invisible.

blockfront: A chest front distinguished by three vertical panels, the center concave and depressed, the ends convex, raised, and flat. Customarily made of mahogany. Found on **Chippendale** furniture.

block printing: *See* woodcut.

Bloom, Hyman (1913–): American expressionist painter who rendered many themes from the Old Testament.

blueprint: A photographic printing of an architectural drawing that produces a white line on a blue background. While this process has been largely replaced by the *ozalid* process, which produces a black or blue line on a white background, the term "blueprint" is still used.

bobbinet: A net of hexagonal mesh made on a lace machine.

bobeche: A slightly cupped ring of glass placed over the cup of a candleholder to catch the wax drippings.

Bohemian glass: Fine-etched glass similar to rock crystal. Introduced in Bohemia in the eighteenth century.

boiserie: An eighteenth-century French term for carved paneling and decorative woodwork on walls.

Bokhara rug: A rug made by Turkestan tribes from very fine yarns or hair, usually having a black-and-white pattern of large and small octagons on a brownish-red or tan ground.

bolection molding: Any molding (but usually one of *ogee* design) that forms a border between two surfaces at different levels.

bolster: A long, cylindrical cushion or pillow for a bed or sofa.

bombé: Curved or swelling in shape. Bombé fronts are most commonly found on late-eighteenth-century cabinets. (Bombé items can bulge on the sides as well.) These pieces are just as much in demand today as they were during the time of **Louis XV.**

Bombois, Camille (1883–1970): French primitive painter best known for his street scenes.

bond: Anything that fastens, binds, grips, or adheres between two objects or materials.

bone china: A fine, naturally white china made of clay mixed with bone ash.

Bonnard, Pierre (1867–1947): French impressionist painter known for his bold and inventive use of color.

bonnetière: A tall, narrow French Provincial cabinet introduced during the seventeenth century. It was devised to accommodate the high bonnets worn by women in Normandy and Brittany.

bonnet top: A **broken pediment** on a piece of furniture that covers the entire top from front to back. Found on American **Chippendale** furniture.

borax firm: A manufacturer of cheap, badly designed, inexpensive furniture of any kind.

Boston rocker: A nineteenth-century American rocker fashioned after the **Windsor chair.** It has a heavy, solid wood seat that curves up at the rear and down in front. The back has delicate spindles.

boucle: A type of yarn with one thread looser than the others, which gives the cloth made from it a curly, tufted, buckled look.

Boulle marquetry: The inlay of brass, tortoiseshell, mother-of-pearl, pewter, or copper on furniture. Originally made and used by the French cabinetmaker André Charles Boulle (1642–1732). The furniture is ornate, with gilt and ormolu mountings.

bowfront: A convex curved front that appeared on chests and commodes during the eighteenth century. Sometimes called a *swell front*.

box beam: A girder or beam that is square or rectangular and hollow.

boxing: A narrow piece of fabric joining the top and bottom sides of a cushion or pillow.

bracket: An angle-shaped support projecting from a wall, designed to hold up a shelf, decorative member, or other weight.

bracket clock: Any clock that sits on a wall bracket.

braided rug: A rug created by weaving together by hand strips or strands of fabrics of various colors. Machine-made braided rugs are also available.

Brancusi, Constantin (1876–1957): Romanian-born French abstract sculptor.

Braque, Georges (1882–1963): French cubist painter and printmaker.

brass: Any of various metal alloys consisting mainly of copper and zinc. *Brass plate* is a thin layer of brass electroplated to steel tubing.

brasses: A slang term designating furniture hardware—handles, pulls, and back plates.

brass furniture: Low brass beds, four-poster beds, and children's beds with canopies made from brass tubing or cast brass were popular from 1850 to about 1900. In recent years there has been a resurgence of their popularity.

breakfront: A cabinet-bookcase combination in which the center section of the front extends a few inches forward of the two side sections. The upper half of the cabinet has glass doors, the lower half, drawers and cabinet doors.

Breuer, Marcel (1902–1981): Architect and furniture designer born in Hungary. He joined the **Bauhaus** as a student in 1920 and became director of furniture design there in 1925. Breuer invented modular-unit furniture and employed bent steel tubing to form frames for tables and chairs, notably the Wassily chair (1925). He also developed some of the first molded plywood chairs. With the advent of Hitler, he left Germany for London, where he practiced architecture for four years. In 1937 he accepted an associate professorship at Harvard University. He was a partner of Walter Gropius from 1937 to 1942. He built all over the United States as well as in South America, Europe, and Asia. One of his best-known projects is the Whitney Museum, New York (1966).

Brewster chair: An early seventeenth-century American **Jacobean** armchair with turned posts and spindles and a plank or rush seat. Named for William Brewster, an elder of Plymouth Colony, who owned such a chair.

bric-a-brac: Small, rare, or artistic objects used as decorative ornaments.

Bristol glass: A thin, fine glass made in Bristol, England. Especially desirable is the glassware in Bristol blue and Bristol milk. The factory was founded around 1750.

broadloom carpet: Any carpet woven on a wide loom and having no seams.

broken pediment: A **pediment** in which the curved lines or scrolls stop before connecting, leaving an open section at the apex.

bronze: An alloy, chiefly of copper and tin. Sometimes small quantities of lead and zinc are added. Bronze is used extensively for furniture ornamentation. Artists and craftsmen also use it for stat-

uary and objects of art. **Ormolu** is gilded bronze.

Brunelleschi, Filippo (1377–1446): Italian **Renaissance** architect and sculptor.

Brussels carpet: A carpet introduced in England in 1740, made with three- or four-ply worsted yarns drawn up in uncut loops to form a pattern. It has a warp and a weft of linen. The carpet is known for its long wearing qualities. It is woven on a Wilton carpet loom and is in fact a Wilton carpet with an uncut pile.

Brussels lace: Net lace with an **appliqué** design.

Buffet, Bernard (1928–): French social-realist painter.

buffet: An item of furniture with drawers or cabinets used for dishes, table linens, silver, etc. The top is often used for serving. It is approximately 33 inches high.

building paper: Also called *roofing* or *sheathing* paper. It is a heavy waterproof paper that is applied over a wall or roof before the outside finish material is applied.

built-ins: Bookcases, headboards, window seats, toy boxes, storage units, cabinets, home offices, television sets, bars, or hi-fi equipment concealed in niches or closets.

bullion fringe: A six-inch, heavy, corded fringe made of twisted gold or silver threads, customarily attached to the bottom of a chair, love seat, or sofa.

bun foot: A furniture foot shaped like a flattened globe or bun. Of Dutch origin, it was introduced in the latter half of the seventeenth century.

bungalow: A modest, one-story house, usually surrounded by a **verandah.**

Burchfield, Charles (1893–1967): American realistic painter.

bureau: In France, *bureau* denotes a desk or writing table. In America, it refers to a **chest of drawers,** generally found in the bedroom.

burl: A tumorous growth on a tree trunk or branch. When cut, it reveals a striking grain with a figured, swirled pattern. Burl wood is available only in small quantities and is in demand as a decorative **veneer** or for the purpose of inlaying furniture.

Burliuk, David (1882–1967): Russian expressionist painter who worked in bright colors and with thick paint.

butler's pantry: A small room situated between the kitchen and dining room. Contains built-in cabinets and drawers for china, linen, and glassware. Usually has a sink and counter as well.

butler's tray: A tray mounted on legs or with an X-shaped folding stand. Developed in Britain in the late eighteenth century. Often used today as a cocktail table.

butterfly wedge: A small, butterfly-shaped piece of wood inserted and glued into adjoining boards to hold them together.

butt joint: A connection of two pieces of lumber or panels in which the squared end of the first is placed against the side of the second, forming a right angle. The joint can be concealed with a decorative or simple **batten.**

buttress: A mass of masonry built against a wall to add extra strength and support to the wall itself. The Romans were the first to employ buttresses. In the medieval church the groined vaults, concentrating their great lateral thrusts at a point along the exterior walls, required buttresses to achieve stability. They were often disguised as **pilasters.**

Byzantine: An architectural and design

style, chiefly ecclesiastical, developed during the years 476–1200. In A.D. 330 Emperor Constantine made the ancient city of Byzantium the new capital of the Roman Empire. He renamed the city Constantinople and moved his court there. (In 1930 the name was again changed, to Istanbul.) The newly renamed capital became a melting pot for a number of races, and the styles and attending arts spread through Greece and the Balkans, to Asia Minor and parts of Syria, and ultimately to Russia and Italy. The Imperial court functioned for more than a thousand years and preserved the culture of the ancients while all of Western Europe was in a state of chaos. The fusing of Greek and Eastern churches resulted in a split between the Roman and Greek orthodox churches. Roman art forms merged with those of the Orient, Persia, and Arabia. From the resultant fusion arose the splendor and ornamentation that we associate with the Byzantine style. Mosaic and glass work reached their zenith in Byzantine architecture. Furniture was heavy, ecclesiastical looking, and profusely ornamented with inlays of gold, silver, ivory, and semiprecious stones. Gold, silver, and purple were the predominant colors used. Turned wood was employed in the construction of armchairs, stools, and couches. All carvings were opulently executed.

To Adam Paradise was home.
To the good among his descendants
Home is Paradise.

Anthony Hare (1863–1933)

cabriole leg: An S-shaped, tapering, double-curved furniture leg that swells outward at the knee and swings inward toward the foot. First used in the late seventeenth century in England, the cabriole leg became a hallmark of eighteenth-century **rococo** furniture.

cachepot: An ornamental ceramic container for a flowerpot.

CADD: Computer-aided Design and Drafting. The application of all aspects of project design and market potential to achieve greater productivity. Computer aids are used by interior designers, architects, and graphic designers. The future of the design and construction industries will be closely linked to the use of computers and computer methods. CADD can be a profitable drafting and data-management tool.

Calder, Alexander (1898–): American sculptor and engineer, best known for his mobiles.

calender: A machine with heated rollers between which cloth or paper is run to give it a smooth or glossy finish. Used in the manufacture of chintzes and other glazed fabrics.

camber: A slight rise or upward curve in an otherwise horizontal piece or structure.

camelback: In English furniture a chair or sofa that curves or arches up in the center.

camelback sofa: A sofa with a raised (humped) back. An eighteenth-century form favored by **Hepplewhite.**

campaign furniture: Portable military furnishings—lap desks, trunks, chests, folding chairs, and the like—that generals and officers used on military campaigns up to the Civil War. Campaign furniture was invented by Napoleon's staff.

campanile: A bell tower, especially one that is detached from the body of a church. The Leaning Tower of Pisa is one example.

canapé: An eighteenth-century French settee, generally upholstered and caned.

Candela, Felix (1910–): Spanish born, world-famous architect. Although not the inventor of the hyperbolic paraboloid, Candela's reputation in Mexico, where he emigrated, was made by his use of the curved shell design.

candelabra: A branched candlestick supported on a single stem.

canopy: Drapery over a bed, attached to posts or suspended from a ceiling.

canterbury: A low, open-topped rack with divisions or partitions. Introduced in England in the late eighteenth century. Originally used to hold books, trays, and sheet music; now popular as a magazine rack.

capital: The top, or head, of a **column** or **pilaster.**

Capodimonte: Italian soft-paste porcelain, first produced at Naples in 1743. The background is usually ivory-colored, with colored decoration standing out in relief.

captain's chair: A nineteenth-century variation on the **Windsor chair** having a rounded back formed by a heavy rail resting on vertical spindles and coming forward to form the arms.

card table: *See* game table.

carnuba: An extremely hard wax obtained from the Brazilian palm. It is much used in furniture polish to impart hardness to a mixture.

carpet graphics: Pieces of carpet arranged in different colors and patterns and used as wall murals as well as to dampen sound and silence echoes.

carpets: Rug weaving is almost 5,000 years old, but more advances and innovations in materials and techniques have been made in the last 20 years than in the past 3,000 years. Today we have not only the traditional wool and cotton fibers, but an overwhelming variety of manmade fibers as well. (See the table on page 29.)

Wall-to-wall carpeting has many advantages. It absorbs sound, cushions one's step, and adds both warmth and a look of luxury. It makes a small room look larger, aids in the reception of high-fidelity music, and lays the foundation for the color scheme of the room. Carpeting of manmade fibers is practical and may be used successfully in schoolrooms, hospitals, libraries, kitchens, and porches.

The most common carpeting problems, and their solutions, are listed below:

Shedding: New cut-pile carpeting often sheds little balls of fluff. Don't worry—these are just bits of fiber and lint working

TYPES OF CARPET FIBERS AND THEIR CHARACTERISTICS

GENERIC NAME	TRADE NAME	SPECIAL PROPERTIES
Acrylic	Acrilan/Orlon/Creslen	Durable, resists soiling, colorfast, cleans easily, fire-retardant, abrasion-resistant, generates static electricity.
Nylon	Antron, Cumuloft, Caprolan, Enkaloft	Exceptional durability, crush-resistant, fade-resistant, cleans fairly easily, quick-drying.
Polyester	Dacron, Kodel, Mylar, Fortrel, Encron	Washable, crush-resistant, soil-hiding, cleans easily, extremely durable.
Olefin	Herculon, Marvess	Lightweight, durable, soil- and stain-resistant.
Rayon	Enkrome, Nupron	Crushes easily, wears well, poor flame resistance, will soil easily.
Polypropylene	Vectra, Polycrest, Mocomilon	Use indoors and outdoors, nonflammable, wears well, soil- and chemical-resistant, cleans well.
Wool	Wool	Excellent durability, doesn't need cleaning too often, crush-resistant, good abrasion- and soil-resistance, warm and soft.
Cotton	Cotton	Cleans or washes easily, but soils quickly, crushes badly, wears well, low-cost, soft.

their way to the surface. Eventually the fibers will all be taken up in the vacuum cleaner. This shedding usually happens more with wool carpeting than with nylon and other synthetics.

Snags: A loose nail on a shoe or a sharp-edged toy might snag some of the fibers and bring them above the surface. If this happens, cut the snag off. Do *not* pull it. If the snag is especially long and covers a large area, call a professional to take care of it.

Shading: Deep-cut pile carpeting will appear darker and lighter in certain areas. This is not a defect. In fact, it is an indication of just how luxurious the carpeting is. All you need to do is vacuum the pile so it's all going in the same direction.

Pilling: Small balls of fibers may appear, depending on the type of carpeting and the amount of traffic it gets. Simply clip off the "pills."

Static: With some carpets, when the temperature outside goes down, the static electricity inside goes up. One way to avoid this is to install a humidifier, which will not only make the static disappear, but will also prevent dust, which is attracted by static, from falling all over the carpeting. Also, higher humidity makes a room feel warmer.

Burns: For cigarette and other small burns, first snip off the darkened fibers. Then use a soapless cleaner and sponge with water.

Rippling: Too much humidity will cause temporary ripples in carpeting. If the ripples don't go away when the humidity returns to normal, you may need to have the carpet restretched.

Crushing: First work the pile back into place. Then hold a hot steam iron about 4 inches above the dented area. Do not touch the carpet with the iron or allow water to saturate the carpet.

Stains: Stains should never be rubbed. Press an absorbent tissue or kitchen towel gently on the stain. Then try lukewarm water with a small amount of carpet shampoo or detergent plus white vinegar. If this fails, try a solvent. Work it in gently with a spoon handle and blot quickly with tissues. *Always* test the effect of a solvent on the carpet by applying a few drops to an area that is hidden from view. Grease stains can be removed by placing an absorbent paper on the stain and ironing the paper for a few seconds. However, a professional cleaner is always recommended for such stains.

Carrara glass: Translucent white glass from Carrara, Italy. Used for tabletops and walls.

cartoon: A preliminary sketch for a rug, tapestry, mosaic, or the like, similar in size to the finished product.

cartouche: A decorative motif used to ornament **baroque** and **rococo** furniture. It represents a shield or partially unrolled scroll with the edges curled or rolled over.

Chippendale applied cartouches to some cabinets.

Cartwright, Edmund (1743–1823): English inventor of the power loom. It was the first machine to make practical the weaving of wide cotton cloth. He also invented a wool combing machine.

Carver chair: A seventeenth-century New England chair of maple or ash whose frame was formed entirely of turned pieces. It had a rush or plank seat, and was similar to the **Brewster chair.** Named for John Carver, the first governor of the Plymouth Colony, who owned such a chair.

caryatid: A draped female figure used as a decorative supporting column. Sculptured male figures used in a like manner are called *atlantes* (plural of *atlas*).

case goods: Furniture built in the form of a box and intended to hold something. Examples include the cupboard, the chest, the cabinet, and the chest of drawers.

casing: A window or door frame set into a wall.

casket: A small box or chest for jewels or letters.

cassone: A large Italian Renaissance

chest with a hinged lid, decorated inside and out with paint and/or carvings.

caster: A small wheel attached to the bottom of an article of furniture that allows it to be moved without lifting.

cast iron: *See* wrought iron.

Castor ware: English pottery made in the second and third centuries A.D. Gray earthenware with incised decorations of human and animal figures.

caulking compound: A flexible adhesive used to fill cracks.

C.B.D.: Cash Before Delivery. An arrangement under which the designer must pay the invoice before goods are shipped. Also known as *pro forma*.

cedar: A fragrant redwood used to protect clothes from moths.

ceilings: A much neglected area for decorative interest. Unusual effects can be obtained with any of the following: plaster, Sheetrock, acoustical tile, paneling, wallpaper, murals, plastic mirror, beams, rafters, suspended ceiling with lighting concealed behind it, skylights, tenting, and fabric.

Celadon: A glaze used on Chinese stoneware. Derived from iron, it ranges in color from putty to sea-green.

cellaret: A small wooden chest lined with lead, made to store and cool wine.

center drawer guide: A wooden, U-shaped track fastened underneath a drawer as a guide for ease of operation.

central air conditioning: *See* air conditioning, central.

central vacuuming: A vacuuming system in which the power suction unit is permanently installed in the basement or garage. Plastic feeder lines are run to outlets in each room. To vacuum, a plastic hose is plugged into the wall outlet and suction begins automatically. Adding a central vacuum system to a house offers many advantages, noise reduction and the elimination of the need to move a heavy vacuum cleaner from room to room being the most important.

ceramic tile: First appeared more than 7,000 years ago. It has proven its durability in such structures as the Alhambra, the pyramids, and the Blue Mosque. Still as magnificent today as it was thousands of years ago.

Hundreds of colors and designs are on the market today in a unique variety of glazed finishes. Flexible pregrouted sheets are available that will go over existing floors or walls. They can be used in entry halls, patios, bathrooms, and kitchens.

certosina: A technique of inlaying light-colored material such as bone, ivory, metal, or any pale wood in elaborate designs on a dark ground. A form of **marquetry** or **intarsia,** popular in Lombardy and Venetia during the **Renaissance.**

Chagall, Marc (1887–1985): Russian painter who spent most of his life in France. His style is personal although it has surrealist and expressionist affinities.

chair rail: A molding around the interior walls of a room at a height of about 30 inches from the floor. The area below this railing is called a **wainscot** or **dado.**

chaise longue: An armchair with a long seat that can accommodate the sitter's outstretched legs. Developed in seventeenth-century France as a variant of the **daybed,** this form reached its height of popularity in the late eighteenth century.

chaise percée: A French chair with a caned back and lift-up seat that fits over a bathroom lavatory.

chalk board: Used in a child's room for drawing on. Watercolors can be hung with a magnetic cube. Also used in corporate offices and boardrooms.

chamfer: A beveled or smoothed-off edge on wood or glass.

chandelier: A branched lighting fixture suspended from a ceiling. Available in bronze, silver, glass, crystal, brass, wood, wrought iron, or porcelain.

channeled or fluted back: An upholstered sofa or chair back with rows of vertical tubular fabric channels.

Chantilly: Factory founded at Chantilly, France about 1725, that produced opaque porcelain decorated with small flowers, usually blue.

Chelsea porcelain: A **soft-paste** porcelain first manufactured about 1732 in Chelsea, England. This porcelain, which often copied **Meissen** and **Sèvres** styles, originally was made with a tin-oxide glaze similar to that used on **Delft** pottery. The finest ceramic ware made in England at that time, Chelsea ware contained bone ash, which reduced the risk of it collapsing in the kiln, a fault to which soft-paste porcelain is prone. The forms included scent bottles, toys, animals, flowers, and birds, as well as traditional tableware. The predominant colors were deep blue and gold. The factory was merged with the **Derby** factory in 1770.

cherry: A **hardwood** that responds well to carving and finishing. It is hard, fine-grained, and strong. Pale brown, darkening to deep brown with age.

cherub: A small winged angel-child, usually gilded and used for decorative purposes. Popular from the **Renaissance** onward.

chestnut: A reddish-brown **hardwood,** frequently used for veneering or inlay work and as wall paneling.

chest of drawers: A large **commode;** a wooden case with drawers.

chest-on-chest: A seventeenth-century English furniture form consisting of a **chest of drawers** resting on another, slightly wider one.

cheval glass: A full-length mirror that pivots from vertical uprights or posts. It usually rests on splayed feet.

chiaroscuro: The technique of using light and shade in painting.

chiffonier: A tall, narrow cabinet or chest fitted with drawers, often with a mirror attached.

chimney breast: The front portion of a chimney stack, which contains the flue and projects into a room.

china: High-quality porcelain ware, so named because it was originally made in China. Also refers to dinner dishes.

china cabinet: A tall cabinet, the upper part of which is fitted with two glazed doors and shelves within. The lower por-tion contains drawers or occasionally doors. An eighteenth-century form.

Chinese calligraphy: Highly decorative handwriting with many flourishes. It is regarded by the Chinese as their supreme artistic achievement. There are fundamental rules concerning stroke order, arrangement of written columns, the use of a writing brush, and other elements that define the basic structures within which the art form developed. The history of calligraphy in China spans a period of more than 3,000 years.

chinoiserie: A French term denoting furniture, fabrics, wallpaper, or other decorative items influenced in style by Chinese art. Chinoiserie had its heyday during the seventeenth and eighteenth centuries. Its influence is still seen today in art, architecture, and furniture design.

Chippendale, Thomas (1718–1779): The most famous English cabinetmaker and designer of the Georgian period. In 1754 he published a book entitled the *Gentleman and Cabinet Maker's Director*, a collection of designs that made his reputation. Its influence spread throughout Europe and America. The majority of his designs and designs done for him include a blending of **Chinese, Gothic,** baroque, and rococo styles. Chippendale's early work followed the **Georgian** and **Louis XV** shapes. Some of his collaborators were **Adam,** Lock, and Copeland. The workmanship was superb. The wood he favored was mahogany. He is also known for lacquering, gilding, and painted finishes.

Chirico, Giorgio de (1888–1978): Italian painter whose works are characterized by unearthly effects with a hint of surrealism.

chrome: Comprised of a layer of chrome-plated tubular steel. Before the chrome is plated to the steel a nickel base is usually applied to the steel. This protects the steel from rusting.

Churrigueresque: Pertaining to the **baroque** architecture of Spain and its Latin-American colonies. Characterized by fantastic and lavish detailing. After the Spanish architect, José Churriguera (1650–1723).

cinnabar lacquer: **Lacquer** colored with cinnabar, a red mercuric sulphide.

circuit breaker: A device for interrupting an electric circuit to prevent excessive current (such as that caused by a short circuit) from damaging the circuit or causing a fire.

C.K.D.: Certified Kitchen Designer. A professional who specializes in designing kitchens and who has been certified to that effect.

clavichord: A medieval musical keyboard instrument resembling a spinet piano.

claw-and-ball foot: A carved foot in the form of a bird's or animal's claw holding a ball. Fashionable in the eighteenth century, it was a favorite motif in **Chippendale's** earlier work. An adaptation from a Chinese decorative motif.

clerestory: That part of a building rising clear of the roof or other parts, whose walls contain windows.

Clichy: Industrial suburb of Paris especially noted for its very fine paperweights.

clocks and clock cases: Clocks have a strong appeal for collectors of antiques.

A *wall*, *table*, or *mantel clock* can be used in any room it fits in aesthetically.

Mechanical clocks, invented in about the ninth century, were driven by weights and were wall-hung; however, until the seventeenth century few were found outside of public squares and cathedral towers. In 1520 a clock driven by springs was invented.

The first *pendulum clock* was made either in Venice in about 1656, or by a Dutchman in 1657; no one is certain. This invention was the inspiration for the tall-case, or grandfather clock.

Grandfather clocks provide a point of

interest for stair landings, libraries, and living rooms.

The grandfather clock first appeared in England in 1660 and was about seventy-eight inches high. It was made of oak (later of walnut), with marquetry inlay work. **Chinoiserie,** lacquered, and inlaid mother-of-pearl clock cases were popular at this time. Some had a piece of glass set into the wood, so that the motion of the pendulum could be seen. Dial faces of brass or silver were beautifully engraved.

The tall-case grandfather clock was in standard use in America by 1744. The early cases were of pine or cherry, later of mahogany, and occasionally oak or walnut. In time they became ornate with the use of lacquering and inlay.

In France the grandfather clock was extremely elaborate, ornamented with gilt, brass, bronze, and marble. **Louis XVI** mantel clocks were elegantly and elaborately styled. Cases were either enameled, ormolu-mounted, heavily carved, gold-leafed, or inlaid with alabaster and ebony.

Eli Terry of Connecticut invented the *shelf clock* in 1790. It had wooden works and sold for $20 to $50.

In 1816 Simon Willard designed the *banjo clock* in a variety of cases: mahogany with brass trimmings, painted and decorated, and even glass. Between 1800 and 1860 there were 850 American clock makers in business.

During the **Empire** period many clocks were made of marble, with gilded bronze figures.

cloisonné: A type of decoration using enamel on a metal base. Delicate metal partition-filaments or *cloisons* are laid on the surface of vases and other decorative objects. Colored enamels are then poured into the *cloisons.* Developed in China during the fourteenth century.

clothes press: *See* wardrobe.

cloth of gold: A fabric consisting of a web of silk interwoven with gold or silver. Used for bed hangings and occasionally for upholstery. Introduced into England in the thirteenth century from Spain and Italy.

Coalport: An English ceramic. The Coalport factory concentrated on reproducing eighteenth-century Sèvres porcelain, going so far as to include Sèvres markings.

coaxial cable: A high-frequency telephone, television, or telegraph cable consisting of a central conductor cable surrounded by and insulated from a second larger cable.

cobbler's bench: An Early American shoemaker's workbench with a seat, last holder, bin, and a compartment for tools. Copies are used today as cocktail tables.

cockfight chair: An eighteenth-century English chair with a narrow back; the user straddled the wedge seat facing the back.

cocoa matting: A doormat made of coconut fiber.

coffer: A decorative sunken panel in a ceiling or **soffit.**

coiffeuse: A nineteenth-century French name for a dressing table.

collage (assemblage): An artistic composition created by gluing together and assembling unrelated objects such as maps, wood, newspapers, bits of cloth, or other materials on a flat surface.

colonnade: A series of regularly spaced columns supporting an **entablature** or superstructure.

color: In 1666 Sir Isaac Newton discovered the spectrum and devised the first color system. Today there are many systems: the Munsell, Ostwald, C.I.E., Ridgeway, Lovibond, and a host of others. All have merit, and all are excellent for color identification, color codes, and standardization of colors. These systems are useful for industry, sign painters, paint contractors, artists, textile mills, architects, and untold others, but interior designers *cannot* accept color as a fixed, unyielding, and rigid factor devoid of emotional content. Interior designers think of color as an art, not a science. It is their foremost tool for creating the perfect psychological environment. There are many good theoretical concepts of color harmony that do not apply to the field of interior design. As scientific color systems lack emotional beauty, no color formula will fit all situations or personalities. In exploring the phenomenon of color, experts have determined that few people are born with an instinctive sense of color values and harmony.

There are more than 100,000 colors that can be mixed or made, though we rarely use more than 100. The need for terminology to describe, measure, and use colors thus becomes obvious. Let us begin with the following definitions:

Hue: The technical term for color.
Tint: Hue (color) plus white.
Shade: Hue (color) plus black.
Tone: Hue (color) plus black and white.
Value: The relative darkness or lightness of a hue.
Chroma or saturation: The pureness, intensity, and brilliance of a color.

You can combine any colors for a harmonious effect—if you follow a number of rules. Here are three foolproof color-scheme formulas:
Monochromatic: The use of one color only, in variations of chroma (intensity) and value (light and dark). Add white to taste and a touch of black if desired to create a delightful, soothing scheme. Use

contrasting textures in fabrics for additional interest. If an accent color is desired, use a high-chroma, deep-value color.

Contrasting scheme: Also called *complementary.* This effect is achieved by the use of one warm and one cool color plus some white. The use of a small quantity of black makes the adjacent colors look richer, more vibrant. Remember to vary the chroma (intensity).

Warm Advancing	Red—Rose—Pink Yellow—Gold—Lemon Orange—Peach—Coral Brown—Beige—Tan
Cool Receding	Blue—Turquoise—Chartreuse Green—Olive—Deep Green Violet White Silver

It is most important that in any scheme of two, three, or four colors *the normal spectrum value must be maintained.*

Lighter	Beige—Oatmeal Yellow Green Orange
Darker	Red Blue Violet Brown—Cocoa

For example, if red and green are used together in a room, the red should be darker than the green. If the red is lightened to pink, then the green should be similarly lightened; otherwise, an inharmonious, clashing color scheme will result. The "big secret" of harmonious color combinations is this: *If you follow normal spectrum values, there cannot be any clash of colors, no matter what the combination.*

Triad scheme: An interesting three-color plan can be achieved by using two warm colors and one cool, or two cool and one warm. Adhere to all the rules for chroma and value. This is the only type of scheme to which spectrum values do not always apply (which only proves that color is not an exact science!).

Personal color preferences are influenced by age, climate, geography, and a wealth of other factors. For example, older persons often prefer strong, bright colors. Introverts tend to like soft, cool, subdued colors; extroverts high-chroma, warm colors.

Listed below are the basic laws of color harmony:

1. Pure color, tint and white look good collectively, and best against a light background.

2. Pure color, shade, and black look good collectively, and best against a darkish background.

3. Tints, shades, and tones harmonize well in conjunction.

4. Tints and receding (cool) colors make a room appear larger.

5. Retain normal spectrum values whenever possible.

6. Contrast light against dark.

7. Contrast bright against dull.

8. Contrast warm colors against cool colors.

9. Black and white are neutrals and harmonize with all colors.

10. Do not use equal areas of tints.

11. Do not use equal areas of shades.

12. Do not use equal areas of contrasting colors.

13. Do not use equal areas of bright or intense colors.

14. Do not use equal areas of dull colors.

15. Do not use equal areas of warm and cool colors.

color and sample boards: Interior design presentation aids showing samples of woods, upholstery fabrics, paint colors, carpets, draperies, and pictures or sketches of furniture.

color flag: A series of clippings attached to a fabric sample showing the complete color line.

color therapy: *See* psychology of color.

column: An upright supporting member generally consisting of a cylindrical *shaft*, a *base*, and a **capital**. *See also* Grecian period.

comb-back chair: An eighteenth-century variant of the **Windsor chair** with a horizontal crest rail. The back with its spindles resembles a comb.

commemorative wallpaper or fabric: Printed designs that memorialize a historic event or person.

commode: An ornamental **chest of drawers.** Available in many sizes, plain or with **bombé** fronts. Also seen with **marquetry** panels and **ormolu** mounts.

companion fabric or wallpaper: A material similar in design and coloring to another and designed to be used together in the same room.

Composite order: One of the five classical **orders of architecture.** As the name implies, the Composite order is a composite of the **Ionic** and **Corinthian** orders. This adaptation was developed by the Romans and is often called the *Roman order.* The first known instance of its use was on the arch of Titus in Rome in A.D. 82.

composition (compo): A molded plastic material attached to cabinets for decoration. It is an imitation and substitute for wood carvings and moldings.

concrete: A manmade stonelike material consisting of sand, pebbles, gravel, cement, crushed stone, and water.

conduit: A pipe or piece of tubing used for conveying electrical or telephone wires.

console table: A narrow table fixed to or placed against a wall. Its top is usually made of wood or marble.

Constructivism: *See* modern art.

consultation: Professional interior designers are available for consultation and design services on an hourly basis. Fees vary throughout the United States from $50 to $150 an hour. The professional's function is to explore a client's tastes and personality; provide drawings, sketches, floor plans, and color schemes; and suggest furnishings, wallpaper, lighting, fabrics, furniture designs, carpeting, and draperies. He will make maximum use of space and solve all technical problems, without imposing his taste on the client. Rather, he will *interpret* the client's needs and wishes. Consultation is excellent for those who are seeking general design advice but do not plan to make purchases through their consulting interior designer.

contemporary style: American furniture of the postwar era. Characterized by simplicity, lightness, and elegance of design.

conversation pit: A part of a room in which the floor has been lowered to create a sunken area and furnished with seating.

converter: A company that dyes or has processed its own greige fabric (i.e., fabric that has come off the loom but has not yet gone through the finishing process) into finished goods.

coquillage: A decorative motif in the form of a scallop shell. Popular during the **rococo** period.

corbel: A bracket support or brace to carry the weight of a shelf or console table.

Corinthian order: One of the five classical **orders of architecture.** The most ornate of the orders (and the last to be developed—in the fourth century B.C.), it is similar in most respects to the **Ionic** but is of slenderer proportions. The first great Corinthian temple is the Temple of Zeus at Athens.

cork: The light, porous, elastic outer bark of a Mediterranean oak tree, the cork oak. Used for insulation, wall covering, and for floors.

corner block: A block or other shape fastened into a corner of a furniture frame, used to strengthen cabinet or chair rails. Also used for bracing legs to chair rails.

corner chair: A square chair with high arms and a seat fixed diagonally so that one of the corners faces front. Popular in the eighteenth century throughout Europe and America.

corner cupboard: A cupboard, usually triangular in design, intended to fit into a corner of a room. It either hangs on the wall or stands on three feet. The upper portion is sometimes glazed for the purpose of displaying china.

cornice: Any continuous horizontal projecting member surrounding a building or wall. Also, an ornamental horizontal molding used to conceal drapery hardware, picture hooks, and the like.

cornice or cove lighting: A lighting fixture concealed behind a wooden **cornice** or **cove** in such a way that light is directed upward.

cornucopia: A decorative motif representing a horn of plenty (a horn overflowing with fruits and flowers).

Coromandel screen: A heavily lacquered Chinese screen, dark-brown or black. The design is cut out in intaglio and usually filled in with gold and other colors. These screens were first made for export in the seventeenth century. They were often shipped from the Coromandel coast of India—hence the name.

counterpane: A coverlet or bedspread; originally made with a reversible fabric.

countersink: To enlarge the top part of a hole so that the head of a nail or screw will fit flush with or lie below the surface.

courting chair: *See* love seat.

Covarrubias, Miguel (1904–1957): Mexican painter and illustrator, best-known for his grotesque drawings.

cove: A decorative concave molding at the top of a wall, forming a junction between the wall and the ceiling.

coverlet: A handwoven or crocheted bedspread.

crackle: *See* crazing.

cranberry glass: Clear, light-red glass used for vases, glasses, small boxes, and the like. Made in England.

crazing: A network of fine cracks on the finish of ceramics or surface of cement or furniture. Also referred to as *crackle.*

credenza: A **Renaissance** buffet consisting of drawers and doors and resting on a carved base, occasionally in the form of lion's feet.

credit memo: An instrument that indicates a reduction in the amount of money owed. Covers returned goods and other allowances.

crewel work: Embroidery done with worsted yarn, usually on linen. Originated during the **Jacobean** period.

cricket table: The collector's name for any simply made version of a high, three-legged stool or tripod stand. Originally, the term referred to an eighteenth-century low wooden hearth stool, which was also known as a **trivet.**

crock: Excess dye that rubs off pile fabrics in deep colors.

croft: A small writing or filing cabinet made of wood. Popular in Britain in the late eighteenth and early nineteenth centuries.

cross banding: A decorative band of veneer whose grain is at right angles, or crosswise to, the face of the veneer.

cross section: A cut-through view drawing of an object at right angles to its longest axis.

cross stretcher: *See* X-stretcher.

crown glass: An old form of window glass formed by blowing a globe and whirling it into a disk with a lump in the center, formed by the craftsman's rod.

cruet: A cut-glass bottle used to hold oil or vinegar.

crystal: High-quality glass of brilliant luster, containing a high proportion of lead. When tapped with a fingernail or a hard object, crystal rings.

cubism: *See* modern art.

curio cabinet: *See* vitrine.

Currier and Ives: Famous nineteenth-century lithographers. Their inexpensive colored engravings were very popular because they portrayed American life of that era. Currier and Ives prints are now considered collectors' items.

Curry, John Steuart (1897–1946): American regional painter and lithographer.

curtain wall: A non-load-bearing external wall attached to a building between columns. It can be made of glass, aluminum, and a variety of other materials. It is usually bolted or clamped to the **columns** or floor **slabs.**

curule chair: An **X-frame chair** with two sets of heavy curved legs. Developed by **Renaissance** furniture makers from medieval thrones, this form ultimately dates back to ancient Rome.

curvilinear: Consisting of or enclosed by curved lines.

cut glass: Glass that has had decorative designs incised into it with an abrasive of sand and water.

cyma curve: An S-shaped curve, used for decorative purposes or as the outline of a structural element such as an **ogee molding.**

cypress: A durable **softwood** of the pine family with a scent like that of cedar.

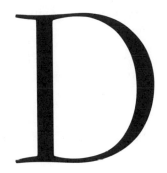

*He is happiest, be he king or peasant,
who finds peace and beauty in his home.*

Goethe (1749–1832)

Dada: *See* modern art.

dado: The lower twenty-seven inches of an interior wall. It can be painted, papered, paneled, or upholstered in one of the fabrics used in the room. It is topped by a wooden molding called either a *chair-rail* or *dado molding*. In architecture, a dado is the section of a **pedestal** between the base and the crown.

dais: A raised platform used in medieval times by the master of the house for his dining area. During the Napoleonic era the raised platform was often used as a place for beds, an idea that is still effective in a large bedroom. Today, the term also refers to a speaker's platform.

Dali, Salvador (1904–): Spanish surrealist painter. He also designs jewelry, glass, furniture, and stage sets.

damascening: Gold, silver, or copper wire inlaid on bronze, iron, or steel for decorative purposes. During the sixteenth century, cabinetmakers mounted or inlaid damascene plaques on furniture.

Danish modern style: A mid-twentieth-century furniture style originating in Denmark, characterized by open-arm, lightweight construction. Danish modern furniture is usually of the highest artistic and quality standards—made for utility and comfort.

Dante chair: A nineteenth-century name for an Italian Renaissance version of the **X-frame chair.** It has two X-frames, one each at the front and rear. The fifteenth-century **Savonarola chair** is fundamentally the same but has a series of X bases. These chairs were normally upholstered in leather or velvet and trimmed with brass nailheads. Named for the great poet, Dante Alighieri, who used a chair of this sort.

davenport: A boxy, upholstered sofa, or a sofa that converts into a bed. Named for a sofa designed around 1900 by the Boston firm Irving & Casson & Davenport. Also, a small eighteenth-century British desk with a slanting, lift-up top that rests on a case, with drawers and cupboards opening on the sides.

Davidson, Jo (1883–1952): American sculptor of portraits who made busts of more than 300 international celebrities.

Davis, Stuart (1894–1964): American cubist and abstractionist.

daybed: A bed used as a sofa, or a sofa-bed used for seating. This dual-purpose furniture form can consist of nothing more than a box spring and mattress on legs, with pillows and bolsters. It can also be an elongated, narrow seating platform with a raised pillowlike end. Daybeds occasionally have high, matching ends made of wood, cane, brass, or wrought iron and are placed lengthwise against a wall.

deal: A British designation for any of the **softwoods,** particularly yellow pine.

decalcomania: A picture or design, printed on specially prepared paper, that is transferred to wood, glass, metal, or other materials. Sometimes used as a substitute for costly hand painting. Very prevalent in America in the early part of the nineteenth century for decorating furniture, such as **Hitchcock chairs.**

decibel: A unit of power ratio employed in measuring the loudness or softness of sound.

deck: In construction, a floor surface without a roof.

deck chair: A folding wooden chair, usually with arms and a full-length leg rest. Commonly used on shipboard. Also known as a *steamer chair*, *desert chair*, and *campaign chair*.

découpage: A technique of decorating a surface with paper cutouts.

deed: A legal document conveying rights to land or a building.

Degas, Edgar (1834–1917): Noted French impressionist painter and sculptor.

de Kooning, Willem (1904–): Dutch-born American abstract expressionist painter.

Delaunay, Robert (1885–1941): French cubist painter and founder of **Orphism** (*see* modern art).

Delftware: Tin-glazed Dutch earthenware. Much of it was made to imitate blue and white Chinese porcelain and Japanese *Imari* ware. Made from the first half of the sixteenth century onwards.

Della Robbia ware: Tin-glazed terra-cotta relief sculpture, originated in Florence by the Della Robbia family in the fifteenth century.

Demuth, Charles (1883–1935): American illustrator and watercolorist.

den: Also referred to as a "library," "study," "family room," or "recreation room," this is a room for both relaxation and a variety of family activities. The essential requirements, including the furniture needed, depend upon the use to which the room will be put, and whether it will be used by adults, children, or both.

Den furnishings may include a game table and chairs, a bar, a soda fountain, a small refrigerator, a high-fidelity unit, a record player or tape machine, and, of course, a television set. If the den is to serve as an auxiliary guest room, a sofa that converts into a bed is a necessity. A fireplace is romantic—a barbecue built into the fireplace is practical. A sewing center can be concealed behind folding doors. If the room is sizable, a raised platform can be built at one end as a stage for children's playacting.

Floor-to-ceiling storage walls or cupboards are handy for storing toys, folding card chairs, card tables, bedding for your convertible sofa, cameras, projectors, and the like. A den is also the perfect room for a home office, in which case it is helpful to have a closet for housing filing cabinets. Provide a desk, chair, and telephone to complete the home office.

If you are a collector of guns, pewter, or other precious possessions, provide a lighted cabinet to house them. The doors should have locks.

Consider a small electric organ or piano if space allows.

A recreation room can be a room for tongue-in-cheek decorating, amusing accessories, and far-out furniture.

It's the room for a personal statement.

Sound- and light-control are extremely important here. It is best to have general illumination plus local lighting; that is, table lamps for reading or writing. Use specific **down-lighting** for game tables, such as ceiling-recessed lights. Bright ceiling lights are particularly important over a bar area. The brighter the lights, the less alcohol will be drunk, but the faster the drinker will feel the effects. Use a light-dimmer for a homey, cozy atmosphere and to encourage intimate conversation.

A bookcase, or preferably a wall of built-in bookcases, is another "must." Books give character to a room; they are practical, colorful, and decorative. Strip-lighting behind frosted glass above the bookcases provides visibility for the books and for any small pieces of sculpture that may be displayed.

Whether you are planning a formal library or a cozy little den with rattan or Early American furniture, comfort is the keynote. The seating should be adequate and commodious, the fabrics durable. For the more formal room, wall-to-wall carpeting, terrazzo, or very dark wood floors with area carpeting are suitable. If the room is informal, waxed brick, vinyl, cork, or ceramic tile may be used. To keep noise down, use a large area rug.

Windows may be shaded, shuttered, or draped. Shades are available of cloth, vinyl, or bamboo. (*See also* draperies.)

Walls can be painted, papered, bricked, paneled, or covered with cork, felt, or murals. (*See also* wall coverings.)

Masses of live plants bring the outdoors in and add a cheerful look.

A two-car garage attached to a house converts easily into a den. A large basement can be transformed into a billiard or bar room, and it is an unsurpassed area for a painting or sculpting studio.

dentil: One of a series of equally spaced small, rectangular blocks used as a cornice molding. Dentils were also used as decoration on fifteenth-century furniture.

Derain, André (1880–1954): French Fauvist painter and illustrator.

Derby porcelain: A fine, often highly ornamented china, manufactured in Derby, England. The earliest specimen is believed to date from 1750, but the years of peak production were 1785 to 1815. The present Royal Crown Derby Company was formed in 1876. The most prominent forms are jars, sauce boats, tableware, and a great variety of ornamental pieces, many modeled after **Dresden** patterns. Human fig-

ures and flowers are prominent decorative motifs.

Derbyshire chair: *See* Yorkshire chair.

De Stijl: *See* modern art.

dhurrie: A flat, woven, fringed rug. Manufactured in India.

diaper work: A regularly repeated surface decoration composed of small checkered or geometrical designs.

Diebenkorn, Richard (1922–): American abstract expressionist.

dining room: Decoration should be planned around the way the occupants live and entertain. A separate dining room is not an emblem of social status. It is for those who would dine graciously and at times formally. Formal dining does not preclude the furniture's being informal Country French, Early American, or any unconventional or bohemian style. The furniture may be made of glass, chrome, Lucite, or wrought iron. A dining room takes to drama; hence, an assembled set is more interesting than an all-matching dining room suite.

One necessary piece of furniture is a wide, long **console table.** It is ideal for buffet supper parties. A traditional buffet will also serve this purpose. The size of the buffet will depend on the storage space required.

Furniture styles, woods, and finishes may be intermixed and still be compatible. This is the room for unusual, daring, and intriguing wallpapers or murals. Since people spend relatively little time in a dining room, treat it with unexpected colors, like red, pink, dark green, or bright yellow combined with large amounts of white. A monochromatic color scheme is a very urbane touch. Drapery treatment will depend on the style of the room. Café curtains, straight-hanging draperies, tied-back curtains, sheers, chintz, lace, or fabric shutters—all are good if imaginatively used. Wall-to-wall carpeting is appropriate, as is an area rug over a dark-planked or parqueted wood floor. Vinyl, terrazzo, or marble in a black-and-white diamond design is elegant.

General illumination and electrified wall sconces can be flattering; however, dimmers should be used. A spotlight can be focused to illuminate just the tabletop for a dramatic effect. Lighted candles play an important role in adding mellowness and charm to any dinner party. Piped-in background music from the den (a good place for a built-in speaker is the bottom of a buffet) transforms an ordinary meal into a banquet.

Diocletian window: A window in the form of a round-headed archway with a narrower section on either side. Also known as a *Palladian* or *Venetian window.*

diptych: A pair of hinged panels that open the way a folding screen does. Both sides of each panel are painted with religious motifs and decorations. Sometimes used as altarpieces.

Directoire style: The furniture style current in France during the revolution that ended the reign of Louis XVI. The actual Directoire period lasted from 1795 to 1799, when Napoleon came into power. It was a time of transition between Louis XVI and the **Empire** period and was characterized by a departure from sumptuousness and overornamentation. The furniture was smaller in scale than Louis XVI-style furniture and much more restrained in terms of ornamentation. Decorative motifs included: oak and laurel crowns, axes, swans, dolphins, lozenges, lyres and wreaths, pikes, and stars. This style was a major inspiration to **Sheraton** and **Phyfe.**

director's chair: A wood-framed folding chair with a canvas seat and back. Also available in chrome or brass with leather seat and back.

distressing: *See* antiquing.

divan: A long, upholstered couch without arms or back, often placed against a wall with pillows. Developed in France in the nineteenth century.

documentary: A printed fabric or wallpaper with a design based on a document dating from the late eighteenth century.

dolphin: A dolphin's head and scaly body was often used as a realistically carved decorative motif on **Renaissance, Louis XIV, Louis XVI, French Empire,** and **British Regency** furniture. A dolphin's head was also used on chair legs and console supports.

dome: A vault of even curvature on a circular base; a circular roof, hemispherical in form.

Dongen, Kees van (1877–1968): Dutch expressionist and Fauvist painter. A superb colorist.

door, window, and room finish schedules: Charts found on working drawings or **blueprints,** giving detailed information about window, door, and room finishes. All information is keyed to the floor plan or elevation drawings.

doorsill: *See* threshold.

Doric order: The simplest and earliest of the Greek **orders of architecture,** characterized by a baseless **column** with twenty flutes. It is found on many Greek buildings, including the famous Parthenon at Athens.

dormer: A window projecting from a sloping attic roof.

dos-à-dos: A eighteenth-century French chair, upholstered in velvet or tapestry, with two attached seats that face in opposite directions, allowing the occupants to sit back to back.

double-acting hinge: A hinge that allows a door to swing in either direction.

double-faced: Reversible. Said of a fabric or material.

double-hung sash window: A window that consists of upper and lower sections (*sashes*), which slide vertically, with a counterweight on each side.

Doulton porcelain: English pottery produced at Lambeth after 1815. The factory produced the Toby Jug, stoneware, pots, mugs, sculptures, terra-cotta statuary, and vases and it included brown stoneware. The factory became the Royal Doulton Potteries.

dovetail joint: A connection of two perpendicular boards by interlocking a fan-shaped **tenon,** or dovetail, into a corresponding **mortise.**

dowel: A short, round wooden pin or peg used in furniture construction. It is glued into a corresponding hole in an adjacent piece of wood to reinforce a joint.

dower furniture: A dowry or bridal chest. The term also refers to a Pennsylvania Dutch "hope" chest, which is decorated with the monogram or initials of the bride.

downlight: A small direct lighting unit that can be recessed, surface-mounted, or suspended.

draperies: Originally, stone walls were draped with tapestries to help keep out the cold. Before separate bedrooms were used, draperies were hung around beds to keep out cold drafts. Later, the utilitarian was subordinated to the decorative, and in the early nineteenth century the tops of windows were ornamented with fanciful carved and gilded cornices that held up the draperies.

The fundamental reasons for draping windows today are to control sunlight, air, view, and privacy and to change the character and personality of a room. Imaginative drapery treatments, of which there are hundreds, can create any mood from traditional to contemporary. Draperies can also be used to give the illusion of more or less space. For example: a room will look larger if the colors of the carpeting and/or the walls are keyed to the major upholstered piece of furniture or draperies. Contrasting and large-printed fabric draperies tend to make a room seem smaller.

Straight-hanging ceiling-to-floor traversed draperies are the most popular today, but draperies that match with period styles are also very much in use.

Draperies should never be skimpy; triple fullness is recommended—that is, the width of the window times three, plus an allowance for the side hems. The headings should contain buckram, a coarse cotton fabric heavily sized with glue, and be pleated.

The major pleats used are: cartridge, accordian, and French. French pleats are the most popular, as they cause the drapery to fall in graceful folds. They consist of three small pleats, which, combined, equal one large pleat. Other headings are: box pleats, pinched pleats, scalloped café pleats, gathering, and smocking.

Beautiful draperies can be created with inexpensive fabrics by using triple fullness and giving attention to styling, color, pattern, and texture.

To black out a room, line or interline the draperies with a blackout lining, which is available in white or gray. If a blackout lining is hung on a separate track at the rear of the draperies, the draperies themselves may be drawn separately for privacy and to allow daylight to filter through. To diffuse direct sunlight, preserve privacy, and soften the hard look of glass, use sheer curtains underneath the draperies. These can be made of nylon, silk, Dacron, voile, organdy, or lace. Alternative window treatments that take the place of sheer curtains include: shutters, very narrow Venetian blinds, woven wooden blinds, and roller shades made of one of the fabrics appearing in the room.

In traditional period rooms, valances or cornices are used as decorative features across the top of the draperies and to conceal drapery hardware. Valances are made of fabric and are pleated, gathered, or shirred, with the bottom straight or scalloped. Cornices are made of wood and are stained, painted, or upholstered in the drapery material or covered in the wallpaper used in the room.

Some suggestions for drapery and other window treatments follow:

1. In an Early American or colonial room, try criss-crossed sheer curtains for a fresh-looking treatment.

2. *Café curtains* will give privacy while letting in light. Café curtains are short curtains—double or triple tiered—hung with brass rings on large, round brass rods. A decorative effect can be obtained by using one lower café curtain and a valance across the top of the window.

3. *Priscilla curtains* are sheer ruffled curtains hung on double rods so that one curtain overlaps the other. The tie-backs used are always ruffled.

4. *Sash curtains* are used over glass inserts in a door. They are made of thin fabric and should be shirred on the top and bottom rods.

5. If a bathroom does double duty as a powder room, conceal the tub by means of straight-hanging or tied-back draperies.

6. A shower stall should have an unbreakable glass door. If there is no shower door, drape the opening with the room's drapery material, which has been waterproofed.

7. Double-faced draperies, or *portieres*, can be hung in an opening between rooms. They are also used as room dividers.

8. *Austrian poufs or shades* are made of accordian rows of scallops. They are formal and feminine and fit well in a powder room. For this type of shade to work easily, it must be made of a thin fabric such as silk or taffeta.

9. *Roman blinds* resemble Austrian shades, except that when drawn up, the effect is one of horizontal accordian pleats.

10. Bamboo or woven wood blinds are ideal for patios, kitchens, informal playrooms, or dens. They are available with bands of colors woven through.

11. Beaded curtains are appropriate for a young person's room. Use with roller shades for privacy. They can also be used to decorate around a tub and as a bed canopy.

12. *Tieback draperies*, as the name implies, are draperies tied back and fastened by hold-backs made of brass, wood, corded tassels, or fabric.

13. *Traversed draperies* can be drawn open or closed with cord pulleys. Electric pulleys are also available, some with remote controls. Remote control switches are available that can be operated anywhere in the room. A switch by the bedside is worthwhile.

14. Frame the three sides of a window with bookshelves, thereby creating a niche; set the draperies inside the recess.

15. *Lambrequin* is a frame or cornice board surrounding a window on three sides. Also called a **pelmet,** it is similar to a picture frame. It is usually covered in one of the fabrics used in the room, or papered to match the walls. Use a lambrequin covered in a floral or stripe and match with a roller shade of the same material. No curtain or drapery is necessary.

16. Allow deep hems for possible future changes in length of draperies.

17. A favorite trick in the living room or dining room is to use two or three paneled screens. They can be freestanding or attached to the window frame with piano hinges.

18. For a distinctive treatment, repeat two or three colors used in a room. This is done by sewing together drapery-weight fabrics of the various colors, resulting in wide alternate-color stripes.

19. Drape windows and walls if necessary to cover up architectural mistakes and to dramatize a room.

20. A narrow room can be made visually wider by draping it from wall to wall and from ceiling to floor.

21. If windows are off center or if there are two different-size windows on one wall, camouflage this architectural fault by extending traverse draperies from wall to wall.

22. Windows need not all be draped alike. An interesting effect can be gained by shuttering one or two windows.

23. French doors are most effectively treated with traversed draperies, if the door is not used too often. Otherwise, install a cornice or valance low enough to just clear the top of the door, and have the draperies draw so that they extend well beyond the door when opened. The simplest way to do this is to shirr the fabric taut on rods at the top and bottom of the glass. The shirred fabric may be trimmed top and bottom with cord or braid and may be banded in the center to create an hourglass effect. One-inch-wide Venetian blinds are also striking.

24. Bay windows can present a decorating problem. Treat them as you would any window, with full-length traversed draperies. Alternatively, you can use continuous glass curtains with side draperies only. A valance can be installed on the inside, or a cornice board can be installed across the front of the bay inside the room. Shutters are also charming.

25. Treat corner windows as a single unit. Do not create the effect of two separate windows.

26. Extra-high windows are attractive if permanent shutters are attached from the sill to the floor, or café curtains are hung slightly above the sill and descend to the floor. Another solution is to use three tiers of café curtains.

27. Clerestory windows accept shutters, café curtains, or simple straight-hanging draperies to four inches below the sill.

28. Dormer windows look best when treated with two-tiered café or priscilla curtains.

29. Kitchen, service area, and breakfast room windows lend themselves to short sill curtains, bamboo shades, plastic roller shades, or shutters. Glass shelves installed in a window provide a place for small plants.

30. View or picture windows with vast expanses of glass can be treated with a solution to eliminate glare and ultraviolet rays, and thus prevent fading. If the view is grand and does not receive too much sunshine, the window may not require draping. Nevertheless, everybody deserves privacy, and unless a window is draped in some manner, an expanse of glass at night is creepy, cold, and foreboding.

31. *Grillwork and latticework* are very decorative if in harmony with the decoration of the room, but they do not always provide privacy. Traversed glass curtains are adequate for this purpose.

32. *Roller shades* are available in light-proof plastic materials of all colors and textures. Patterned shades can be made to match wallpapers, curtains, or bedspreads. They can be made of lace, silk, chintz, or ticking, and can be painted or stenciled. They can be vinyl-impregnated for durability.

33. Hang a drapery on a ceiling track and use it as a room divider.

34. *Shoji screens* with panels of translucent plastic offer the flavor of the Orient. While allowing light in, they keep prying eyes out.

35. The modern one-inch, very thin Venetian blind provides more than total privacy. It also produces total visibility when necessary. No tapes are needed, as the louvers are supported by nearly invisible polyester cords. These blinds are available in many colors. When hung from the ceiling they may also be used as room dividers.

36. *Shutters* are available with vertical as well as the usual horizontal louvers. Louvers can be eliminated and fabrics installed, repeating one used in the room. Mirrored shutters are handsome and will magnify the size of the room.

37. For an unusual look, provide an underdrapery or glass curtain of the same material as the overdrape.

38. For children's rooms, economical draperies, bedspreads, window shades, canopies, and slipcovers can be made out of ready-made colored and patterned bed sheets.

Deciding on drapery fabrics: A large room can stand large floral patterns, heavy casement fabrics, even velvets. Draperies can be topped with festoons and cascades. A small room calls for simple solid-color fabrics or modest stripes, which add height to a room. A formal room requires antique satins, silks, taffetas, damasks, brocades, or failles. An informal room calls for rough cottons, plaids, chintzes, linens, denims, and novelty textures. Using the same floral pattern for draperies and at least one upholstered piece helps tie the room together. When combining two printed fabrics in one room, the size of the patterns must be different; one must be considerably larger than the other. Fiberglass, when available, is a sun- and soil-resistant fabric, and works well in a library or den.

Fabrics must relate in weight, feeling, scale, and texture to the period style and furnishings of a room. For example, use a rough texture, a linen, or a **crewel**-embroidered fabric in a den or room with a heavy or masculine feeling.

If the walls are covered in a patterned paper, the draperies should be plain or striped, although small dots or an inconspicuous self-pattern is permissible.

An open-weave fabric, or a *casement cloth*, does not need lining, but fabrics like chintzes and satins do.

Draperies deteriorate for a number of reasons:

1. Sun: Line the draperies or have windows treated to eliminate ultraviolet rays.

2. Fading: Caused by fabrics not being vat-dyed and being exposed to sunlight.

3. Shredding: This hazard is as recent as smog. Tobacco smoke and natural chemicals in the air, combined with humidity, can cause it.

4. Rise and fall: Preshrinking the fabric helps, but moisture or dryness in the air will cause up-and-down changes in the length of the draperies.

draw table: *See* refectory table.

Dresden: *See* Meissen.

dresser: A **Gothic** sideboard with a high back and shelves, used for preparing food. Today, the term refers to a low **chest of drawers,** five or six feet long and normally thirty-six inches high.

dressing table: A table or stand, usually surrounded by a mirror, in front of which one sits while applying makeup.

drop-in seat: *See* slip seat.

drop-leaf table: Any table with hinged flaps or leaves at either end, which when raised, extend the length of the top.

drop shipment: A shipment made to a client or any address other than that of the interior designer.

drum table: A British **neoclassical** style **pedestal table,** circular or polygonal in shape, with a deep apron, often with drawers. The top usually rotated on the pedestal.

dry point: A technique of engraving in which a fine, hard needle incises lines on a copper plate without using acid. Also, a picture printed from such a plate.

dry rot: A fungous disease that causes lumber to become brittle and crumble into a powder.

dry sink: A nineteenth-century American kitchen cupboard with a sink lined in zinc, generally with cabinets below. Today it is often used as a bar or a planter.

dry-wall construction: The application of Masonite or other prefabricated paneling to walls. Used as an alternative to costly plastering.

du Bois, Guy Pène (1884–1958): American satirical genre painter.

Dubuffet, Jean (1901–): French modernist painter and sculptor. Difficult to classify as to style.

Duchamp, Marcel (1887–1968): French-American artist. A founder of **Dada.**

duchesse: An eighteenth-century upholstered **chaise longue,** consisting of two **bergères** and an **ottoman.** The separate elements could be attached to one another or used separately.

duck foot: *See* pad foot.

duct: Any tube, canal, pipe, or conduit in which a fluid or cool or warm air is conducted or conveyed.

Dufy, Raoul (1887–1953): French Fauvist painter, lithographer, and fabric designer.

dumbwaiter: An eighteenth-century English invention consisting of several re-volving tiers or trays affixed to a central post. Used as a serving table. Also a small elevator used for transporting food from the kitchen to upper floors.

dust board: A thin horizontal wooden panel set between the drawers of a chest or dresser, for protection against dust.

dust ruffle: A shirred or pleated skirt that hangs from a box spring to the floor.

Dutch colonial style: Massive, stolid, heavy, **baroque**-type furniture of the late seventeenth and eighteenth centuries, found in New York and along the Hudson valley. Perhaps the best-known form of this period was the **kas,** a large, painted cabinet whose doors were primitively carved with fruits and flowers. Painted finishes were the most common decorative medium. The term *Dutch colonial* also applies to an American building with a **gambrel roof.**

Dutch cupboard: A large buffet with attached open shelves above it, resembling a **Welsh dresser.** Used to display china and plates.

Dutch door: A door divided in half horizontally so that either half can be opened separately.

dutchman: A piece of wood inlaid to fill

in a defect or large chip in another piece of wood.

Dutch metal: An alloy of copper and zinc, used in place of gold leaf.

Dutch settle: An eighteenth- to nineteenth-century **settle** with a hinged back that can be converted into a table.

eagle: A decorative motif adopted as the seal of the United States by act of Congress in 1786. Employed since the days of antiquity as a carved ornament and symbol of military power. Revived in the eighteenth century in **baroque** work. During the Napoleonic period, the eagle was made use of in carvings and bronzes and printed on fabrics. It has been popular in America as a patriotic design for furniture decoration since 1788. It is used profusely as a **finial** on mirrors and to top off **banjoclocks.**

Eames, Charles (1907–1978): A highly innovative and influential American furniture designer. Particularly noted for his chair designs, which influenced furniture production on an international scale. In 1940 Eames collaborated with Eero Saarinen in designing a revolutionary chair of molded, curved plywood—the famous Eames chair. Other Eames contributions include: a modular storage system (1950), the Eames lounge chair and ottoman (1956), and a number of experimental films.

Early American style: When the colonies were first founded, each colony made furniture and built houses in the style of the country from which they had emigrated. These styles were simplified for economic reasons and lack of technical know-how. Later, craftsmanship became very fine; nevertheless, the informal, casual look remained. The native woods used were those that were plentiful, such as pine, maple, oak, and birch. Dutch tiles were popular. Colors were bright and gay. The favorite fabrics were chintzes, the favorite floor covering, hooked rugs.

ears: The wings of a **wing chair.**

earthenware: Any object made of clay that has been baked or hardened by fire. That is, all pottery except **stoneware.**

easement: A legal right-of-way for use of another's property for a specific purpose. It cannot be sold or disposed of without consent of the legal owner. An easement is usually given without remuneration.

Eastlake, Charles Locke (1836–1906): English writer and designer whose 1868 book, *Hints on Household Tastes*, greatly influenced American tastes. His style was adapted from **Japanese** and **Gothic** furniture. The patterns were specifically designed for manufacture by machine. The wood he used most often was cherry.

easy chair: Any large chair conducive to comfort and lounging.

eave: The lower, overhanging portion of a sloping roof, near the walls.

ébéniste: A seventeenth-century French cabinetmaker who worked with ebony wood. Today it denotes a master cabinetmaker particularly distinguished in fine veneering.

ebony: A hard, black, tropical wood. Dense in texture, this heavy wood takes a high polish. Used for piano keys, novelties, and for various types of furniture.

eclecticism: The effect achieved in a room by selecting and mixing forms and motifs from various schools of design and period styles.

egg-and-dart: A carved decorative border ornament, common in classical architecture. Introduced in the sixteenth century, it is composed of a running pattern of ovals alternating with arrowheads or darts.

eggshell china or porcelain: An extremely thin variety of porcelain ware originating in China during the fifteenth century. Today it is manufactured by Japanese, British, and Irish factories.

Egyptian style: The architectural style developed by the ancient Egyptians (4000 B.C.–A.D. 300) featured pyramids, obelisks, monoliths, pylons, and lotus columns. Furniture forms included chests, tables, folding chairs, and X-legged stools, the tops covered with leather or rush. Upholstering as such was unknown. Various conventionalized animal forms were used as legs. Woods used included acacia, sycamore, cedar, and olivewood. Common motifs were the scarab, the solar disk, sphinxes, rams, reeds, and lilies. The style is a curiosity now; however, it was revived temporarily during the **Empire** period.

Eilshemius, Louis (1864–1941): American "mood" painter.

elevation: A drawing representing a vertical right-line projection of a building, an exterior, or interior wall.

Elgin marbles: Fifth-century Greek sculptures and friezes removed from the Parthenon by Lord Elgin (1766–1841) during the years 1801 to 1803. They are now located in the British Museum in London.

Elizabethan style: An outgrowth of the classic **Renaissance** style that prevailed during the last phase of the **Gothic** period, the Elizabethan style of furniture, developed in the years 1558–1603, is characterized by massive, bulbous cabinet and table supports, Italian Renaissance carving, baluster turnings, and **gadroons.** Stretchers on tables were placed low and were square. Also typical of the period were **finials** carved in the form of human heads. Characteristic decorative motifs were acanthus leaves, caryatids, scrolls, the Tudor rose, interlacing straps, masks, and swags. Important rooms were paneled in oak; fireplaces were elaborate. Ceilings were of plaster, with relief decorations. This style is rarely found in America today.

elm: A tough, resilient **hardwood** used in cabinetmaking, especially as a decorative **veneer.** The heartwood is lightish brown in color. White elm is used for flooring, boat building, and bentwood work.

embossing: A raised effect created when metal rollers impress a design in the back of a wallcovering, metal, leather, or fabric.

embrasure: A splayed enlargement of a door or window toward the inner face of a wall outward from the window frame.

embroidery: The ornamentation of fabric with needlework. First practiced by the Egyptians.

Empire style: A French **neoclassical** style of the early nineteenth century, named for France's First Empire, created by Napoleon in 1804. Indeed, Napoleon hired two architects, Fontaine and Percier, to create a style in his honor. They did a straight job of copying antique Greek, Roman, and Egyptian forms and motifs. The furniture was massive and imposingly grand, decorated with symbols of imperial pomp. Its elegant severity was offset by brass mountings and classical ornamentation such as wreaths, swags, swans, laurel branches, sphinxes, bees, crowns, and the initial ''N.''

Fabrics were woven with the same symbols and ornamentation, plus medallions and stripes. The colors favored by Napoleon were brilliant greens, reds, and yellows. Marble was used extensively, especially for the tops of pedestal tables. Rosewood, mahogany, and ebony were the woods used, and they were often inlaid with bronze and silver. This grandiose style swept through Europe and America and influenced the designers of those countries. In Germany, a bourgeois adaptation of the Empire style was called **Biedermeier.**

The Empire style is still popular today.

enamel: A glossy substance applied by fusion to the surface of metal, pottery, or porcelain.

encaustic: A method of painting or decorating in which colored beeswax is applied and fused with hot irons.

encoignure: A French corner cupboard of the eighteenth and nineteenth centuries. It stood on three or four feet and had a diagonal or curved front.

end table: Any type of small table used at the end of a sofa or beside a chair.

English Regency style: This style, which was popular in the years 1805–1835, coincided with the **Empire** style in France, **Biedermeier** in Germany, and Duncan Phyfe's **Federal** style in America. Furniture was modeled after the French Empire and **Directoire** styles. **Neoclassicism** set in as the style evolved. Decorations embraced everything from Egyptian sphinxes to Chinese motifs. **Thomas Hope** was the foremost designer during this epoch.

English silver: *See* silver.

engraving: A print obtained by the process of incising lines into a plate.

entablature: The upper section of a classical **order**, including the architrave, cornice, and frieze.

entasis: In architecture, the almost imperceptible swelling of the shaft of a **column** in the middle so that the column appears perfectly straight.

entrance: Whether called a foyer or an entry hall, an entrance creates an important first impression. Even the most diminutive entrance hall should be an impressive prelude to the rest of the house and should be decorated to give an illusion of space and a feeling of welcome. If an entry hall does not exist, the effect of one can be created by the use of a screen, a room divider, or a translucent plastic or glass partition. Many times a sofa in an adjoining room can be placed in such a manner that its back helps to create the illusion of a separate entryway.

An entrance hall is unique in that it is a room where appearance is most important. It can be formal or informal, elegant or beautifully understated. It can be the focal point of a collection or impart a clue to the style of the rest of the house. From a practical standpoint, a closet for wraps and a small-scale console or cabinet with a mirror above are advisable, as are a chair, bench, or a live plant. A table lamp or unusual center light fixture adds glamor. If the inner hallway is wide enough, build bookcases with cabinets from a height of thirty inches down to the floor; invaluable storage space will thus be acquired. Build shelves above to house books, objects of art, or a hobby collection. The opposite wall is often a good place for family pictures.

If spacious enough, the foyer is an excellent place for a bar; however, traffic patterns must not be impeded. Aside from wall-to-wall carpeting, practical flooring materials are: tile, terrazzo, cork, spatter-dash-painted floor, flagstone, marble, stone, slate, wood planks, vinyl, brick, or black and white squares of rubber. A sensational result is produced by inlaying brass stripes or decorative inserts of contrasting colors into vinyl, cork, terrazzo, marble, or rubber.

Regardless of the size of the entry, wallpaper can be overscaled and dramatic. If the entry is small, a space-expanding scenic or mural will give the impression of spaciousness. A mirrored wall also creates the illusion of space. If there is no guest closet, antique coat racks, pegs, unusual brass coat hooks, or antique hat racks are useful. Victorian hall trees can be used to hold coats, hats, and umbrellas.

epergne: An elaborate, tiered table centerpiece of glass or silver, with arms supporting small dishes for flowers, candies, and nuts. Some epergnes are also fitted with candle holders.

Epstein, Jacob (1880–1959): British sculptor, born in New York City, who specialized in portraits and figures.

ergonomics: *See* biotechnology.

Ernst, Max (1891–): German-born American surrealist painter and sculptor.

escritoire: An early English **Georgian** writing desk that contained many compartments, pigeonholes, and secret and standard drawers.

escutcheon: A decorative metal plate surrounding a keyhole or door handle and protecting the edges of the veneer.

espagnolette: A small wooden or bronze sculpture in the form of a female bust, used as a mount at the top of a furniture leg or as a terminal ornament at the top of a cabinet column or post. Found primarily on **Régence** and **Louis XV** style furniture.

étagère: A cabinet of open shelves, sometimes pyramidal in shape, which is used for the display of curios or accessories. It is frequently designed to fit into a corner of a room and is sometimes called a *whatnot*. Étagères date back to the **Louis XV** period but are very much in use today, in such materials as glass, chrome, brass, and Lucite.

etching: A method of **engraving** or

drawing on a metal or glass plate by the action of acid on a wax coating. A print is then made from the etched plate.

Evergood, Philip (1901–1973): American social protest painter.

ewer: A large, wide-mouthed pitcher or jug used during ancient times to hold water for washing the hands after eating.

It usually rested on a decorated dish or basin.

expansion joint: A joint between two parts of a structure that allows expansion or contraction, as from heat or cold, without structural damage.

expressionism: *See* modern art.

*This is the true nature of a home—
it is the place of Peace; the shelter,
not only from all injury, but from
all terror, doubt, and division.*

Beardsley Ruml (1894–1960)

Fabergé, Peter Carl (1846–1920): Russian goldsmith and jeweler of note. His workmanship in translucent enamel and gold is unsurpassed to this day. He was best known for his gold and jeweled Easter eggs made for the czar.

fabrics: *See* textiles.

façade: The face or front of a building. Also, the front of a chest or cabinet that resembles an architectural exterior.

facing: The finishing material applied to the outer surface of a building, such as glass, brick, stone, or wood.

faience: Fine, cream-colored terra cotta or earthenware covered with a decorative glaze to simulate fine porcelain. First made in Faenza, Italy, hence its name.

family room: *See* den.

fan-back chair: A **Windsor chair** having a back of vertical spindles fanning out from the seat to the top rail. Also, an upholstered high-backed chair with a back shaped like a half barrel.

fanlight: A semicircular window above a door or window in **Georgian** and **Regency** buildings, often with sash bars arranged like the ribs of a fan.

farthingale chair: A **Jacobean** period chair, low, upholstered, and made without arms in order to accommodate the farthingales or wide-hooped dresses of the era.

fascia: A wide board used as a horizontal facing, nailed under the eaves of a building.

F.A.S.I.D.: Fellow of the **American Society of Interior Designers.**

fauteuil: A French, open-sided upholstered armchair, first made in the seventeenth century and still popular today.

Fauvism: *See* modern art.

faux: French word meaning imitation, false. Said of imitation wood, tortoiseshell, marble, etc.

Federal period: The first half century in the United States following the American Revolution. In terms of furniture design, this marked the end of the colonial period and the beginning of **Duncan Phyfe's** most fruitful years. Another important designer of the period was the architect Samuel McIntire, who did excellent copies of the **Adam** style.

The Federal period in America coincided with the **Regency** in England and the **Empire** in France. Phyfe, an American cabinetmaker born in Scotland, borrowed design elements from and adapted the forms of the English and French cabinetmakers. **Adam, Hepplewhite, Sheraton,** and the **Empire** styles were his inspirations. Phyfe's favorite motif was the American emblem, the eagle. Other Federal motifs were the lyre, the acanthus leaf, the cornucopia, and the trumpet.

Brass was employed extensively for feet, casters, and hardware, with glass and china knobs used as drawer pulls later in the period. American designers favored mahogany, cherry, maple, and rosewood. The popular fabrics were silk, taffeta, satin, and printed cottons. In a more simplified form this style is still in great demand today.

fees and compensations: There is no regulatory body of interior designers that sets fees and compensations. Professional interior designers (for instance, members of the **A.S.I.D.**), when working in the residential field, charge fees that are competitive with local retail prices. For that reason, even a family of modest income can often avail itself of the services of a recognized professional interior designer. If budget considerations do not permit doing an entire home at one time, the professional designer will work out a long-range plan, beginning with one room, or even one piece of furniture.

The professional interior designer is available on an hourly or per diem basis. This practice is particularly helpful when a client is seeking general design advice but does not plan to make purchases through the designer. An hourly charge basis is used for services rendered in collaboration with architects, contractors, and tradespeople. This is money well spent, as it can help the client avoid costly mistakes.

For commercial jobs, the designer usually charges a flat fee, which compensates for travel, design talent, layouts, specifications, working drawings, consultation and shopping time, research, installation, and supervision. The interior designer receives an advance of $33\frac{1}{3}$ to 50 percent at the signing of the contract and before work commences.

Feininger, Lyonel (1871–1956): American watercolorist, influenced by cubism and orphism.

fender: A low, decorative metal guard placed before an open fireplace to keep cinders or logs from falling out.

fenestration: An architectural term denoting windows and their arrangement.

ferrule: A metal cap or band fitted over or around a furniture leg to strengthen it and prevent the wood from splitting. Ferrules made of brass can be decorative features.

festoon: A decorative carving or painting in the form of leaves, fruits, flowers, or fabric arranged in scalloplike swags or loops on draperies or poster beds.

fiddle back: A chair back with a single **splat** that resembles a violin. Originally found on **Queen Anne** side chairs in the early eighteenth century.

F.I.D.E.R.: Foundation for Interior Design Education and Research. The accreditation program for interior design schools sponsored by **A.S.I.D.,** the American Society of Interior Designers.

filigree: Intertwined gold or silver wire worked into an interlaced ornamental pattern, often resembling lace. Found on traditional furniture, as well as on jewelry, small boxes, and other novelties.

finial: An ornamental knob placed at the top or apex of a piece of furniture such as a bedpost or a lamp. In architecture, an ornament at the top of a gable, pinnacle, or newel post; customarily in the form of a knob, pineapple, or foliage.

finishing and refinishing: The process of applying stain, paint, varnish, lacquer, polish, shellac, oil, wax, or various chemicals to raw wood to preserve and protect it and to bring out its beauty.

Gold leaf and other metals can also be applied, as well as *faux* marble, tortoiseshell, porphyry, and malachite. These effects are generally best left to experts. For the nonprofessional finisher, there are many products on the market for quick and easy finishing and refinishing of any wood surface. An oil finish, for example, is a fast, easy way to create that professional handrubbed appearance on wood. Such a finish is easily maintained. It is imperative, however, to do the finest possible sanding job before applying the oil.

No valuable antique should ever be restored except by an expert. To preserve furniture, dust regularly and wax occasionally. Before waxing, the wood must be perfectly clean, free of any stickiness caused by the buildup of old wax, dust, and oil. Wash the surface lightly with a mild soap solution and dry thoroughly. Wax should be applied very thinly over a small area at a time. Polish with a soft flannel, rubbing with the grain. When many thin coats of wax have hardened and built up, a **patina** will result, and the wood will become water-, alcohol-, and heat-resistant.

fir: The wood of various evergreen trees, most of which grow on the west coast of the United States and Canada. It is soft but durable and is used for interior construction and interior parts in furniture. Unfortunately, it does not take a finish well. Called *deal* in Europe, where it is used mainly for interior structures and ship building.

fire brick: A refractory brick made of special clay hardburned to resist heat. Used for lining furnaces, chimneys, fireplaces, etc.

firedogs: *See* andirons.

fire door: A one- or two-hour fireproof door, generally metal-faced on one side. Customarily used between a garage and the dwelling on which it abuts.

fireplace: Once used for cooking and protection from frigid temperatures, today a fireplace may be one of the aesthetic focal points of a room, because it is a center of interest or activity. It also determines the positioning of furniture. In a small den, a raised hearth or sitting platform surrounding the fireplace imparts a feeling of intimacy. If a room does not have a built-in fireplace, pre-fabricated factory-built units are available and cost about half as much as all-masonry fireplaces. Any fireproof facing can be used, from simulated masonry to real rock. Factory-assembled, freestanding, cast-iron fireplaces are economical and are easily installed. They can be placed island-fashion in the center of the room, with seating around them, or they can be located against a wall or in a corner. They are designed to burn wood, gas, or electric logs and are available in many pleasing colors. Fireplace walls can be of stone, marble, wood paneling, copper, brick, antique mirror, tile, travertine, or plaster. Decorative overmantel treatments are limitless—a painting, a planted **lavabo,** a mirror, a hood, a piece of sculpture, carvings, a clock, a candelabra, a barometer, plates, a tapestry, an Oriental screen, or a family coat of arms. Accessories for a mantel shelf include candlesticks, vases, clocks, figurines, plants, sculpture, antique toys, obelisks, and porcelain birds.

To determine the proper width of a fireplace opening, calculate the sum of the length and width of the room, then allow one inch to the foot. For example: if a room is fifteen by twenty feet, the sum is thirty-five feet; thus, the width of the fireplace opening should be thirty-five inches.

fire screen: A metal protecting screen placed in front of a fireplace to act as a spark arrester and to protect those seated nearby from excessive heat. The *cheval screen*, developed in the Middle Ages, is a low panel placed in front of the fire. The *pole screen*, developed in the seventeenth century, has a sliding panel of wood with a needlepoint, tapestry, or leather insert. It can be adjusted to any height and is set between the fireplace and a seated person to protect the face from the heat of the fire.

flammability: Under Federal Standard DOC FF 1-70 (issued under the authority of the Flammable Fabrics Act), all carpets and rugs manufactured for sale in the United States or imported into the United States must meet the following standard: no more than one of eight specimens shall burn a distance of three inches from the point of ignition when tested according to a prescribed method. This standard is generally believed to provide an adequate measure of the hazard where carpet is the first item ignited.

flashing: Sheets of metal or other material used to exclude water from a junction between a roof and another surface.

flatware: Utensils such as knives, forks, spoons, and flat dining dishes and plates.

Flemish scroll: A **baroque** furniture motif found on chair legs, consisting of two intersecting and oppositely curved C scrolls.

fleur-de-lis: A decorative motif in the form of a lily, used as a heraldic device since medieval times. The coat of arms of past French royalty, it is still a national emblem in France.

flex: A flexible metal channel for conveying electric wiring.

flint glass: A soft, lustrous, lead-oxide glass developed by George Ravenscroft about 1674. It has high refraction and low dispersion. Also called *lead glass*.

flip-top table: A table top that unfolds, doubling the size of the top area.

flitch: A longitudinal cut from the trunk of a tree.

flocking: *See* wallpaper.

flooring: A wealth of materials is available for this purpose. Flooring is considered the "fifth wall," for it relates to the room as much as the walls. Choice depends on the purpose of the room, the period of the furniture used, and the amount of traffic it will have to withstand.

Resilient flooring is available in two basic forms: sheet goods and nine- or twelve-inch squares (and various odd shapes). Some resilient flooring does not lend itself to installation on or below grade:

TILE ESTIMATOR		
SQUARE FEET	NUMBER OF TILES 9″ × 9″	NUMBER OF TILES 12″ × 12″
10	18	10
20	36	20
30	54	30
40	72	40
50	89	50
60	107	60
80	143	80
100	178	100

Vinyl comes in a permanent polished finish that eliminates the necessity of waxing. Cushioned vinyls are available; they have a layer of rubber under the surface, which makes it easy to walk on. It also muffles sound but does not recover from heel marks or denting very easily.

Asphalt tile is inexpensive, but it is brittle, cracks easily, and is noisy.

Linoleum is the most economical, if not always the most decorative form of resilient flooring. It is acid-resistant.

Plastic-coated cork tile is soft underfoot, wears well, and has the advantage of warmth.

Rubber tile is warm, quiet, very durable, and easy to maintain, as is all resilient flooring. All that is required is damp-mopping and waxing with a water-based, self-polishing wax twice a year. The amount of resilient floor tile needed depends on the area of the room. Allowance must also be made for waste. The following table will serve as a quick estimating guide.

Nonresilient flooring is also available in many forms.

Glazed or *quarry tiles* come in a variety of shapes, sizes, and colors, and last indefinitely. All they need for upkeep is soap and water. Ceramic tiles are perfect for areas like foyers and patios where there is a great deal of traffic, but they are cold, slippery, and noisy.

Brick floors are appropriate for country rooms, entry halls, or kitchens. Brick can be sealed and polished with a nonslip wax.

Slate and *flagstone* are suitable for entrance halls. *Marble* and *terrazzo* can be used in any room of a house.

MAINTENANCE OF TILE, MARBLE, BRICK, AND SLATE

Glazed and unglazed ceramic floors: Damp mop with soapless detergent. If badly soiled, make a paste with powdered household cleanser. Apply and let stand for five minutes, then rub with a stiff brush and rinse. Scouring powder on a toothbrush cleans joints (grouts). Use washing soda on grease- or oil-stained joints. On quarry tile, add a protective coating of an oil-base sealer.

Marble and terrazzo: Protect with a penetrating sealer compound. Clean with very soapy warm water. Rinse, then wax.

Brick: Damp mop glazed brick. Rough-cut brick requires a sealer. Use silicone or a liquid acrylic sealer, then wax.

Slate: Dry mop and clean with a mild liquid soap and water.

Wood floors: Wood floors are strong and actually become more beautiful with age. For warmth, beauty, durability, and low maintenance, prefinished, plastic-impregnated wood flooring is recommended. Luxury woods are offered in a wide variety of pattern arrangements. Strip flooring, plank flooring, and parquetry are the major types used.

Strip flooring: Strips that are **tongue-and-grooved** and can be purchased in several widths.

Plank flooring: The same as strip flooring, but wider.

Parquetry: Mosaic work of wood. Easily laid over most flooring. Unlimited possibilities for designs and patterns. Adaptable to both commercial and residential use because of high wear resistance combined with low maintenance cost. Some of the patterns available are: basket weave, basket weave diagonal, herringbone, diamonds, squares, brick, and checkerboard.

MAINTENANCE OF HARDWOOD FLOORS

Food spots: a damp cloth will often do the job. If a cleaned-up spot looks dull, apply a little wax.

White spots: Rub lightly with fine steel wool that has been dampened with wax or mineral spirits. Wipe dry and wax lightly.

Water spots: Try *white spots* remedy first. If no results, rub with fine sandpaper, wipe with mineral spirits, touch up with stain, and then wax.

Dark (or dog) spots: Try *white spots* or *water spots* treatment. If no results, try applying household bleach or oxalic acid to spot and let stand one hour. Rinse with wet cloth, wipe dry, smooth with fine sandpaper or steel wool, touch up with stain, and wax.

Ink stains: Use household bleach or oxalic acid, or sand lightly. Wash with mineral spirits. Retouch with stain, then wax.

Greasy spots: Rub with fine steel wool dipped in mineral spirits.

floor plan: A horizontal section drawing showing the arrangement of passages and apartments, the placement of doors and windows, and the thickness of walls and partitions.

floor slab: A reinforced concrete floor, customarily four inches thick.

flounce: A gathered or pleated strip of fabric used for the bottom of upholstered seating pieces to conceal the legs. Also, the bottom part of a two-piece bedspread.

flue: A passage or duct to carry smoke up a chimney.

fluorescent lamp: A discharge lamp with a fluorescent phosphor coating on the inside of the bulb that transforms ultraviolet energy into visible light.

flush door: A door that fits into the face or framework so that the surface is level and flush.

flutes, fluting: Narrow vertical grooves carved on classical columns, pilasters, bedposts, furniture legs, and cabinet or table aprons. It was a popular feature on furniture designed by **Adam, Chippendale,** and **Phyfe.** It is commonly used on pressed glass as well.

flying buttress: A **buttress** connected with a wall at some distance from it by an arch or part of one. It serves to resist outward pressure.

F.O.B.: Free On Board. This term indicates the point of origin from which the interior designer is to pay freight or any other shipment charges.

focal point: The point of emphasis in a room, such as a fireplace, an armoire, a bar, a music center, a view, or the central axis of a wall.

foil wallpaper: A thin sheet of flexible metal foil laminated to a paper back.

footcandle: A unit for measuring illumination. It is equal to the amount of direct light thrown by one candela on a square foot of surface every part of which is one foot away.

RECOMMENDED FOOTCANDLE LEVELS

OFFICE AREA	FOOTCANDLES ON TASKS*
General Offices	
Reading poor reproductions, business machine operation, computer operation	150
Reading handwriting in hard pencil or on poor paper, reading fair reproductions, active filing, mail sorting	100
Reading handwriting in ink or medium pencil on good-quality paper, intermittent filing	70
Private Offices	
Reading poor reproductions, business machine operation	150
Reading handwriting in hard pencil or on poor paper, reading fair reproductions	100
Reading handwriting in ink or medium pencil on good-quality paper	70
Reading high-contrast or well-printed materials	30
Conferring or interviewing	30

OFFICE AREA	FOOTCANDLES ON TASKS*
Accounting Offices	
Auditing, tabulating, bookkeeping, business machine operation, computer operation	150
Drafting Rooms	
Detailed drafting & designing, cartography	200
Rough layout drafting	150
Conference Rooms	
Critical seeing tasks	100
Conferring	30[a]
Note taking during projection	30[b]
Washrooms	30[a]
Elevators, Escalators, Stairways	20[a]
Corridors	20[a,c]

*ANSI standards are given in ESI (Equivalent Sphere Illumination). If there are luminaires or windows located where their brightness can reflect specularly in the task, more footcandles may be required to provide the recommended ESI. For more favorable lighting and task geometry, recommended ESI can be achieved with lower footcandles. For further information see ANSI #A132.1—1973.

Notes
[a] Footcandles rather than ESI.
[b] Controllable (dimmer).
[c] But no less than 20% of illumination in adjacent areas.

footing: A foundation to a wall or the projecting base of a column.

footlambert: A unit of luminance equal to the luminance of a surface emitting a luminous flux of one lumen per square foot.

foot warmer: A portable hot-water container made of copper or other materials.

formica: *See* laminate.

formwork: Forms of plywood or steel into which wet concrete is poured. When the concrete is set, the forms are stripped away to be used again. Used for building foundations.

four-poster bed: A bed having four posts or pillars, one on each corner. Introduced during the middle of the eighteenth century. Often hung with decorative curtains or draperies.

frame: The understructure of an upholstered piece.

framing: In a new structure, the bare skeleton of a building; the $2'' \times 4''$ vertical members.

Franklin stove: A cast-iron stove similar in appearance to a fireplace but employing metal baffles to increase its heating efficiency; invented by Benjamin Franklin.

French doors: Two adjoining doors that have glass panes from top to bottom and are hinged at opposite sides of a doorway so that they open in the middle, like an ordinary pair of doors.

French polish: A high-gloss furniture finish consisting of numerous coats of **varnish,** each rubbed for hours. Introduced in France in the late eighteenth century.

French Provincial style: Country furniture modeled after the prevailing Paris fashions of the seventeenth through the twentieth centuries. The copies in the provinces were simpler, without any ornamentation, gilding, or inlay. The workmanship was honest and sturdy. The **Louis XIII** style was the first to be copied, followed by the **Louis XIV, Louis XV,** and **Louis XVI** styles, but with a definite tendency toward functionalism. The furniture was made of solid walnut, wild cherry, oak, beech, and fruitwoods. Finishes were honey-colored. Styles varied from province to province. In the mountainous areas, enclosed built-in beds (*lits clos*) were popular for protection against cold. In Alsace, the Swiss influence was felt in the appearance of painted furniture. The most common forms were cabinets, wardrobes, buffets, and cupboards. The **armoire** (a cabinet for the storage of clothes) was the piece of furniture in which home owners took the greatest pride. Those made in Provence and Limousin had large, handsome steel hinges and hardware made by the local steel workers. The charm and subtlety of French Provincial furniture still appeals and is held in great esteem by many people today.

French window: A window similar to a **French door;** usually hung in pairs.

fresco: A painting executed on wet lime plaster. The earth and mineral pigments used are mixed with water. Perhaps the most famous fresco is Michelangelo's in the Sistine chapel in Rome.

fretwork: A geometric border motif carved in low relief. Chinese in origin, it was a favorite theme of **Chippendale** and all eighteenth-century cabinetmakers, especially as **galleries** for tables and **commodes.**

frieze: Any sculptured or richly ornamented band below a ceiling or ceiling cornice or along the upper part of a piece of furniture.

fringe: A decorative edging or trimming of cord, thread, or the like, hanging loose or tied in bunches at the top. Used as trim on draperies and upholstery.

fruitwood: A general term applied to woods of fruit trees such as apple, pear, cherry, lime, and lemon. Widely used in **French Provincial** cabinetmaking. The finished wood was always pale or natural color.

Fulham stoneware: Transparent earthenware and stoneware first manufactured in England in 1671. It is regarded as the link between earthenware and porcelain.

Fuller, Richard Buckminster (1895–):

Renowned American inventor, designer, developer, architect, engineer, cartographer, philosopher, and mathematical genius. His name is synonymous with the future. As early as 1930 Buckminster Fuller foresaw pollution and energy problems. He invented the geodesic dome, which uses the tetrahedron as its basic structural system. It does not derive stability from outside sources but from the support that is integral to its form. Fuller believes that someday great transparent domes may cover entire cities, providing total pollution-free climate control. His portable geodesic domes can serve as living quarters and can be air conditioned by sun power. Thousands of these structures have been built throughout the United States.

fumed oak: Oak wood given a dark, antique appearance with more distinct markings by exposing it to ammonia fumes.

functionalism: The doctrine that an object's function should determine its design and materials, rather than decorative considerations.

furniture arrangement: The ultimate success of a room depends on two essentials: furniture arrangement and color. A desirable arrangement is one that suits the lifestyle of the occupant(s), provides for the proper functioning of each area, has more than two focal points, and cre-

ates a mood. There are simple rules to follow when arranging furniture and seeking formal balance. Planning a room on paper first helps prevent disastrous and costly mistakes. Allowing one square to equal one foot, sketch in on graph paper the length and width of a room, indicating all doors, windows, fireplace, and other architectural features. Next, draw two center lines, one down the length of the room, another across the width, bisecting each other and dividing the room into four equal parts. The object is to place the furniture in such a manner that weight, bulk, and height are well distributed and will balance equally in each half or quadrant. If one side of a room is heavier, it will give the impression of tilting, and must be corrected by adding weight on the other side. The effect of weight can be achieved by a contrasting color, a mirror, a wall of pictures, a larger piece of furniture, a fireplace, a **highboy,** or bookshelves. Experiment by arranging the room with pieces of cardboard cut to one-quarter scale equaling one foot, and representing various pieces of furniture. Ready-made cutouts of furniture are available at most art-supply houses. When arranging templates (cutouts), give thought to conversation units, hobbies, music centers, writing areas, television viewing, entertaining, and reading.

There are two basic kinds of groupings:

1. Two matching pieces of furniture, such as a pair of tables or upholstered pieces, that are identical in style, finish, or fabric. This is called a *symmetrical arrangement.*

2. A grouping of two pieces of furniture that balance each other and are pleasingly related but are not identical. This is called an *asymmetrical arrangement.*

The first arrangement is formal, the second informal. Use both in one room.

The following terms describe weight, dimensions, and shape:

Scale: The relative dimensions of a piece, in comparison to other objects in a room.

Proportion: The relationship of size to the artistic harmony of a piece of furniture or object.

Balance: Equal distribution of weight, size, and height.

To be attractive, the arrangement of furniture against walls must also be in balance. Each wall has an imaginary line running down the middle of it from ceiling to floor. This imaginary center line is called an *axis.* Every wall must have an axis, for the eye recognizes that spot as a focal point. Arrange furniture around this axis in either a symmetrical or asymmetrical fashion. If a wall is broken up by a window or door, the axis is found in the center of the space remaining. Always put decorative emphasis up high on the very center of the axis so that the eyes look up. Keep the room uncrowded and uncluttered.

Hints on furniture arrangement:

1. Be sure to have a floor plan. It is the end result of an interior designer's planning and expresses the personality of the homemaker. It is the only way to anticipate and solve problems.

2. Avoid using massive furniture in a small room. Keep all pieces in scale with each other.

3. Do not place a large piece of furniture so that it obstructs a view window. Place a grouping on either side of the window with a low bench in front of the window or a cocktail table between.

4. Make a room seem larger by placing mirrors in the corners.

5. Decide beforehand if you want a formal or informal room.

6. If a corner cannot be brought into the scheme of the room, create a unit of interest of its own in that place: a high plant, a paneled screen, a corner **étagère,** or a corner table flanked by two chairs.

7. You can change the architecture of a room with color. Shorten a room by painting the long end darker than the other three walls. To lower a ceiling, paint it a darker color than the walls; paint it lighter than the walls, and the ceiling will appear higher. To make a room appear larger, install wall-to-wall carpeting and paint the walls and woodwork the same tone as the carpeting.

8. To make a room more restful, make sure that *line follows structure.* Lines run-

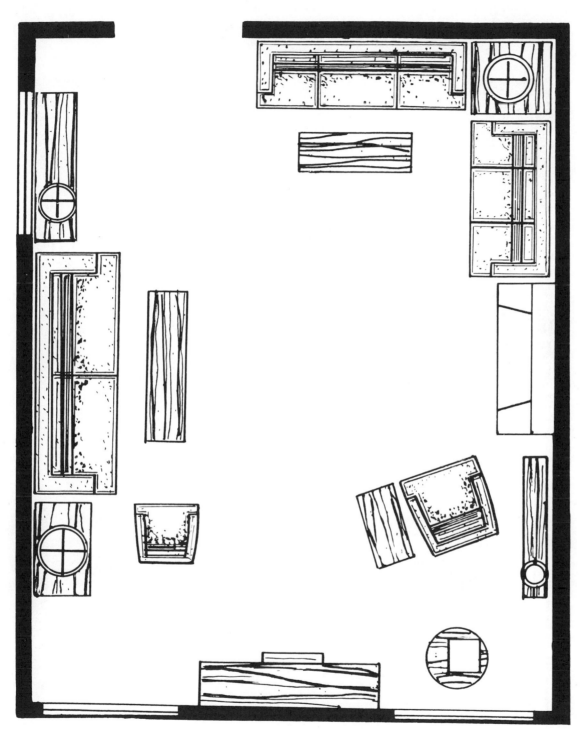

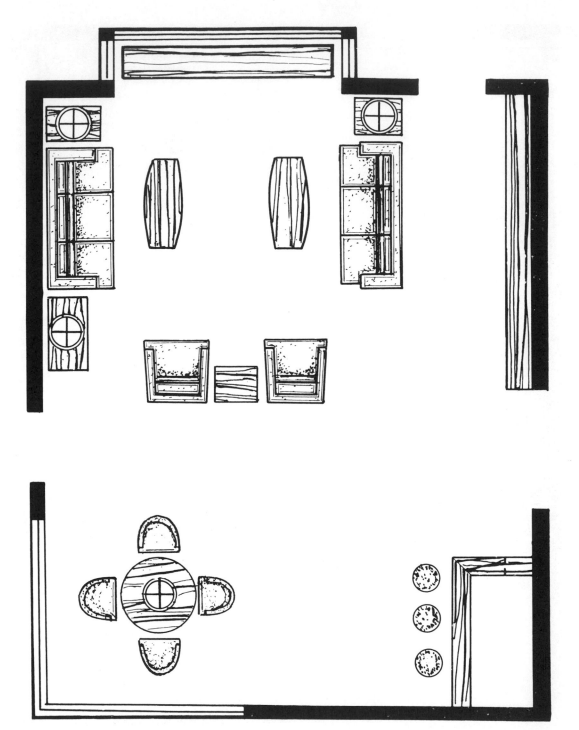

ning in all directions are confusing, so avoid cater-cornering. Place large, straight pieces parallel to a wall or at right angles to it.

9. Don't use low groups around an axis. There must be a high point on the central line of the axis. A triangular arrangement is usually the best.

10. In an extremely contemporary room, create an island of seating places in the center of the room, leaving the walls free for large paintings, and the corners free for statuary and plants.

11. Accessories are among the most important finishing touches for an interior, but they should be considered last and placed when all the furniture has been installed.

12. In many of today's apartments, living rooms are L shaped, the alcove serving as a dining room. Use strong, saturated colors on the walls, or a dramatic wallpaper to make the dining area an entity. The alcove can be closed off by a ceiling-traversed drapery, a folding screen, or shuttered doors.

13. In a very long, narrow room without a fireplace, install a bookcase or music unit two-thirds of the way down the room and at right angles to the long wall. Use an L-shaped sofa, and, on the other side of the bookcase or music unit, a desk and chair or a row of tall plants.

14. If you have extra dining room chairs, use them around a game table in the living room or den.

15. The conversation grouping is the starting point when planning the living room or den. Provide two or more intimate seating groups, if possible.

16. In a bedroom with a bow window, a kidney-shaped desk is often appropriate.

17. For a short wall between two windows or a window and a door, a small cabinet, a wall-hung **console,** a Chinese scroll, a carving, or a clock is practical and useful.

18. For a small space used as a dining area, place the table at right angles to the wall. Hang an unframed mirror the width of the table and extend it up even with a door frame or window, or have it run up to the ceiling. Alternatively, the table can be placed against a window to save space.

19. The problem of getting as much seating space as possible in a corner of a room is best solved by the use of two sofas or love seats flanking a square corner table that is sofa-arm height. Add a cocktail table and two low, square benches, and a corner conversational group is created.

20. Use a pair of matching chairs or love seats to flank a window that frames a view.

21. Do not have all the bright colors and patterns on one side of a room; distribute them.

22. If occupants enjoy games, a permanent game table and chairs are appropriate in the most formal or informal settings.

23. Traffic lanes should be at least

thirty inches wide. A cocktail table should be set back approximately fifteen inches from the edge of the sofa. Allow thirty-six inches of space for a desk chair. If a television is installed in a wall, the middle of the screen should be forty inches above the floor. Bar height is forty-two inches. Maximum height for whiskey or wine bottles is fifteen and one-half inches. Long halls should be at least forty-eight inches wide. Comfortable staircases are usually fifty-two inches wide, and the handrails are thirty-four inches high. The maximum distance at which people can converse comfortably is about twelve feet apart.

24. In calculating the seating capacity of a dining room table, allow twenty-two inches per person.

25. Allow seven square feet of floor space for a permanent game table and four chairs; five feet when the chairs are pushed in.

Finally, design any decorative arrangement so it is functional for the occupants' lifestyle.

furring: Attaching strips of wood to a wall or other surface to provide an even support for metal, lath, plaster, or paneling.

*For where there is love of man,
there is also love of art and home.*

Hippocrates (460–377 B.C.)

gable: In architecture, the triangular upper portion of an end wall with a ridged or sloping roof. Also, any gablelike appurtenance on an article of furniture.

gadroon: A carved-edge ornamental molding of continuous ridges and flutings found around the edge or rim of furniture, silver, or glass. A characteristic decoration on bulbous Elizabethan furniture legs, and a familiar treatment of borders and edges of **Chippendale** furniture.

gallery: A small, decorative, protective railing attached to the outer edges of a table, shelf, or cabinet. Generally made of pierced wood or metal. **Chippendale** used **fretwork** galleries on many of his tables.

Also a wall, room, or long hall that is used to display paintings and other works of art.

In architecture, a covered walk, verandah, or balcony.

galloon: A plain, ribbonlike braid used in trimming upholstered furniture and draperies.

gambrel roof: A ridged roof with two slopes. The lower slope has a steeper pitch than the upper. Known in England as a *mansard roof.*

game table or gaming table: A small table for playing board games, having a permanent place in a room. It first appeared early in the seventeenth century, with a top covered in needlepoint. By the eighteenth century the top was designed for playing chess and backgammon. The early game tables were made with folding tops and often contained "wells" in the four corners, which were used for counters, money, or candlesticks.

garden stool: A barrel-shaped seat of porcelain, stone, or wood. Garden seats are highly decorative and often come with perforated openwork designs. The wooden ones are generally of rosewood and are used in the interior of a house.

gargoyle: In medieval architecture, a grotesque carved human or animal figure projecting from a parapet or roof. Usually made of stone, it was employed as a rainspout, with water flowing out of the mouth.

gate-leg table: A table originally made of oak, with folding, hinged leaves supported by legs that swing closed like a gate, allowing the leaves to hang down. Invented in England in the late sixteenth century, it is still popular today.

Gaudí, Antoni (1852–1926): The Catalan architect Gaudí is to Spain what Frank Lloyd Wright is to the United States. Gaudí was ridiculed, scorned, and actually considered abnormal by critics in England and the United States, but the cultured as well as the common people of Spain loved his showy, florid, but harmonious work.

He was the greatest, most innovative modern architect of his time. Influenced by Gothic, Moorish, and Moroccan elements, his buildings are pieces of fantastic sculpture—radical, revolutionary, fairytale **baroque.** He was a brilliant engineer, builder, designer, architect, and sculptor. He used concrete in an unconventional, untraditional, abstract manner. The façades of some of his concrete buildings look like waves that rise and fall. Now and then he purposely warped his columns. Wrought-iron balconies are masterpieces of ornamental invention; their free-form serpentine lines are not only decorative but structural. Gaudí did not believe in symmetry. He was concerned with the effect of light and shade on the façades of his buildings. Because his buildings were conceived and developed as sculpture, one must walk through and around them, as one would while viewing a piece of sculpture. Among his best-known works are the Milà house, Güell palace (1895–90), the Güell park (completed 1914), and the unfinished Sagrada Familia church (begun 1883).

Gauguin, Paul (1848–1903): French postimpressionist painter and sculptor, a forerunner of the **Nabis** (*see* modern art).

gazebo: A small circular or octagonal outdoor shelter located in a garden or on a knoll overlooking a garden. It is a place in which to read, relax, entertain, or enjoy a view. The architecture or design should match or blend with the surroundings or harmonize with the house.

general lighting: Lighting designed to provide a substantially uniform level of illumination throughout an area.

genre: A category of art in which subjects from everyday life are treated realistically. A good example is the American realist **Ashcan school.**

Georgian period: This period of British history encompasses the reign of the three Georges:

Early Georgian	1714–1750
Middle Georgian	1750–1770
Late Georgian	1770–1811
Prince of Wales, Regency, and early Victorian	(1811–1860)

The architecture at the beginning of the early Georgian period was strongly classical in feeling, a carryover from the influence of **Christopher Wren, Andrea Palladio,** and **Inigo Jones.**

This was a period of prosperity, and is often regarded as the "golden age" of British architecture. **Palladian** exteriors, based on the Roman classical style of the sixteenth century, were extremely popular. Next in importance was the architecture of **Robert Adam,** who also designed furniture for his wealthy clients, as did such architects as William Kent, Thomas Hope, and Thomas Langely.

This was also a time of increasing wealth, culture, and "good taste." Great country mansions were built with interiors more elaborate than the exteriors. Literally thousands of furniture makers, cabinetmakers, and designers throve and prospered in the Georgian period.

English cabinetmaking reached its zenith during the eighteenth century. The skill and superb craftsmanship of designers and makers like **Hepplewhite, Chippendale, Sheraton,** and **Adam** were at their highest. Less familiar cabinetmakers and designers of the highest order were Shearer, Manwaring, Kent, Lock, Ince, Mayhew, Vile, and Seddon. The Georgian style embraces all these designers and all articles of furniture made in the eighteenth century.

Early in the period, **Queen Anne, baroque,** and **rococo** styles influenced furniture designs; the latter two were decorated with much gilding.

Between 1735 and 1765, Chinese designs were very much in vogue. Lacquer in many colors was used as a decorative finish. **Coromandel screens** were cut up and used as tops, sides, or doors on cabinets and chests. Many times an affluent home owner sheeted the walls of an entire room with Coromandel lacquer panels, replacing the pine, cedar, or mahogany previously used. During the middle-Georgian period, imported wallpapers were introduced. Shortly afterward, England began producing its own Oriental papers, using woodblocks. Around 1755 Wilton and Axminster began making carpets by machine, replacing the arduously handmade needlework ones. Painted and gilded furniture came into fashion toward the end of the middle-Georgian period. Josiah Wedgwood produced the finest china of the period, which is much sought after today. **Wedgwood** medallions showed up as inserts into furniture. Outstanding articles of silver were fabricated. Sheffield plate, the first substitute for wrought silver, was developed.

Chairs in the middle-Georgian period

had **lyres** or **Prince of Wales plumes** carved on the backs. **Ladder-back** and **Windsor** chairs made their appearance, as did chairs with shield-, oval-, and heart-shaped backs. At this time England exported a great deal of furniture to the colonies and throughout Europe. At the beginning of the late-Georgian period, the age of realism in portraiture, landscape painting, and sculpture flourished. The outstanding portrait painters were Thomas Gainsborough, Sir Thomas Lawrence, Sir Joshua Reynolds, George Romney, and Sir Henry Raeburn. The prominent landscape painters were John Constable and J. M. W. Turner.

Dining-room tables were made in sections. Sofa tables, Pembroke tables, breakfronts, sideboards, secretaries, dressers, china cabinets, four-poster beds, chests of drawers, and dressing tables were originated, developed, and produced. Mahogany and satinwood with inlays became commonplace, with satinwood continuing to be used to the end of the Georgian period. The chief motifs were: laurel leaves, acanthus leaves, swags, festoons, eagle heads, lion heads, human masks, shells, honeysuckle, and ball-and-claw feet. The favorite upholstery fabrics were: velvet, damask, and needlepoint. Wall mirrors were prominent in late-Georgian decoration. Mirrors were used as architectural features, with the frames becoming an integral part of the wall paneling.

In the final phase of the Georgian period, factory mass production put the handcraftsman of furniture out of business. Standards of quality and design in furniture were lowered during the Industrial Revolution. With inventions like the mechanical loom and steam power, unemployment and poverty were rampant, while at the same time the wealthy lived better than ever.

In 1807 Thomas Hope, perhaps the first interior designer, published a book entitled *Household Furniture and Interior Decoration.*

About this same time, Sheraton's style changed and influenced the **Regency** period which followed.

German silver: A hard, corrosion-resistant, malleable alloy of copper, zinc, and nickel. Also called *nickel silver.*

gesso: A preparation of plaster of Paris, linseed oil, and glue, which came into use in the seventeenth century. It is applied to a surface for raised decoration prior to gilding or painting.

Giacometti, Alberto (1901–1966): Swiss surrealist sculptor. Known for his elongated, minimalist human figures.

Gibbons, Grinling (1648–1721): English **baroque** wood and stone carver, sculptor, and designer. After Christopher Wren employed him, he became the most sought-after carver in England. His carvings adorn many of England's finest country houses, palaces, castles, and churches. Typical of his distinctive work are carved foliage, flowers, birds, animals, fruit, and shells, all characterized by exquisitely executed minute details.

gilding: A wood or metal finish of thin sheets of gold leaf. The practice of gilding goes back to the time of the Pharaohs. However, it was not until the **Gothic** period that it was used to decorate furniture.

gimp: A flat, narrow, decorative braid used in trimming upholstery, draperies, or clothing. Gimp is also glued over upholstery tacks to conceal them on wood-framed chairs or sofas.

ginger jar: A Chinese ceramic jar with a wide mouth, a globular body, and a dome-shaped cover. Used to preserve green ginger, this form dates back to ancient times.

girandole: An elaborate, **rococo,** carved and gilt wall bracket, sconce, or chandelier. Frequently found with a mirrored back, which serves to reflect the candle flames. Girandoles were generally surrounded by candle arms of bronze or silver, adorned with crystal pendants. They first appeared during the early part of the eighteenth century. The most typical ornamental motif was the eagle. Some-

times the mirror was convex and was referred to as a *bull's-eye* mirror.

girder: A large horizontal wood or steel beam used over a wide span as a main support for a vertical load.

girls' rooms: *See* teenagers' rooms.

Glackens, William James (1870–1938): American realist painter, a member of the group called the "eight" or Ashcan school.

glass: A material composed chiefly of silicates and alkali fused at high temperatures. By varying the degree of heating and the method of cooling, innumerable kinds of glass can be produced.

Lead is added for brilliance, and metallic oxides are added to impart color.

Glass has been made since prehistoric times in India, the Far East, and Egypt. The first American glass was made in 1608.

glass blowing: A method of producing glassware by injecting air under pressure into molten glass and then shaping the material within the mold. Even today, very fine pieces are still blown by hand.

glazing: In furniture finishing, the wiping and brushing out of a thin wash-coat of paint or stain that has been applied over a dry or existing color-coat, thereby changing and modifying the base color into a two-toned or antique effect. Unusual patterns and highlights can be attained by wiping this layer off with different materials such as crushed newspaper, a sponge, or a piece of carpeting. Glazing also refers to the use of a glossy transparent liquid applied to ceramics, which, when baked at high temperatures, is fused to the surface, leaving it shiny. Glazing not only adds to the beauty of the article but makes the porous body impervious to liquids, and imparts depth and richness. (*See also* porcelain.)

Gobelins: A dye factory established in Paris in the fifteenth century by the brothers Gobelin. Approximately 100 years later a tapestry works was added. The Gobelin family controlled it until Louis XIV purchased it in 1662. It then became state controlled, and all tapestries were considered the property of the king. Fine furniture and upholstery fabrics were also manufactured. Louis XIV's tapestry works' first job was for the Palace of Versailles. Court painters prepared designs, borrowing freely from famous frescoes. In 1826, after the Revolution, they began production of handmade carpets. Toward the end of the nineteenth century another tapestry works opened at Beauvais, also administered under the patronage of the state.

Goddard, John (1724–1785):   Early American furniture designer and cabinetmaker. Originator with **Job Townsend** of **blockfront** cabinets, chests, and secretaries. Goddard developed two motifs: carved shells and the **ogee**-curved bracket foot.

gold leaf: *See* gilding.

Gorky, Arshile (1904–1948):   American abstract artist.

Gothic style: The dominant style of the Middle Ages (1150–1500). Architectural features include the pointed arch, the flying buttress, and the rib vault.

Furniture, made chiefly of oak, was heavy and crude. Details were borrowed from church architecture. They included: tracery carving, trefoil and quatrefoil carving, and cluster columns. Articles of furniture were few, and each served more than one purpose. Chests, cupboards, beds, and benches were the principal articles made.

Gottlieb, Adolph (1903–1974):   American artist who painted in a variety of naturalistic and modern styles.

gouache: An opaque pigment made by mixing zinc white with watercolors. First used during the Middle Ages for illuminated manuscripts.

graining: In cabinetwork, a method of painting a surface to resemble the natural grain of wood or marble. The graining process dates back to ancient Egypt.

grandfather chair: *See* wing chair.

grandfather clock: A pendulum clock enclosed in a tall, narrow cabinet, usually more than 6-feet tall. A smaller version is called a *grandmother clock.*

granite: A hard igneous rock, consisting chiefly of quartz, feldspar, and mica, used for monuments and in building.

graphic arts: Nonpictorial line drawings or paintings used as decoration on walls. Also refers to various printing processes that produce etchings, drypoints, engravings, and woodcuts.

grass cloth: *See* wall coverings.

Grecian period: It is possible to reconstruct some of the furniture made during this period (1200–320 B.C.) from vase paintings. Beds, couches, and chests made of cedar, yew, and ebony existed, sometimes ornamented with gilt work and inlaid of precious stones and ivory. Bronze was used on some chairs for legs and feet. The perfectly proportioned classic chair had a shoulder-height, sweeping, curved, narrow, wooden back that also served as arms; its legs were saber type and curved outward. This chair was the inspiration for the **Directoire** and **Regency** styles.

The Greek architectural style of 480 to 320 B.C. left a strong imprint on civilization. It was distinguished by its purity of form. Grecian architecture was based on the three great **orders of architecture:** Doric, Ionic, and Corinthian. Buildings were of simple column-and-lintel construction. Masonry was laid without mortar.

The Acropolis in Athens represents the acme of Greek architectural beauty.

Greek key: A **fretwork** pattern formed by a geometrical repetition of intertwined hook-shaped square forms.

griffin: One of the most ancient of all grotesque devices deriving from the mythological bestiary. It has the head, wings, and forelegs of an eagle and the rear quarters of a lion. It was widely employed as a decorative motif during the late Italian Renaissance, during the **Louis XIV** period, and by **Adam** and **Sheraton.** Griffins were also used as supports on **Empire** and **Regency** console tables and sideboards.

grille: A wood or metal grating used as a divider, a barrier, or for decorative purposes (e.g., on the front of bookcases or for ornamental screens).

Gris, Juan (1887–1927): Spanish-born French cubist painter.

grisaille: A style of monochromatic painting in shades and tints of gray.

groin vault: In architecture, the curved line formed by the intersection of two **vaults.**

Gropius, Walter (1883–1969): German-American architect; a pioneer of the **International** style. In 1919 Gropius became the head of the **Bauhaus,** where he revolutionized the teaching of architecture and industrial design, by encouraging artists, artisans, and architects to collaborate in creating the perfect environment.

In 1928, after Hitler assumed power, Gropius left Germany, emigrating first to England and then to the United States. He taught at Harvard while continuing his private practice in partnership with **Marcel Breuer.** Three important Gropius projects are the United States Embassy at Athens, the Harvard Graduate Center, and New York's Pan-Am building.

Gropper, William (1897–1977): American painter and illustrator who first established his reputation as a political cartoonist.

gros point: A coarse needlework technique done with wool cross-stitched on a canvas ground. Gros point is used for upholstering furniture.

Gross, Chaim (1904–): American sculptor working principally in wood.

Grosz, George (1893–1959): German-born American expressionist painter.

grout: A thin mortar used to fill chinks and cracks between masonry and to consolidate the adjoining objects into a solid mass.

Gruen, Victor (1903–): Austrian-American architect and urban designer. He studied with Peter Behrens.

guilloche: A classical ornamental border, carved, painted, or inlaid, consisting of interlaced curves or circles enclosing foliate rosettes. Used on furniture from about 1550 to 1800.

gum, gumwood: An American wood used for inexpensive cabinetwork. The wood is not durable and has a tendency to warp. It is used a great deal in the making of plywood. It finishes fairly well with a mahogany or walnut stain but is best painted.

Hadley chest: A late-seventeenth-century American **dower** chest made in Hadley, Massachusetts. It had a hinged top. The front had three sunken panels with two drawers below. Carvings of tulips, vines, and leaves covered the entire front. The center panel often had the owner's initials carved into it.

half-timber: In architecture, having a wooden framework with plaster, brick, stone, or another material filling in the spaces.

hall: *See* entrance.

hallmark: In England, the mark stamped on silver or gold as a guarantee of official approval of the standard of purity. The date made and the maker are thus identified. Hallmarks were introduced in 1300.

hand-block printing: A method of imprinting fabric with a series of wooden, metal, or linoleum blocks.

handkerchief table: An American drop-leaf table consisting of a triangular top with a triangular leaf. When the leaf is raised, the table has a square top.

hanger: A metal strip used to support a gutter, suspended ceiling, etc.

hard-paste: A pottery clay made with a base of kaolin, a material first used by the Chinese in making true porcelain.

hardware: All metal fittings on furniture, such as locks, keyhole plates, hinges, hasps, handles, and drawer pulls. Hardware should be harmonious in style with the furniture itself.

hardwood: Any compact, textured wood produced from deciduous trees, such as mahogany, walnut, oak, teak, maple, or birch.

harewood: *See* sycamore.

harpsichord: A forerunner of the grand piano. The English harpsichord had two keyboards. Single-keyboard instruments were also made.

Hartung, Hans (1904–): French abstract painter.

Harvard chair: A three-legged armchair of the late seventeenth century that has been used by the president of Harvard University when conferring degrees since the eighteenth century.

harvest table: A crude, dining room-type table, often with **drop leaves.**

hasp: A hinged strap used with a lock to secure a door or chest.

Hassam, Frederick Childe (1859–1935): American impressionist painter and graphic artist.

hassock: An upholstered footstool or thick cushion, used for kneeling or sitting.

hatching: The shading of black and white in drawings or etchings, accomplished by crossing and recrossing parallel lines close together.

Haussman, George Eugène (1809–1891): A French public official who planned and rebuilt nineteenth-century Paris, including streets, buildings, sewage systems, cemeteries, and all landscaping.

Haviland: Porcelain tableware made in **Limoges** but designed for the American trade.

header: A horizontal wood or steel beam placed between two long beams and supporting the ends of one or more tailpieces. Also, a brick laid across rather than parallel to a wall.

hearth: The masonry or tiled floor area directly in front of a fireplace.

heart-shaped chair: An open-backed **Hepplewhite** design, whose back resembles two interlaced hearts.

Hepplewhite, George (d. 1786): English cabinetmaker and furniture designer. *The Cabinet Maker's and Upholsterer's Guide,* which made him famous, was published by his widow two years after his death.

   The Hepplewhite style was an elegant one, based on **Adam** and **Chippendale** designs but much lighter, more delicate, and more graceful. His later output took on a classical look. Perhaps his best-known designs are his chairs with shield backs and turned or square tapered legs. Hepplewhite favored mahogany or satinwood with inlaid or painted designs. Characteristic motifs were: Prince of Wales plumes, ribbons, classic urns, rosettes, fans, acanthus leaves, honeysuckle, wheat ears, lyres, and swags. The fabrics used were silk, satin, and formal striped upholstery materials. Hepplewhite dining room chairs are today the most popular of all English traditional chairs.

Herculaneum: The Roman city whose

excavations inspired the classic styling of the **Adams** brothers and **Sheraton.**

hex sign: A sign often seen on buildings by Pennsylvania Germans, in the shape of a circle enclosing a six-pointed star. Variously regarded as conferring good or bad luck.

H.F.C.:   Hold for Confirmation. Refers to orders that cannot be processed without confirmation from the designer.

H hinge: A hinge in the form of the letter H, used on the butt end of doors. When the door closed, a decorative acorn or other object would appear on the exterior of the door butt. Extremely popular in the sixteenth century.

H.I.D. lamp: High-intensity Discharge lamp. This is a general term used to denote all high-pressure sodium mercury and metal halide lamps.

highboy: A tall chest of drawers, mounted on a low chest or stand, with drawers. The top is flat and has a **bonnet** or a **broken pediment.** Early examples were painted or lacquered. Popular in England in the late seventeenth century. Introduced in America during the early part of the eighteenth century. The American version showed **Queen Anne, William and Mary,** and **Chippendale** influence. The woods used were mahogany and maple.

high-low cocktail table: A table on a swivel base that raises up from cocktail to dining height.

hipped roof: A roof with sloping ends and sides.

historic preservation: The preservation of exteriors and interiors from the point of view of their historic value and with an eye toward practical reuse.

Hitchcock chair: A chair named after Connecticut chair maker Lambert Hitchcock (1795–1852). It featured straight, turned, or splayed legs, a caned seat, and a "pillow back" or oval-turned top rail. It was invariably painted black and stenciled with fruit and flower designs on the back splat and top rail.

Hoban, James   (1762?–1831): Irish-American architect. He designed and built the White House in 1792–1799 and rebuilt it after its destruction by the British in 1814.

home office: Can be combined with a den without sacrificing a great deal of space. For a homemaker's office, all that is needed is a corner in the kitchen or breakfast room.

A small wall-hung desk or shelf with drawers attached underneath, a wall telephone, and a bulletin board above the desk are all that is necessary. A breadboard-type pull-out leaf supported by the open doors of a cupboard below will carry a portable typewriter.

honeysuckle ornament: A design motif consisting of a stylized cluster of honeysuckle flowers and leaves. Originating in ancient Greek art and architecture, this motif was popular in European **neoclassical style** furniture. Also known as *anthemion* motif.

hoof foot: A carved foot in the form of an animal's hoof. Dates back to ancient **Egyptian** furniture.

hooked rug: A handmade rug formed by drawing narrow strips of wool or yarn through a canvas or burlap backing.

Hope, Thomas (1770–1831): English architect, collector, and furniture designer, largely responsible for the development of the **Regency** style in England. Hope published several books on furniture and interior decoration, most notably the 1807 work, *Household Furniture and Interior Decoration.*

Hopper, Edward (1882–1967): American realist painter. Member of the **Ashcan school.**

horn furniture: Furniture such as chairs, small sofas, and hatracks that is made from the horns or antlers of elk, deer, buffalo, and other animals. First made in the Middle Ages, horn furniture ex-perienced a revival in Europe in the mid-nineteenth century and in America in the late nineteenth century.

horsehair: A stiff fabric made from the mane or tail of a horse. Because of its durability, it has been used for upholstery since the middle of the eighteenth century.

Hudson River school: A group of American romantic landscape painters in the years 1825–1875, who drew their inspiration from the Hudson River valley and the Catskill Mountains. Among the group were Thomas Cole, Samuel F. B. Morse, and George Inness.

hue: *See* color.

Hunt, Richard Morris (1828–1895): American architect; a conspicuous exponent of nineteenth-century eclecticism. He worked on the Capitol in Washington, D.C. and was one of the organizers of the A.I.A. (American Institute of Architects), of which he became president in 1888. His works include the Fogg Museum at Harvard University and the main section of the Metropolitan Museum of Art in New York.

hunt table: A crescent-shaped table, sometimes with end **drop leaves.** Used as a bar or wine table in the late eighteenth century in England.

hurricane glass or lamp: A tall glass

cylinder open at both ends. When placed over a candle it protects the flame from being blown out.

hutch: A cupboard or cabinet, usually with a superstructure of wood doors concealing storage space, or open shelves used for the display of plates. Originating in seventeenth-century England, it was first used for storing food and clothing. Usually made of oak.

hyperbolic paraboloid roof: A double-curved shell roof that resembles a butterfly. It was developed from a parabolic arch.

A man builds a fine house; and now he has a master, and a task for life; he is to furnish, watch, show it, and keep it in repair the rest of his days.

Ralph Waldo Emerson
(1803–1882)

icon: In the Eastern Orthodox Church, a religious image painted, carved, or sculpted, of Christ and the Virgin Mary. Today it refers to any religious subject executed on a portable plaque of wood. It may also be a mosaic on a metal plaque. Icons date back to the **Byzantine** era.

I.D.E.C.: The Interior Design Educators Council. The I.D.E.C. was formed in 1962 for the purpose of establishing and strengthening lines of communication between individuals, educational institutions, and organizations in the field, so as to improve the teaching of interior design, and thereby raise the professional level of the field.

I.E.S.: Illuminating Engineering Society. The purpose of the I.E.S. is to promote the optimal use of light to benefit sight and comfort.

illuminated books and manuscripts: Works in which the initial letters or opening phrases of a chapter are enlarged, colored, gilded, and decorated. The text is sometimes illustrated with brilliant pictures and complex linear and abstract patterns. Illumination is believed to have begun in the seventh century. In the fifteenth century, when printing was invented, hand illumination was discontinued.

Imari ware: *See* Arita porcelain.

impasto: In painting, the application of thick layers of pigment.

impressionism: *See* modern art.

incandescent lamp: An electric lamp in which a filament is heated to incandescence by an electric current.

Ince & Mayhew: English firm of cabinetmakers who published an important pattern book of some 300 furniture designs entitled, *The Universal System of Household Furniture*. Some of the designs were obviously cribbed from **Chippendale's** *Director*. Ince and Mayhew were in business from 1759 to 1810.

indirect lighting: Lighting produced by fixtures distributing 90 to 100 percent of their light upward.

industry foundation: An organization composed of companies engaged in supplying products and services to the interior design profession.

inglenook: A built-in wooden **settle** in a chimney corner or recess beside a fireplace.

inlay: A decorative design formed in wood or metal by insetting, flush with the surface, different colored woods, ivory, bone, tortoiseshell, mother-of-pearl, or pewter.

intaglio: The process by which a carved pattern or design is cut or stamped beneath the surface of a hard material like a gemstone.

intarsia: A form of **marquetry** using small pieces of wood to create mosaics. Found on Italian **Renaissance** furniture.

International style: An architectural movement that emphasizes space instead of mass. This modern, functional trend began in the United States and Europe in the late twenties and spread throughout the world. Typical of the style are rectangular volumes defined by light, and taut, undecorated, planar and linear geometric components that are asymmetrically balanced by equivalent voids and solids. The chief exponents of this style are Walter Gropius, Louis Sullivan, Le Corbusier, Philip Johnson, Adolf Loos, Henry Russell Hitchcock, and Ludwig Miës van der Rohe.

Ionic order: A classical Greek **order of architecture,** characterized by two opposed **volutes** in the **capital.**

Ironstone china: A hard, durable white English earthenware that contains slag of ironstone. First manufactured in 1813.

ironwork: Ornate indoor and outdoor iron furniture was the vogue in **Victorian** times. In the eighteenth century, English decorative ironwork appeared in the form of grilles, balconies, gates, stair balusters, railings, window guards, and fanlights over entrance doors. **Gothic** and **chinoiserie** designs were popular, as well as some that reflected the **Adam** brothers' influence. In the nineteenth century, iron castings were decorative, with an overabundance of carved effects. Cast-iron stoves and beds were elaborate, with applied simulated carved ornaments.

isometric projection: A method of drawing a room and furniture so that three dimensions are roughly shown, not in perspective but in their actual measurements to a preset scale.

Italian furniture periods: There are essentially six recognized substyles:

1. *Pre-Renaissance:* The Middle Ages (1100–1400). Furniture (what little there was) was based on **Gothic** and **Byzantine** art. The most important article was the chest (*cassone*).

2. *Quattrocento:* The early **Renaissance** (1400–1500). The Renaissance originated in Italy, but its style influenced all of Europe. Furniture of this period was architectural in detail and scale, simple and classical in line.

3. *Cinquecento* (1500–1600): The high Renaissance. A rich and opulent period of soft chairs, four-poster beds with elaborate carvings, decorated chests, silk velvets, and carved and tooled leathers.

4. *Baroque* (1560–1700): Overscaled, exaggerated, and ornate furniture that reflected the French, Spanish, and English influence. Distinctive features included quantities of gilded cherubs attached to walls and ceilings and flamboyantly carved sideboards, tall cabinets, and console tables. A profusion of curves, scrolls, pediments, swags, and sculptured bases were developed and used during this period, as well as the **cartouche,** scroll work, and ornamental detail on and over doors and ceilings. Furniture was painted and gilded. Table tops were of colored marble and mosaic work. The most popular wood of the period was walnut.

5. *Settecento, rococo* (1700–1750): A vivacious theatrical style; the outgrowth of baroque. Furniture was lighter than in the baroque period but still lavishly elegant, with elaborate decoration and **C scrolls.** The most popular decorative motifs were: shells, bowknots, ribbons, foliage, and wreaths, with much gilding, painting, and carving. Mirrors, lacquered furniture, and **bombé** commodes were popular. Rococo furniture attained its greatest production in Venice. Consequently, most Italian rococo furniture is called *Venetian.*

6. The styles that followed were copies of **Louis XVI, Hepplewhite, Adam,** and **Directoire.** A newly revived interest in designs of a classical nature was seen after the excavations at Pompeii. In the present century, Italian designers have stressed classically inspired modern designs and have emerged as a dominant force in contemporary design.

ivory: The smooth, hard dentine forming the tusks of elephants and other animals. Ivory has been used for decorative purposes since before recorded history. Eskimos used walrus tusks for carving trinkets. Furniture makers have used ivory as an inlay material for many centuries.

The Chinese, who have been producing carved ivory objects of art since 1100 B.C., are known for their delicately pierced ivory carvings, statuettes and figurines, and carved and painted snuff bottles. The

Chinese use elephant tusks and rhinoceros horns (*see* netsuke).

Ivory can be cleaned with ordinary rubbing alcohol. Do not try to remove "yellowing"; it is part of the natural **patina.** *Never* use water, as it will cause the ivory to split or crack. Lemon oil will bring up a high shine.

J

jacaranda: *See* palisander.

Jacobean period: The period of the reign of the Stuart kings in the seventeenth century.

Early Jacobean (early Stuart): James I (1603–1625); Charles I (1625–1649)
Commonwealth, Cromwellian, Protectorate: (1649–1660)
Late Jacobean (late Stuart), Carolean (Charles), Restoration: Charles II (1660–1685); James II (1685–1688)

As far as furniture design is concerned, the first forty years of the Jacobean epoch differed very little from the preceding **Elizabethan** period. It was only after that, when great changes in decoration and furniture design occurred, that the passing of the oak age in furniture became manifest.

The **gate-leg table** and **Welsh dresser** were developed during this period, together with cupboards of carved oak; settle-tables had tops attached to the back of the settle arms, which, when swung up, transformed the piece from a settle to a dining table. The clothespress (wardrobe cabinet) was customarily of walnut, the doors decorated with inlay. These wardrobes were quite tall, some reaching over six feet, and showed up in most living rooms and bedrooms. **Joint stools,** chairs, and benches remained basically the same during the Jacobean period. James I was the patron of Inigo Jones, who introduced the Palladian Renaissance style of architecture in England. Jones's innovations include built-in picture frames above a mantelpiece and circular wreaths in the centers of ceilings.

Jacobean furniture was the first to be made in the colonies; therefore, it is sometimes referred to as *Pilgrim furniture.* Decorative motifs used were: arabesques, medallions, and geometric designs.

After the Restoration in 1660, there was a revolution in taste. English furniture designs began to reflect the **baroque** influence. There was a demand for luxury. During this period, walnut, **veneering, marquetry,** and gilt **gesso** were in high favor. Upholstered furniture was covered in the finest silks, tapestries, velvets, leather, wools, brocades, and embroideries. Furniture was trimmed with large nail heads and gold fringe. Cane chairs, turkey carpets (Oriental-type carpets made in Turkey), **wing chairs,** desks, and case clocks materialized during Charles II's reign. Colorful lacquer of red, black, green, and gold, in the Chinese theme, was in demand. Scrolls were used in the design of legs and arms. Other decorative features were masks, coronets, cherubs, birds, **cartouches,** and leaves. Cherubs were to be found everywhere, even suspended from ceilings.

Extension dining room tables with draw leaves, and chests resembling buffets were introduced. The latter were paneled and elaborately carved. Legs on stools, benches, and dining tables were the turned **baluster**-type with plain stretchers for support. Massively carved four-poster beds with paneled headboards were surrounded by costly hangings.

Jacobsen, Arne (1902–1971): Internationally known Danish architect and designer. His architectural style was *International Modern:* simple classical lines without clichés and theatrical effects. During the 1950s he designed and marketed the Ant, Egg, and Swan chairs, which are in demand to this day.

Jacquard, Joseph (1752–1834): French inventor of the mechanical loom. The Jacquard loom was the first machine to weave in patterns.

jade: Either of two different species of minerals. The rarer variety is called *jadeite.* The less costly and more abundant variety is called *nephrite.* Jade comes in all colors: green, white, gray, red, cream, yellow, black, and lavender. Both the Chinese and Japanese prize jade highly, but the Chinese excel in the art of carving it.

jalousie: A louvered shutter or angled slat set into a frame, designed to regulate the passage of air and light. They originated in the sixteenth century. The Venetian blind is a type of jalousie.

jamb: The straight or vertical side posts of a door or window frame.

japan: A furniture finish used in Europe during the seventeenth and eighteenth centuries, intended to simulate the appearance of **lacquer.** (During the seventeenth century, the Japanese ceased shipping lacquered goods to the Western world.) Like lacquer, japan was employed in many ways on furniture, objects of art, and the interior walls of houses: plain, or mixed with gold, silver, or mother-of-pearl. Polished glossy black and cinnabar red were the colors most in demand, with painting and calligraphy applied as decoration. In 1688 Stalker and Parker wrote

A Treatise of Japanning and Varnishing, a technical, practical guide and witty "how-to" book still worth reading today.

Japanese architecture, gardens, and interiors: The earliest Japanese buildings were religious edifices such as the Shinto shrines, which appeared about A.D. 500. After the seventh century, Buddhist monastery buildings with **pagodas** and projecting cantilevered roofs were built.

Wood has always been the major building material in Japan. Wooden pillars, interior walls of light, sliding wood or paper panels, and verandahs all around the building, are traditional, standard design elements. In addition, each house had a *tokonoma* or alcove built for the display of a single flower or **kakemono.**

Rather than using chests for storage, cupboards were built in. Instead of beds, mattresses were stored in the cupboards and rolled out at night on the **tatami**-covered floors. (A *tatami* mat measures three feet by six feet and is used as the basic unit of measurement to determine the size of a room.) Tables were few, and those used were low and finished in highly polished lacquer, often painted with floral motifs taken from nature. At the beginning of the twentieth century, reinforced concrete, steel, and glass were introduced in construction.

Because Japanese gardens are considered extensions of a house, they are integrated with the architecture and treated as works of art. A tea house in the garden is an essential part of Japanese tradition, and it is built like a miniature private house. Ponds, stones, moats, bridges, and raked sand represent in miniature the large natural forms of nature. Stone lanterns, evergreen trees, and shrubs complete the garden and make it a traditional place for contemplation and peace.

After 1858 Japanese building was influenced by Italian **Renaissance** architecture. Today, construction is influenced by Western techniques, Western architecture, and modern technology, with roots in past national traditions.

Japanese painted screens: Used both as partitions and as works of art, these folding screens are actually a blending of literature, calligraphy, and painting. The silk-, paper-, or leather-covered frames are painted with Japanese deities, birds, mythological subjects, cherry blossoms, chrysanthemums, and the like. Heights range from 3 to 7 feet; the individual panels are available in 12-, 18-, or 24-inch widths.

jardinière: A large, decorative stand or pot designed to hold flowers or indoor plants. The jardinière is fitted with a metal-lined well and mounted on four square or round tapered legs.

jasper ware: A fine, close-grained stoneware invented by **Josiah Wedgwood** in the late eighteenth century. Can be stained throughout with metallic oxides to blue, lavender, green, and black.

Jawlensky, Alexei von (1864–1941): Russian-German expressionist painter.

Jeanneret, Charles Edouard: *See* Le Corbusier.

Jenny Lind style: Late-nineteenth-century American designation for **spool furniture.** So named because the famous opera singer Jenny Lind was said to have slept in a spool bed while touring America.

jig: A clamp or other device used as a guide or template for making parts of furniture.

jigsaw: A saw with a narrow vertical reciprocating blade used to cut scrolls, fretwork, or lattice work.

John, Augustus Edwin (1878–1961): British portraitist and landscape painter. An impressionist.

Johns, Jasper (1930–): American expressionist and pioneer of pop art.

Johnson, Philip (1906–): American **International** style architect. Designer of urbane, dramatic modern buildings. He was greatly influenced by Ludwig Miës van der Rohe, Sir John Sloan , and Marcel Breuer. In 1949 he designed his now famous all-glass house, which established his reputation. Following the Japanese tradition, he always tried to integrate the house and garden. Johnson's buildings and houses are beautifully detailed and finished. He calls himself a modern traditionalist. His best-known works include the New York State Theater for the Lincoln Center (1962–1964) and the AT&T building (1978) in New York.

joint: An arrangement whereby two pieces of wood are connected or *joined* together by one of many methods, rather than being glued or nailed. The making of various types of joints is known as *joinery.*

joint stool: A sixteenth- and seventeenth-century **Jacobean** stool with turned legs, **mortise-and-tenon** joints, and pegged construction.

joist: A wood or steel horizontal beam supporting a floor, the underside forming the framework for a ceiling.

Jones, Inigo (1573–1652): Renowned English architect, furniture and set designer. He appropriated the principles of the classical style from Italy, and many of his buildings show the **Palladian** influence. He was the first to build a house with a **hipped roof** and **dormer windows.** His furniture designs were executed exclusively for the crown.

Juhl, Finn (1912–): Danish architect and furniture designer noted for his unusually lightweight wooden chairs, known as "floating seats." They have a distinctly sculptural form and are suspended on crossbars slightly raised above the main structure, rather than on the chair frame.

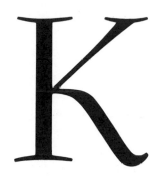

Kahn, Louis (1901–1974): American architect whose creed can be summed up in his statement that "architecture exists not for itself but for man's needs." Kahn's love of structure, great open spaces, texture, light, and shadow, together with his highly ordered sequence of space and unusual structural systems, earned him his international reputation. Some of his buildings plainly expose the web trusses that provide support for each floor of a building.

kakemono: A Japanese hanging scroll made of silk or paper with a painting or inscription on it. It is attached to wooden dowels top and bottom. They were hung in the *tokonoma*, a shallow alcove, and are used today as decorative hangings or pictures.

Kandinsky, Wassily (1866–1944): Russian expressionist painter, a leading member of *Der Blaue Reiter.*

K'ang: A platform in a Chinese living area on which are placed various pieces of furniture. It is also used as a sleeping platform and is customarily covered with woven mats.

kaolin: A fine clay, white, yellowish, or gray (in powder form it is pure white), used in the manufacture of fine porcelain.

kapok: A fiber obtained from the fruit of the silk-cotton tree, used as a stuffing for pillows, mattresses, and sleeping bags.

kas or **kast:** Seventeenth-century Dutch wardrobe or **armoire;** enormous in size, with a large overhanging cornice. Made in America from 1670 to 1770. The doors were paneled and the case mounted on ball feet. It was often elaborately painted with bright fruit designs; otherwise, it was given a simple fruitwood finish.

Kauffmann, Angelica (1741–1807): Swiss decorative artist who worked in England for **Robert Adam.** She painted furniture, ceilings, and murals. Her subject matter was usually groups of figures in mythological or idealized pastoral settings.

K.D.: Knocked Down. Designates furniture that is unassembled.

keeper: A striking plate, device, or guide for a bolt in a door.

Kent, William (1685–1748): English architect and interior designer; a leader of the British **Palladian** style. His furniture was massive and architectural in feeling, designed specifically for the **baroque** and classic mansions he furnished. It was heavily carved and gilded, with thick marble tops for all his tables.

Kerman or **Kirman rug:** A Persian rug with an elaborate border pattern and muted colors.

keystone: The central, wedge-shaped topmost stone of an arch, which locks and holds the others in place.

kidney table: A **kneehole desk** shaped like a kidney, with a bank of drawers on either side.

kilim: A flat handwoven rug of wool.

kiln: A furnace or oven for firing ceramics. Also, a heated room used for drying lumber, thereby removing moisture.

kinetic sculpture: Sculpture incorporating some aspect of motion, sometimes including movable works.

kitchen: A cooking room should be an efficient, pleasant, working area and reflect the personality of the user as much as any other room in a house. Some people enjoy eating and entertaining in the kitchen; others use the kitchen primarily for preparing and cooking food.

The cooking room has changed in recent years. There are no longer typical kitchen colors, wallpapers, fabrics, or decoration. Any wallpaper or fabric can be treated so that it is washable. Colors can be bold and bright. Careful planning is the keynote to the successful building or remodeling of a kitchen. It should not be designed as a laboratory but as a meticulously planned area that is convenient and attractive, saves steps, and minimizes drudgery. It is important to allow adequate storage space and to work out a scientific traffic-work pattern which, in order of importance, revolves about the sink, food preparation area, refrigerator, and cooking appliances.

Kitchens fall into five types:

1. *U-shape:* Ideal, especially with a center island.

2. *L-shape:* The most practical.

3. *Corridor:* Two walls of appliances and cabinets with walking space between. Efficient. An allowance of four and one-half feet should be allotted between cabinets.

4. *Island:* Ideal solution if space permits. It is most efficient when combined with a U-shaped kitchen.

5. *Single wall:* Least efficient.

Counter tops: Laminated plastics, linoleums, ceramic tile, vinyl, stainless steel, laminated hardwood, marble, mosaic tile, or alberene stone. Laminated plastics are available in many colors, patterns, and stripes.

Paint and paper: Many washable vinyl wallpapers in an array of colors and patterns are available. The use of two or three alternating paint colors for cabinet doors is a way of creating unusual interest. Different colors are often used to define the various work areas.

Walls: Brick, tile, washable vinyl wallpaper, paneling, vinyl tile, plastic laminate, fieldstone, siding, plastic-coated fabric, stainless steel, or paint.

Floors: Brick, tile, vinyl, flagstone, travertine marble, marble, linoleum, wood, washable carpeting, braided or rag rugs, terrazzo, or cork tiles.

Ceiling: Beams, vinyl wallpaper, paneling, or paint. Wallpaper can be used on the ceiling in a pattern, and the walls may be in a plain coordinated color or a stripe.

Window treatments: Bamboo shades or curtains, laminated shades, fabric that matches the wallpaper, textured roller shades with appliqués, draperies or curtains of companion fabric to the wallpaper used, shutters, mini-sized louvered Venetian blinds, awnings, café curtains, Roman shades, washable draperies of linen, sailcloth, or permanent-press fabrics.

Lighting: No room deserves closer scrutiny than the kitchen when it comes to lighting. Remember that light must be in front of the worker if she is to avoid working in her own shadow. As in most rooms, general as well as local and specific illumination must be provided. General lighting can be in the form of a complete luminous ceiling or just the soffit area above the work stations. It can be a central chandelier or a close-to-the-ceiling center light fixture. For local or task lighting, the level of light should be concentrated on work areas such as the sink and range. Under counter cabinets, fluorescent lighting is effective and easy to install. To blend with incandescent light and flatter the food as well as the worker, *warm-white* fluorescent tubes must be used. In addition to an overall ceiling light, spotlights for special working areas are recommended.

Compact kitchens. Storage is the most important consideration for a small kitchen. A compact kitchen, through scientific planning, can be more efficient than a large one. Integrate equipment and working counters and do not hesitate to remove a wall between the kitchen and the service area or porch. A small kitchen is an excellent room in which to use plain unframed mirrors to expand the space.

Gourmet kitchens. Three ovens are necessary, or two with a portable electric broiler-oven. Two separate sinks will be needed and a large wooden counter space. A gourmet kitchen usually calls for two or three ventilating fans. Pots and pans are invariably in plain sight. Many cooks like to have their knives hung on the wall as well. The true gourmet cook equips his or her kitchen with commercial restaurant-type equipment.

Kitchen Cabinet Dimensions:

Counter height	36 inches
Counter depth	24 inches
Highest shelf in upper cabinet	
	6 feet off floor
Utility closet:	Maximum height
	84 inches
	Depth
	13 to 25 inches
Distance between upper and base	
cabinets	15 to 19 inches
Distance between upper cabinet	
and sink	22 inches, minimum
Distance between upper cabinet	
and range	30 inches, minimum

Reminders:

1. When planning a new house, locate the kitchen so that it can serve the dining room on one side and the patio, terrace, or garden on the other side.

2. Stencils, découpage, decals, and wallpaper borders can rejuvenate old cabinet doors and transform the room.

3. Allow a minimum of twenty-four inches next to the range, for stacking serving dishes and dinner plates.

4. Create a kitchen greenhouse by opening up part of one wall or extending a window outward.

5. The refrigerator door should open toward the preparation area, which should be a minimum of twenty inches wide, and near the sink.

6. When the laundry center must be included in the kitchen, provide an extra ventilator.

7. When space is minimal, a **drop-leaf table** or a thick pull-out shelf can be used as a snack table or breakfast table for two.

8. A snack table can also be created by placing the range or sink at right angles to a wall and backing it with a counter.

9. A few shelves or an open cupboard can house a collection of mortars, bottles, tankards, old glass, copper molds, pepper-grinders, cruets, apothecary jars, or candy jars.

10. A pot- and pantry-closet is convenient for canned goods and cereals as well as pots and pans.

11. Handy built-ins include: chopping boards, intercoms, can openers, coffee-makers, radios, mixers, blenders, and clocks.

12. Extending a counter as little as three feet can provide a compact snack area.

13. A hanging desk, a telephone, and a portable typewriter make a home office and food-planning desk.

14. Ordinary cabinets can be given a custom look by adding moldings around the fronts of drawers and cabinet doors.

15. A closed-circuit television can be beamed at the children's play area.

16. Soapstone, if varnished and waxed, makes an excellent counter top that can withstand slicing and chopping.

17. Wall space between kitchen counter and overhead cupboards is a convenient place for a collection of spices. A rack attached to the back of a cupboard door is another place for spice containers.

18. In a small kitchen, a center island on casters is convenient. The top can be a chopping block, or it can be covered in marble and serve as a candy-making surface. It can even double as a snack bar.

19. An extra sink, a small work counter, and a cupboard for the storage of vases makes a flower-arranging area. It can also be used as a package-wrapping center.

20. Silver-drawers lined in Pacific cloth will help prevent silver objects from tarnishing.

21. When building a new kitchen or remodeling an existing one, a sewing center can easily be built into a deep closet.

22. Provide a place for magazines and cookbooks.

23. Fine art is not out of place in a kitchen.

24. Wine cupboards should be kept out of the kitchen unless the space provided for the wines is temperature-controlled. (*See* wine.)

25. Adding a skylight will flood the kitchen with sunshine and daylight.

26. Kitchens can vary widely in mood and style. For example, cabinets are available in the following styles: Contemporary, Early American, Oriental, French Provincial, Pennsylvania Dutch, and Spanish.

Klee, Paul (1879–1940): Swiss surrealist and Dada painter.

Kline, Franz (1910–1962): American avant-garde abstract painter.

klismos: A Greek chair that was particularly popular in the fifth century B.C. The legs are concave and splay toward front and back. Above the seat frame, at the back, curving **stiles** continue the lines of the rear legs and support a concavely curved board at shoulder height.

kneehole desk: A desk or writing table that has an opening or space for the knees and a bank of drawers on either side of this opening.

knife case: An eighteenth-century English container made of mahogany. Knife cases were customarily used in pairs, one on each side of a sideboard. They have sloping lids, serpentine fronts, and contain slots for silver flatware. Later versions appeared in the form of urns and had a rod in the center to prevent the top from being removed. These were placed on pedestals at either side of a buffet or sideboard. They were frequently made of satinwood, usually inlaid, sometimes painted.

knotty pine: *See* pine.

Kokoschka, Oskar (1886–1980): Austrian expressionist painter.

Korean furniture: The emphasis is on clean lines with the minimum number of glued joints necessary to ensure solidity. Korean furniture tends to be heavily ornamented, often with mother-of-pearl inlay, and is rather clumsy in comparison with Chinese furniture. The most fre-quently used decorative motifs are flowers, birds, butterflies, and the "ten longevities" (moon, sun, mountain, cloud, pine tree, water, bamboo, crane, deer, and the longevity plant).

Kuan-yin: A pure creamy-white porcelain figure with brilliant glazing. It represents the Buddhist goddess of mercy standing on a cloud base. Very popular as an art object and as a base for table lamps.

Kuhn, Walt (1880–1949): American painter of clowns and acrobats.

It takes a heap o' livin' in a house t' make it home.

Edgar A. Guest
(1881–1959)

lace: An open-work fabric made of fine threads of silk, cotton, gold, or silver. Lace-making originated in Italy during the fifteenth century. Lace was made by hand until the late eighteenth century, when machine-made lace became available. During most of the eighteenth century, the finest lace was made in Belgium. Nottingham, England was the center for machine-made lace.

lacquer: A varnish used as a finish on Oriental furniture since ancient times. It comes from the sap of the Asian *lac* tree, *Rhus vernicifera*. Lacquer is extremely resistant to wear. It comes in all colors and can be polished to a high gloss. Modern lacquers are compounds of cellulose derivatives. They dry on contact and must therefore be sprayed on.

ladder-back chair: In English and American cabinetwork, a chair back resembling a ladder, with several horizontal rails equally spaced. Very popular from 1750 to 1800. The **Chippendale** variety often had pierced rails.

Lalique: A French decorative glass made by molding, pressing, engraving, and frosting. Some pieces are obscure with low-relief designs of foliage, flowers, birds, animals, and figures. Originated by René Lalique of France (1860–1945).

Lally column: A tubular steel cylinder, usually filled with concrete, used as a structural column in residential and light commercial construction.

lambrequin: *See* draperies.

laminate: Wood, plastic, or one of a group of vinyl compounds bonded together to form a surface material that can be used as a covering for furniture, counters, or walls. Laminates are available under various trade names, such as Formica, Nevamar, Micarta, Parkwood, Textolite, and Laminart. High-pressure laminates are resistant to high temperatures, water, acids, and alkalis. They are more durable than painted, varnished, stained, or lacquered wood surfaces. Laminates are used for walls, doors, kitchen cabinets and counters, bar tops, bathrooms, and in public areas. Laminates can be had in hundreds of solid colors, wood grains, and patterns.

lamps and lampshades: A wealth of objects can be used as bases for table lamps: porcelain vases, bronze figures and vases, antique urns, buddhas, brass and silver candlesticks, antique Sheffield oil lamps, terra-cotta objects of art, and crystal vases and candlesticks. Indeed, any object of art may be electrified and converted into a table lamp. Lamp shades should be white most of the time. In bedrooms, very pale yellow or peach is acceptable. To avoid too much contrast, an opaque shade is recommended when a table lamp is placed against a very dark or paneled wall. Translucent shades reflect unpleasantly in windows, so opaque shades are recommended here as well. *See also* lighting.

lanai: A Hawaiian term for a covered terrace or verandah.

landing: A platform at the middle or end of a flight of stairs.

landscape architecture: The art of laying out a garden by arranging trees, shrubs, flower beds and borders, and fountains, in the interest of beauty and according to the principles of composition, balance, form, and color. It also involves the use of garden furniture and sculpture.

landscape painting: A representation of nature in paint. This genre flourished in seventeenth-century Holland, with Ruysdael and Hobbema being the foremost proponents. In nineteenth-century England, Turner and Constable were renowned for their landscapes, and in France, Rousseau and Corot were representative of the **Barbizon** painters.

lantern: A light fixture consisting of a glass receptacle for holding a light. It is suspended from a ceiling or attached to a wall. It first became fashionable in the eighteenth century, when a candle or an oil lamp was placed inside the lantern.

lap joint: A connection between two pieces of wood made by lapping one piece or part over another and fastening them together by gluing or nailing.

Larsen, Jack Lenor (1927–): Distinguished American textile designer, writer, and teacher. His innovations include: the first printed velvet upholstery fabric, the first stretch upholstery fabric (1961), and Interplay, a saran monofilament (1960). He has developed upholstery fabrics for Pan American and Braniff airlines; upholstery collections for Cassina and Vescom; and quilted silk banners for the Sears Tower in Chicago.

lath: A narrow strip of wood or metal nailed to studs and ceiling joists as a base for receiving plaster.

lathe: A machine used for shaping and carving a rotating article of wood or metal.

Latrobe, Benjamin (1766–1820): American architect. Considered the first professional architect in the United States, he introduced Greek forms, an important element of the classic revival. He designed the first Roman Catholic cathedral in the United States in Baltimore in 1804–1818, the Capitol at Richmond, Virginia, and interiors of the Washington Capitol.

lattice: An open framework made of narrow strips of wood, metal, or other materials, interwoven to form regular, patterned spaces. Latticework of thin slats of wood used in gardens as walls or ceilings is referred to as *treillage.*

latticinio: White opaque Venetian glass chiefly used in thread form to decorate clear glass pieces and paperweights.

lavabo: An eighteenth-century washbowl or basin attached beneath a wall-fountain. Also, a wall-mounted water container provided with a spigot.

lazy Susan: A revolving tray for food and condiments, usually placed in the center of a dining table. Today, cocktail tables are available with the entire top revolving.

lead glass: *See* flint glass.

leather: Leather is made from animal skins with the hair removed and the hide tanned. It has been used since the Middle Ages for wall hangings. In medieval England, traveling trunks were made of leather. In the sixteenth century, decorated leather was used for the first time for upholstering and cushions. Later, table tops were covered in morocco leather that was gilded, tooled, and embossed. Chests, chairs, and screens were covered with leather and studded with nail heads in a decorative pattern.

Steers are the usual source for furniture upholstery leathers. Morocco leather made from goatskin is the softest and finest leather available. The most pliable steer leather is called *top grain.* It is the first cut next to the hair. There are four other cuts: buff, split, skivers, and shoe. Leather is sold on a square-foot basis, in whole or half hides. A whole hide averages forty-five square feet. Use the following table to estimate quantities needed:

CONVERSION TABLE—FABRIC TO LEATHER

50–54 INCH FABRIC	SQUARE FEET IN LEATHER
1 Yard	17 square feet
2 Yards	34 square feet
3 Yards	51 square feet
4 Yards	68 square feet
5 Yards	85 square feet
6 Yards	102 square feet
7 Yards	119 square feet
8 Yards	136 square feet
9 Yards	153 square feet
10 Yards	170 square feet

MAINTENANCE

Leather should be protected from sunlight, moisture, and dirt. Saddlesoap is a good cleaner, as is a 60-40 blend of lanolin and neetsfoot oil. A neutral-color shoe wax also works well.

Lebrun, Charles (1619–1690): French architect, furniture designer, painter, and interior designer. He was made Director of the **Gobelin** tapestry factory under Louis XIV in 1667. He acted as artistic arbiter to the king, directing all decorative works. He decorated Versailles and the Apollo gallery at the Louvre.

Le Corbusier (1887–1965): Pseudonym of Charles Edouard Jeanneret, Swiss architect and leader in the development of modern architecture. Among his better-known works is the Chapel at Ronchamp, characterized by its sculptural and organic feeling. He designed many housing developments in France and worked on the United Nations Building in New York. He was also a painter, writer, urban planner, and designer of chairs and tables supported by tubular steel bases.

lectern: A reading desk, pulpit, stand, or pedestal made of wood or metal.

Léger, Fernand (1881–1955): French cubist painter.

Lenox: Fine American china, first manufactured in 1889. It was considered to be the first American china that could compete with European tableware.

Lescaze, William (1896–1969): American architect born in Switzerland. He helped develop the skyscraper as we know it today.

Libbey glass: An American glass company, specialized in cut glass during the late nineteenth century.

library steps: A set of two to four steps that fold into another form, such as a table, chair, or bench. Designed to provide access to high bookshelves. First made by eighteenth-century English cabinet-makers.

Liebes, Dorothy (1899–1972): American designer of fabrics. At one time or another she designed textiles for most major mills in America.

lighting: Even a well-designed room can be greatly improved with the proper illumination. Appropriate lighting will enhance the colors, forms, line designs, textures, and mood, and will create an atmosphere of spaciousness. Inadequate lighting can cause headaches, nervousness, eyestrain, and accidents due to poor visibility.

Two basic kinds of lighting are required in a house; *general* and *local* or *task lighting* placed at work centers. General lighting can be achieved in several ways: cove lighting, perimeter lighting, underlighted valances, or hanging, recessed, or wall fixtures. Local lighting is provided by portable lamps or equivalent fixtures.

Light is measured in units called *foot-candles*. A footcandle is the amount of light falling on a surface one foot from a candle. General illumination should be from seven to ten footcandles; local lighting (depending on the task) from fifteen to two hundred footcandles.

Circuit breakers can be installed at the entrance to each room so that lights will be turned on automatically upon a person's entering a room.

Artificial lighting does unexpected things to colors, because incandescent light adds yellow. Accordingly, if incandescent light falls on blue, it gives it a greenish cast; red takes on an orange cast. The specific use, purpose, and design of a room, as well as the personalities of the occupants, determine the proper intensity and distribution of light.

Avoid having a "daytime-only" attractive room. The color of upholstery and drapery fabrics should always be checked under the same lighting conditions in which they will be used. It is wise to keep a stock of spare bulbs, fluorescent tubes, flashlight batteries, and candles in a handy location for emergencies. With an eye to the future when building or remodeling, provide a larger switchboard than actually needed for immediate use.

The recommended minimum light levels are as follows:

- *Entry halls* (small, 50 to 75 square feet)
1 100-watt hanging fixture
1 150-watt R 40 floodlamp for a recessed fixture

- *Passageways*
1 75-watt fixture for every 10 feet of hallway
1 100-watt recessed fixture for every 10 feet of hallway

- *Closets*
Average size: 1 100-watt fixture
Walk-in: 1 100-watt recessed fixture for every 10 feet

- *Living rooms:*
General lighting, such as a chandelier of low wattage, may be used for decorative purposes. Local light is needed for casual reading, simple sewing, or knitting. The minimum requirement for a very small living room is four table lamps or a mixture of table and floor lamps. Two hundred watts of light are needed on each wall so that the local light is balanced in the room.

Lampshades should be white or off-white. The only place a pale color is used is in a bedroom. The inside of the shade should always be white. The bottom of the shade should be about thirty to forty-two inches off the floor. If a lamp is on a corner table, it should be pushed toward the corner and carry at least 200 watts of light.

Wall-light dimmers and track-lighting offer additional flexibility and mood control. For dramatic effects, additional fixtures can be used over a piano, a furniture grouping, or a game group. Keep the light fixture over a piano at least twenty-four inches in front of the keyboard, to avoid shadows. A wall of artwork can be shown to advantage by the use of spotlights or wall-washers.

There should be no harsh contrasts or deep shadows between local and general lighting. Subtle shadows are necessary to delineate form.

Accent lighting supplies a dramatic touch. It is used to light plantings, displays, or collections of objects of art. Bookshelves may be lighted by wall-washers recessed in the ceiling.

• *Dining rooms:*

A central fixture that is too bright causes glare and visual discomfort. A dimmer switch used judiciously, plus candlelight, will add drama, warmth, and graciousness. The soft light from the chandelier and the flicker from the candles will create sparkling highlights on crystal stemware and silver. To add further dramatic quality, provide two low-wattage recessed downlights on either side of the center chandelier. Candles should be high, so that guests will not be looking into the direct glare of the flames.

• *Bedrooms:*

A center ceiling fixture well shielded against glare is employed for general illumination. The recommended wattage is about 200. For reading in bed, the night-table lamp should be no more than twenty-five inches away from the book. Minimum wattage is 200. An extended swinging-arm wall lamp should be attached twelve inches from the bed and in line with the shoulder of the reader when in a semireclining position. A fluorescent wall bracket covering the entire width of the bed or beds is highly recommended for reading. Use only deluxe warm-white tubes. A table lamp or lamps are needed on a long dual dresser.

• *Bathrooms:*

For shaving and applying make-up, it is necessary to supply high-wattage lighting near the mirror behind the sinks. **Soffit** lighting is best when one or two sinks are installed in a pullman counter. If the counter is less than four feet long, two rows of warm-white or deluxe warm-white tubes are satisfactory. If the counter is between four and eight feet in length, three rows of fluorescent tubes are called for. A decorative hanging fixture on the opposite side of the room, with a minimum of seventy-five watts, will complete the illumination. If the bathroom has a freestanding sink with a medicine cabinet above, place a pair of brackets or light sconces on either side of the mirrored cabinet. Use at least 100 watts of light for each fixture. Another treatment is the theater dressing-room device, in which three sides of the mirror are surrounded by bare frosted bulbs. These lights come in strips and are available by the foot. For any partitioned area, use a recessed ceiling unit; for the shower, use a vaporproof light unit.

• *Den, study, or family rooms:*

Table lamps and downlights are needed to ensure desirable amounts of lighting for card playing, reading, sewing, and other taskwork. Two hundred watts is sufficient for studying and reading; 300 watts for sewing or embroidering.

Recessed or surface downlights are suitable for a specific area such as a game group or a bar. Provide 250 to 300 watts for adequate lighting. When entertaining around a bar, turn up all the lights. It is psychologically stimulating to guests and enhances the gay mood of a party. For conversations, turn off all downlights, using only table lamps. The light level should also be lowered for relaxing, listening to music, or watching television. Color television is not designed to be enjoyed in a dark room with strong contrasts between the screen and the general illumination of the room.

• *Kitchens:*

The ceiling fixture should provide a good overall level of illumination. A lu-minous ceiling provides impressive, shadowless, overall general lighting. The fluorescent tubes must be warm-white. Strip fluorescent lighting, mounted under cabinets, provides excellent illumination for local work surfaces. To avoid working in your own shadow, install soffit lighting over the range and sink. If this is not feasible, employ recessed incandescent fixtures that accommodate 200 watts of light each. The amount of wattage needed will vary with the wall color and reflecting value of porcelain or tile surfaces in the kitchen. Avoid dark colors on the counter tops, as they absorb too much light.

• *Outdoor lighting:*

The garden is the only place where one does not strive for even illumination. Make it a point to light the outdoors dramatically, not evenly. Ensure safety by lighting all entrances, steps, walks, service areas, and the driveway.

Well-lighted terraces, patios, swimming pools, tennis courts, and play spaces increase the hours of outdoor living. Spotlight flower beds, statues, water fountains, bird baths, or other points of interest. Mount floodlights on the roof, under the eaves, and in trees or telephone poles, if allowed. A gas or electric post lantern is desirable at the driveway and the main entrance walk. Keep in mind the post's architectural relationship to the house. Install weatherproof electrical outlets on all sides of a house, plus two additional ones on a terrace, porch, or patio. They will be useful for appliances and electrical yard tools. For patios, flower beds and general ground lighting, use low-wattage lamps.

Limoges: A city in France where fine hard-paste china and porcelain are made. Manufactory established in 1770. The decoration of Limoges porcelain is similar to that of Paris and **Sèvres** porcelain.

Lincoln rocker: A high, straight-back, upholstered rocker with padded elbow rests. The back is continuous with the seat.

linear perspective: A technique of representing three-dimensional objects and depth relationships on a two-dimensional surface using actual or suggested lines that converge in the background, thereby creating the illusion of distance.

linenfold: A decorative motif on walls or carved furniture resembling a scroll or fold of cloth. Flemish in origin; very popular in Northern Europe in the fifteenth through the seventeenth centuries.

linen press: A seventeenth-century wooden contrivance for pressing linen when damp. The linen was placed between two boards, with pressure applied by a spiral screw. Also, a cupboard for storing linen.

lining paper (blank stock): Plain paper applied underneath the wallcovering to ensure a smoother surface and better adhesion.

lintel: A horizontal beam over an opening such as a door or window that supports part of the weight above.

lion motif: An ancient decorative motif used in furniture design as far back as ancient Egypt. Popular during the Renaissance, Gothic, and Empire periods.

Lipchitz, Jacques (1891–1973): French sculptor, born in Lithuania, who worked in different modes and styles. He favored cubism and surrealism.

lit clos: French term for "closed bed." Typically, a **French Provincial** bed built into a niche and partially enclosed by paneling and draperies. Occasionally used in a corner, and often referred to as a *Breton bed*. These beds were common in all colder regions of France. They date from the sixteenth century and were often made with an upper berth.

lites: Panes of glass in the opening between the **mullions** of a window.

lithography: A printing process in which the image to be printed is rendered on a flat surface (originally a stone, nowadays usually a sheet of zinc or aluminum), and treated so that it will retain ink, while the nonimage area is treated so that it will repel ink. The end result resembles a pencil or crayon drawing.

living room: *See* furniture arrangement; color; lighting.

load-bearing: Referring to walls that support an upper floor, roof, or joist loads.

local lighting: Lighting designed to provide illumination over a relatively small area or confined space, without providing any significant general surrounding light.

Loewy, Raymond (1893–): American industrial designer. He studied electrical engineering and fashion illustrating. In 1929 he was appointed Art Director to the Westinghouse Electric Company. His best-known designs include the Studebaker "Avanti" car; the Coca-Cola dispenser; the Schick razor; the Lucky Strike cigarette pack; and the Electrolux vacuum cleaner. The firm Loewy-Snaith, Inc. is the largest industrial design firm in the world.

loggia: A roofed but open gallery or arcade adjacent to a building.

lost wax process: A method, dating back to antiquity, of reproducing in bronze an exact copy of an original model. A mold taken from the original is lined in wax. Molten bronze is then poured in to replace the wax. Today, this method has largely been replaced by the *sand-casting method.*

Louis XIII style: Furniture of early seventeenth-century France, during the reign of Louis XIII (1610–1643). The furniture had no national character but was a potpourri of many Flemish, Spanish, and Italian elements as well as most characteristics of the **Renaissance.** The furniture was heavy, massive, and ornately carved, especially with spiral turnings. Ornamental motifs were: cartouches, swags, cherubs, marquetry, tortoiseshell, and gilding. Upholstery in the form of leather was introduced.

Louis XIV style: French **baroque** style, named for the king who reigned during this period (1643–1715). Furniture was on a grand scale—majestic, elaborate, flamboyantly decorated, and richly carved and gilded with animal, plant, and floral forms. Musical instruments were used as carving motifs. **Boulle marquetry**—inlays of brass, pewter, tortoiseshell, tin, ivory, and mother-of-pearl—was popular. Furniture was painted, gilded, or silvered. Woods were varied; almond, holly, box, ebony, pear, and chestnut were used. The **Gobelin, Aubusson,** and **Savonnerie** factories were producing richly colored upholstery fabrics, tapestries, carpets, and furniture. Comfortable upholstered furniture was introduced in this era, as were **console tables, bonnetières,** and bookcases with doors fitted with wire grilles. Beds grew huge and draperies very elaborate, for the king was a lover of pomp and splendor. France rose to the place of first power in Europe. The early period of Louis XIV's reign was one of lavish display, marked by the building of the Palace of Versailles, but when Louis XIV died, he left France impoverished and practically bankrupt.

Louis XV style: French furniture style of the years 1730 to 1765, encompassing both the **Régence** and late **rococo** eras. Louis XV was five years old when he inherited the crown from his grandfather, Louis XIV. There were no distinguishing changes in style during the regency of Philippe II, Duc d' Orléans (1715–1723), although the **commode** was first introduced, heavily decorated with **ormolu** on corners, feet, and even on the surface. These eight years ushered in the blossoming of the rococo period.

Rococo Period: This gay and frivolous period produced extravagant, charming, graceful, and smaller-scaled furniture. It is the most popular of all French styles. Furniture was slender, decorative, curved, delicate—and comfortable. Wood frames were gold-leafed or painted. Rocks, birds, shells, foliage, musical instruments, and baskets of flowers were used for decoration and carvings. Many highly carved,

decorated, and unusually shaped mirrors and sconces appeared. **Marquetry** and inlay work could be found on most cabinet pieces. A finishing technique known as *Vernis Martin* was developed by the Martin brothers. Its quality rivaled that of Oriental lacquers. Marble, onyx, and alabaster showed up as covers for **console table** and commode tops. Cane, straw, and rush bottoms for chairs were popular. This was the era of intrigue, and secret rooms existed that were entered through the backs of wardrobes or through sliding panels in walls. Rooms were artistic and charming but smaller than heretofore. Walls were upholstered in silk, satin, damask, taffeta, moires, or printed cottons called *toiles de Jouy*. Louis XV was notorious for his circle of female friends, and the furniture of his time reveals the influence they had upon it. Madame de Pompadour, the King's Lady, a cultured person of great taste, popularized Oriental silks, porcelains, and wallpapers, and was responsible for the feminine grace prevalent during the years 1740–1760. She was also a dominant influence in restraining the exuberant rococo style.

Louis XVI style: French furniture style of around 1765–1790. The excavations at Pompeii and Herculaneum profoundly influenced French furniture designers of the time. There was a return to simplicity in this classical revival period. Straight lines and the use of classical architectural forms were the order of the day. The **ro-coco** curve gave way to the simple oval, the circle, and the ellipse. Wall paneling was unaffected and unadorned. Legs were round and tapered, with **fluting** or grooves. Ornamentation consisted of classical motifs, including: laurel, acanthus, egg and dart, palm leaves, lyre, urn, wreath, fretwork, ribbons, oak leaves, swans, and bound arrows. The style was a refinement of the **Louis XV period** but more graceful, restrained, and severe. Mahogany was the preeminent wood, but ebony returned to favor along with satinwood and tulipwood. Typical fabrics were silks with restrained small patterns, simple tapestries, and *toile de Jouy.*

louvers: A series of slanting slats set in a window or frame to provide air, light, and privacy. Outdoor louvers can be adjusted to shed rainwater.

love seat: A sofa for two persons. It was very popular in eighteenth-century England, when it was called a *courting chair.*

lowboy: A low, tablelike chest of drawers. Very popular in America throughout the eighteenth century. The lowboy is essentially the lower section of the **highboy** and was used as a companion piece to the latter.

Lowestoft porcelain: Soft-paste English porcelain manufactured since 1757. Con-tains bone ash. A great deal of it is in the blue and white chinese style.

low relief: *See* bas-relief.

lozenge: A diamond-shaped decorative motif.

Lucite: A tradename for a transparent, acrylic, manmade plastic. (It is also known by the name Plexiglass.) In making the acrylic, it is slowly cooled to forty degrees, then it is fitted into metal corner joints or sleeves. When the acrylic returns to room temperature, it expands to hold the joints securely, precluding the necessity for screws or bolts. Lucite is used to make elegant chair and sofa frames as well as tables.

Luks, George (1867–1933):   American painter of portraits and of New York City's East Side. A member of the **Ashcan school.**

lumen: The international unit of luminous flux, equal to the luminous flux emitted within a unit solid angle by a point source having an intensity of one candela.

lunette: A semicircular or crescent-shaped opening or space, usually over a door or window, filled with fan-shaped carving or inlay. In architecture, an opening set in a dome, or a semicircular window set deeply into a wall.

lusterware: English ceramic ware coated with either copper, silver, platinum, or gold, creating a luster.

lyre-back chair: A chair whose back is in the form of a lyre, often with metal rods representing the strings. The lyre motif, which was also used on table pedestals, was a feature of **Louis XIV** and **Louis XV** furniture.

lyre form: Pierced wood with the outline of a lyre, usually found on open chair backs and table bases. Metal rods are often used to represent the strings. First designed by **Robert Adam** in about 1770.

MacDonald-Wright, Stanton (1890–1973): American abstract painter.

machine-printed wallpaper: Wallpaper produced on a rotary press. The printing rollers are made of brass and felt, and the design is routed out or engraved.

McIntire, Samuel (1757–1811): American architect, builder, wood carver, sculptor, and musician. He is noted mainly for his skilled **neoclassical style** carvings on furniture executed by others. His favorite motifs were baskets of fruit, grapes, wheat sheaves, festoons, rosettes, and cornucopias. His mantels, curved stairways, and cornices are especially noteworthy. He also sculpted figureheads for clipper ships out of Salem.

McKim, Mead & White: The most influential architectural firm during the 1890s in New York. They used Roman Renaissance forms and built such edifices as the Metropolitan Museum of Art, Madison Square Garden, Bellevue Hospital, and the University of Virginia.

macramé: Lacework made by knotting cotton, silk, or linen into various designs and fringes.

Madeira: Fine needlework designs of embroidery made by nuns on the island of Madeira.

magic realism: *See* modern art.

magnolia: A pale hardwood used in furniture making, primarily for framing and interior linings.

Magritte, René (1898–1967): Belgian surrealist painter.

mahogany: A very hard, brown or red-colored wood of attractively figured grain. It is very valuable in the manufacture of furniture because it is easy to work and finishes well. Mahogany is imported from Honduras, Brazil, Africa and, at one time, from Cuba.

Maillol, Aristide (1861–1944): French sculptor of heroic female nudes.

majolica: Tin-glazed earthenware, richly embellished with painted decoration, made in Spain and Italy since the fourteenth century.

manifest: A document, similar to a **bill of lading**, showing consignor, consignee, and gross weight. The term is normally used in connection with shipments made to foreign countries.

Mannerist style: A European decorative style of the sixteenth and seventeenth centuries characterized by grotesque, distorted human figures and other bizarre motifs. This style was a revolt against rational classicism and was short-lived, forming a transition between **Renaissance** and **baroque** styles.

mansard roof: *See* gambrel roof.

mantel: In architecture, the structure surrounding the fireplace. Also, the shelf over a fireplace.

Manwaring, Robert (active 1760s): English **rococo** cabinetmaker and furniture designer specializing in chairs. Known for his pattern books, especially the 1765 *Cabinet and Chair Maker's Real Friend and Companion.*

maple: A hard but easily workable wood used in furniture making. Its natural color varies from beige to reddish brown. Generally found in northeastern United States and Canada. Available in highly figured bird's-eye or **burl** grains.

marble: A beautiful and durable metamorphic rock that polishes and wears well. Marble is divided into four grades: A, B, C, and D. A and B are for exterior use, C and D, the most decorative, for indoor use only.

Travertine marble, characterized by irregular cavities, is beige in color, but the cavities can be filled in with any color. It polishes well, is easily available, and is used for floors, walls, table tops, and counters. It is lower in cost than regular marble. During the eighteenth century, it was customary to stain common white marble in imitation of the more rare and costly varieties.

Upkeep of marble is quite simple. For polished marble with a glossy finish, apply marble wax. Dust regularly and use a damp cloth occasionally. If stained, use hot water and a soapless cleaner. For honed marble (marble with little gloss), use an abrasive powdered kitchen cleaner. Oil stains must be washed with a detergent, or a 50/50 mixture of ammonia and water, and then treated with a poultice of equal parts of whiting powder and acetone. Leave the poultice on overnight. If the stain is not completely removed, try a poultice of equal parts of whiting powder and hydrogen peroxide, plus two drops of ammonia.

marbling: In bookbinding, a decorative

imitation of marble patterns on endpapers and page edges. Originally done by stirring colors mixed with gums in a flat pan and floating them on. Today, most marbelizing is done by silk screening.

marquetry: A furniture inlay of variously colored thin woods, ivory, shells, brass, pewter, or mother-of-pearl. **André Boulle** brought this artistic expression to its highest point during the reign of **Louis XIV.**

Marquise chair: An eighteenth-century French chair. It is a very wide, deep armchair—the French version of a narrow **love seat** or **courting chair.**

Martha Washington chair: A mid-eighteenth-century American open-arm chair with a shallow upholstered seat and high back. The legs are square or round and tapered.

mastic: A pliable material similar to a **caulking** compound, used for sealing small openings or narrow joints.

Matisse, Henri Emile (1869–1954): French postimpressionist painter and sculptor. A leader of the Fauvist movement (*see* modern art).

media room: A home sound studio, screening room, music and television room all in one.

Mediterranean style: A twentieth-century label for a conglomeration of fifteenth-century **French Provincial, Directoire, Spanish, Italian,** and **Moorish** furniture. It is commercial-looking—heavy and boldly scaled. It has much crude carving and grillwork, with leather and wrought iron used for trimmings.

Meissen: A delicate porcelain, first made in Meissen, Germany, in the early eighteenth century. Also known as *Dresden.*

member: Part of a structural assembly, such as a stud, a joist, a beam, a girder, or a column.

mercury vapor lamp: A lamp in which ultraviolet and yellowish-green to blue visible light is produced by sending an electric discharge through mercury vapor.

méridienne: A short **daybed** of the **Empire** period having ends of unequal height connected by a back with a sloping top.

Metric System:

TABLE OF EQUIVALENTS

UNITED STATES	METRIC
1 inch	2.54 centimeters
1 foot	0.3048 meter
1 yard	0.9144 meter
39½ inches (1.0936 yards)	1 meter

Metzinger, Jean (1883–1957): French cubist painter.

mezzanine: A partial floor located between two main floors of a building.

mezzotint: A technique of engraving a copper or steel plate by scraping and burnishing areas to produce various tones of black and white. Devised in the eighteenth century and used principally to reproduce portraits. The process lends itself to hand coloring.

Michelangelo (1475–1564): Florentine sculptor, painter, and architect whose genius in sculpting the human figure influenced cabinetmakers of the sixteenth century to introduce **baroque** carvings of human figures on furniture. His full name was Michelangelo Buonarroti.

Miës van der Rohe, Ludwig (1886–1969): German-American architect and furniture designer—a pioneer of the **International** style. He had no formal training but worked for the architect **Peter Behrens,** alongside **Gropius** and **Le Corbusier.** Miës became director of the **Bauhaus** in 1930, but soon after, Nazi pressure forced him to move to the United States. His design credo was "less is more." He believed in honesty of construction, even in exposing parts of the steel framework of his furniture. His designs are of classic severity, with great use of glass and steel. He was a stickler for purity of form and dramatic simplicity. Miës's best-known designs include the **Barcelona chair** (1929); the Tugendhat chair (1930); and the X-based table (1930).

milk glass: An opaque or translucent white glass.

millefiori: Decorative glass made by fusing multicolored glass canes together, cutting them crosswise, joining them together, imbedding them in clear glass and then blowing the mass into the shape desired. Used in glass paperweights. *Millefiori* means "a thousand flowers" in Italian.

miniature: A small painting. Also, a miniature (ten-to-fourteen-inch) furniture cabinet used as a sample model by eighteenth-century cabinetmakers.

Minton porcelain: Earthenware, usually white decorated with blue in the Chinese manner. The factory was established in 1793. By 1825 fine-glazed porcelain was being made. Decorations consisted of medallions of flowers, Chinese landscapes, and much gilding.

Miró, Joan (1893–): Spanish abstract and surrealist painter.

mirrors: The first mirrors to become fashionable were made of highly polished metal, silver, gold, and obsidian. **Tudor** style mirrors were made of steel and were enclosed by sliding doors or draperies, to prevent oxidation. Mirrors of silvered glass appeared during the **Renaissance** in Murano, near Venice, Italy. Frames were overly large and elaborate, for the mirrors were costly and, at first, available only in small sizes.

Materials used for framing included: carved walnut or mahogany, **marquetry,** tortoiseshell, embossed silver, ebony with silver, Chinese lacquer, and cut glass. Frames were sometimes painted or decorated with gilt and gesso. Some had candle brackets at each side.

Very elaborate overmantel mirrors, in all shapes and sizes, were made popular by **Chippendale.** The French overmantel mirror, known as a **trumeau,** consists of a mirror and a painting combined in one frame.

mission furniture: When the Spanish missionaries settled in California and Mexico they built their missions with Indian labor. Clumsy, crude furniture was constructed with native oak, which was readily available. Upholstery was of coarse-grained leather. Large-headed copper nails were used for trimmings. There was a resurgence of this style in the early 1900s. By 1910, the style was nonexistent.

miter, miter joint: A connection between two pieces of wood made by beveling an edge of each piece and placing the beveled edges face to face.

mobile: A metal or wire sculpture that, because of its finely balanced construction and arrangement, will move or oscillate with natural air currents. Often suspended from a ceiling.

modern architecture: Modern buildings are areas of space resting on slender piers or concrete slabs and enclosed by large areas of glass and thin **curtain walls.** Modern technological contributions include: air conditioning, sound control, synthetic wall and floor materials, steel, reinforced concrete, suspended roofs, space frames, and prefabrication. European and American architects who were active innovators and vigorous contributors to modern architecture include:

Alvar Aalto
Max Abromovitz
Gunnar Asplund
Pietro Santi Bartoli
Pietro Belluschi
Marcel Breuer
Felix Candela
Ray Eames
Buckminster Fuller
Antoni Gaudí
The Greene brothers
Walter Gropius
Victor Gruen
Arne Jacobsen
Philip Johnson
Albert Kahn
Benjamin Latrobe
Le Corbusier

William Lescaze
Charles Rennie Mackintosh
Laszlo Maholy-Nagy
Ludwig Miës van der Rohe
Pier Nervi
Richard Neutra
Oscar Niemayer
I. M. Pei
William L. Pereira
Henry Richardson
Eero Saarinen
Rudolf Schindler
Skidmore, Owings & Merrill
Edward Durrel Stone
Louis Sullivan
Henri van de Velde
Robert Venturi
Frank Lloyd Wright
William Wurster
Minoru Yamasaki

modern art: Artwork ranging from simple, formalized structures, to geometric improvisations, to abstract art. While many find the techniques employed by modern artists to be elusive, the work itself cannot be condemned. When understood, it is exhilarating and inspiring. This revolution in art began in the 1860s with the Impressionist movement. A survey of the most important modern movements follows.

IMPRESSIONISM

A French movement whose chief aims were to emphasize the transitory and portray overall visual impressions. The impressionists tended to disregard perspective, detail, and form. They popularized painting directly from nature, out of doors. They used broken color, with each brush stroke distinct, thus achieving a certain luminosity and effect of light and atmosphere. Colors were bright and pure. The major artists associated with the impressionist movement were: Monet, Manet, Degas, Renoir, Sisley, Pissaro, Morisot, Cézanne (for a brief period), and Cassatt.

NEOIMPRESSIONISM— POINTILLISM

A late-nineteenth-century movement heralding the beginning of postimpressionism. The pointillists applied tiny dots of pure primary colors to a white ground, and the eye automatically blended them into secondary and tertiary colors. A certain luminosity was also achieved in this way. The chief practitioners included Signac and Seurat.

POSTIMPRESSIONISM

The era following 1880—an interim period between impressionism, the Nabis group, and Fauvism in 1905. The artists Cézanne, Seurat, Gauguin, Signac, Van Gogh, and Redon are often termed postimpressionists. They were dissatisfied with the objective point of view of the impressionists and placed emphasis on the subjective viewpoint—on form, space, and color.

NABIS

A late-nineteenth-century group that painted simple, intimate genre subjects using the impressionistic technique. The group consisted of Denis, Vuillard, Bonnard, and Valloton. These artists are sometimes known as *intimists*. *Nabi* is the Hebrew word for *prophet*.

FAUVISM

The Fauves were the nihilists of the art world at the turn of the century. The name, which means *wild beasts,* was adopted by a group of French painters, including Matisse, Rouault, Dufy, Derain, Vlaminck, Braque, Van Dongen, Valtat, Kirchner, Kandinsky, Jean Puy, and Manguin. The movement was characterized by flaming, brilliant, vivid colors, bold distortion, abstract, decorative forms, and a generous use of paint. The total effect is both sensuous and emotional. Fauvism was short-lived (1905–1906) and preceded cubism.

CUBISM

A French movement that arose in revolt against representational art. It lasted from 1906 through 1921. Cubism was a new means of pictorial expression that stressed abstract, three-dimensional, geometric forms. Objects were portrayed by the use of cubes, cones, and geometric solids rather than by realistic representation. Forms were broken up into angular planes, thus creating a new visual ex-

perience. In portraiture, the face was painted from many angles, all at one time in one canvas. Among the cubists were Picasso, Braque, Léger, Gris, Mondrian, Derain, Metzinger, Delaunay, Klee, Gleizes, Lhote, Duchamp, Marin, Macdonald-Wright, LeFauconnier, Lipchitz, Archipenko, Laurens, Weber, and Duchamp-Villon.

ORPHISM

A French art movement of 1912, best described as lyrical abstract cubism, closely associated with abstract expressionism. It relied on the use of highly saturated pigments. The leading artists of this group were Marc, Macke, Feininger, S. MacDonald-Wright, and Delaunay, who created this style of painting.

CONSTRUCTIVISM

An art movement and style that originated in Russia during the 1920s. Constructivists used untraditional materials such as hair, wood, rags, and pieces of glass, assembled in nonobjective, geometric, and abstract forms. Vladimir Tatlin created the first works of this kind. Others that followed were: Picasso, Gabo, Pevsner, Malevich, and Moholy-Nagy.

EXPRESSIONISM

An early-twentieth-century central European movement in which the artist, through a purposeful distortion of color, form, and space, practiced free expression to reveal his inner emotions and experiences. This style was typified by the paintings of two German schools, the *Bridge* (*Die Brucke*) and the *Blue Rider* (*Der Blaue Reiter*). Expressionists tried to paint the soul—the truth of existence, the analytical essence of life—in revolt against academic painting. They tried to interpret their philosophy through distortion, exaggeration, and shock—sensation for the sake of drama. Artists of the Bridge were: Nolde, Pechstein, Van Dongen, Heckel, and the organizer of this group, Ernst Ludwig Kirchner. The Blue Rider group, which was formed in 1911, was headed by the Russian Wassily Kandinsky. Artists associated with this school included: Kokoschka, Klimt, Marc, Jawlensky, Munch, Delaunay, David and Vladimir Burliuk, Klee, Macke, Gontcharova, Beckman, and Feininger.

DADA

A violent revolutionary cult among European and American artists during the years 1916–1924. All conventional and traditional forms and aesthetics were attacked in the belief that all art movements of the past had to be completely discarded. This movement was initiated by Jean Arp in Zurich, in revolt against World War I, and was expressed by fantastic, formless expressions of satire against the horrors of war. It was an exercise of protest against the inhumanity and materialism of reasoned order. In actuality, it was more of a philosophy than an art, although Dadaists took an active stand against cubism and traditional art. Artists involved were: Arp, Tzara, Janco, Man Ray, Arensberg, Ernst, Grosz, Picabia, Duchamp, and Archipenko. This movement was the forerunner of *surrealism*.

DE STIJL

A Dutch art movement initiated by Theo van Doesburg in 1917, based on the theory that all must be kept to a minimum. The only colors used were the primaries and black and white. Composition was based on asymmetrical arrangements, and form was confined to the rectangle.

SURREALISM

A modern French art movement founded in 1924, influenced by the work of Sigmund Freud. Surrealists are concerned with portraying the workings of the subconscious mind as revealed in dreams and nightmares. Marc Chagall pioneered this style, but it was Salvador Dali who exploited its shock value. Other surrealist artists were: Miró, Tanguy, de Chirico, Duchamp, Ernst, Magritte, Giacometti, Masson, Arp, and Man Ray.

Dali, Tanguy, and Magritte painted representational, symbolic, dreamlike objects such as melting watches. The composition was excellent and the painting meticulously done. Chagall and de Chirico arranged their figures in an irrational, noncontextual manner and claimed that their work was done entirely under the domination of the subconscious. Masson and Arp did not paint in a representational way but were whimsical, even humorous, in their works. Miró's works were more abstract than those of the other surrealists.

MAGIC REALISM

America's answer to French surrealism, magic realism refers not to visionary art but to paintings done with a faithful adherence to nature—meticulously reproduced down to the last realistic detail. This group included: Andrew Wyeth, Ben Shahn, George Grosz, and Otto Dix.

ABSTRACT EXPRESSIONISM

This nonobjective manner of painting arose during World War II. It combined elements of expressionism, cubism, Dadaism, and surrealism in abstract, nonrecognizable forms, lines, and colors. The chief practitioners include: Gorky, Pollock, Albers, Motherwell, Rothko, Kline, Gottlieb, de Kooning, Baziotes, and Hans Hofmann.

THE ASHCAN SCHOOL

A group of American painters (1890–1929), also referred to as "The Eight," that painted contemporary, socially conscious subjects, particularly scenes of city life, in a highly realistic manner. The group included: William J. Glackens, Arthur B. Davies, Ernest Lawson, Robert Henri, Everett Shinn, George B. Luks, John Sloan, and Maurice Prendergast.

AMERICAN SCENE PAINTERS

A realistic genre school of the 1930s, that concentrated on rural life and landscape. Its membership included: Charles Burchfield, Edward Hopper, Thomas Hart Benton, John Steuart Curry, and Grant Wood.

THE NEW YORK SCHOOL

The American version of abstract expressionism as practiced in the years 1945–71 by Hans Hofmann, Joseph Albers, Franz Kline, Robert Motherwell, Frank Stella, Jackson Pollock, Arshille Gorky, Willem de Kooning, Mark Tobey, Elsworth Kelly, William Baziotes, Mark Rothko, and Larry Rivers.

POP ART

A broad movement (1960s) of antiart, happenings, insanities, and biomorphic fantasies. Preoccupation with the common object was de rigueur. Hard-edge studies of food cans and hot dogs were raised to the level of art. Practitioners include: Claes Oldenburg, Roy Lichtenstein, and Andy Warhol.

OP ART

Commercial kinetic illustration in which the tricky use of luminous color, perspective, and X rays are combined to produce optical illusions of space and motion. A form of Neo-Dadaism. Among its adherents are Roy Lichtenstein, Robert Rauschenberg, and Jasper Johns.

modern interior design: In every era, what is deemed "modern" in terms of interior design is essentially a transition from the previous modern period. Each period segues into the next, and each new "modern" movement contains adaptations from old themes.

Today's modern design had its genesis in the early stages of the industrial revolution. It is noteworthy that today's modern is not a recycling of a previous period's style or styles. Modern furniture has kept pace and developed along with modern architecture. In modern interior design, contemporary materials and techniques are used to create environments suited to today's lifestyles. Furniture forms are not imitative of past designs and have a minimum of ornamentation. Furniture is made by machine, not by hand. The modern furniture designer understands technology, new materials, and industrial techniques. There are a number of distinct schools or styles of modern design:

Scandinavian Modern combines modern technology with old-fashioned craftsmanship and materials.

Contemporary is an umbrella term for all current modern designs, but especially traditional furniture modernized.

Modern interior designers create the illusion of space by using mirrors and other reflective materials, including glass, chrome, trompe l'oeil murals, and graphics. Color is an important factor in liberating space. Modern interiors emphasize comfort, openness, and lightness. There is no "organized clutter." Much of the furniture has an architectural feeling, with some of the structural skeleton exposed. Illumination, both natural and artificial, becomes a significant factor in designing a room. Walls of glass slide open to gardens and terraces in temperate climates. Emphasis is on the use of natural materials: linen, cotton, unstained woods, plants, and fur. However, manmade materials are not forgotten. Structural and decorative materials include tubular steel, molded plywood, plastics, caning, foam rubber, vinyl, chrome, aluminum, bronze, glass, rattan, fiberglass, canvas, and Lucite.

Designers who left an indelible mark on modern furniture design were:

Alvar Aalto
Ward Bennett
Harry Bertoia
Marcel Breuer
Charles Eames
Owen Jones
Finn Juhl
Kaare Klint
Florence Knoll
The Lavernes
Le Corbusier
Paul McCobb
Bruno Mathsson
Ludwig Miës van der Rohe

William Morris
George Nelson
Isamu Noguchi
Jens Risom
Eero Saarinen
Kipp Stewart
Louis Tiffany
Michael Thonet
Henri van de Velde
Hans Wegner
Edward Wormley

modesty panel: A panel set into the back of a **kneehole desk** in order to secure privacy for the sitter.

Modigliani, Amedeo (1884–1920): Italian painter and sculptor of the human figure, particularly portraits. Known for his elongation of face, form, and neck.

modular furniture: Upholstered furniture units that can be arranged to suit the designer's or client's seating ideas. Wooden modular case goods are also available.

module: In architecture and building, a unit of measurement or proportion.

molding: Any of various ornamental, shaped wooden members used on tables, cornices, frames, or between a ceiling and a wall.

Mondrian, Piet (1872–1944): Dutch abstract painter.

monochromatic: *See* color.

moon gate: A circular opening in a wall used instead of a door in traditional Chinese architecture.

Moore, Henry (1898–): British abstract sculptor.

morocco: A fine pebble-grained leather originally made from goat skin tanned with sumac.

Morris, William (1834–1896): An English artist, poet, pseudoarchitect, painter, writer, interior designer, and manufacturer of stained glass, textiles, wallpaper, tapestries, and furniture. Morris was a leader of the British **Arts and Crafts movement.** In 1861, in association with several friends, he established a firm to manufacture furniture, Morris & Co. This firm played a large part in reforming the decorative arts of the **Victorian** era. The firm produced simple, clean, but meticulously crafted furniture, devoid of the elaborate decoration popular at this time. It was decorated, instead, with stylized botanical designs or painted with Pre-Raphaelite depictions of medieval scenes. A socialist, Morris was a firm believer that all art should be "by the people and for the people," and not just for the moneyed class. Some believe that his design philosophy culminated in the **Modern** movement. The *Morris chair*, a large wooden lounging chair with an adjustable back and loose cushion seat was actually designed by Philip Webb, a partner in the firm Morris & Co.

mortar: A mixture of sand, cement, water, and occasionally lime, used in building.

mortise and tenon: A method of joining two pieces of wood. A hole or notch is cut in a piece of wood called a *mortise*, to receive a projecting part called a *tenon*, which has been shaped to fit it.

mosaic: A picture or decorative design made by arranging in cement, small squares or fragments (*tesserae*) of multicolored stone, wood, glass, or marble. Usually incorporated in a wall or a floor.

Moses, Grandma (1860–1961): American primitive painter. Her full name was Anna Mary Robertson Moses.

mother-of-pearl: The hard, lustrous inner layer or lining of marine shells such as the pearl oyster or abalone. In the West, it has been popular as a decorative inlay in furniture since the sixteenth century. Used in the Orient since about the ninth century.

Motherwell, Robert (1915–): American action and abstract expressionist painter.

motif: A dominant theme, idea, symbol, or feature of design or ornament used to embellish furniture or architecture.

muffin stand: A small table with shelves for holding plates and a tea service.

mullion: A vertical strip dividing bars in a window into two or more sections, lights, or panes.

muntin: A sash bar.

mural: A decoration or picture painted directly on a wall or, by extension, onto a ceiling. It is possible to paint a mural on canvas that is attached to a wall and that can always be removed and hung elsewhere. Murals should have a matte finish to avoid glare and reflections. Permanent murals, called **frescoes,** are created by painting with watercolors on wet plaster. Other methods and media exist, including oil, tempera, encaustic, and painting on porcelain enamel.

Murano: An island off the coast of Venice, Italy. Home of the Venetian glass industry.

museums: A selective list of the world's outstanding museums and art centers arranged by countries and cities follows. Included are those museums whose superb works of art are of universal significance. A visit to these institutions will prove a truly rewarding experience for the tourist, sightseer, student, or the most enthusiastic art lover.

MUSEUMS

Austria

Modern Galerie	Vienna
Albertina Museum	Vienna
Kunsthistorisches Museum	Vienna
Akademie der Bil- den Kunste	Vienna

Belgium

Art Ancien	Brussels
Musée Royal des Beaux-Arts	Brussels
Musée Royal des Beaux-Arts	Antwerp

Denmark

Carlsberg Glypothek	Copenhagen
National Museum	Copenhagen
Royal Academy of Arts	Copenhagen

France

Louvre	Paris
Musée de Jeu de Paume	Paris
Luxembourg Palace	Paris
Musée du L'Art Moderne	Paris
Cluny	Paris
Estampes	Paris
Versailles Museum	Versailles

Germany

Alte Pinakothek	Munich
National Gallery	Berlin

Great Britain

British Museum	London
National Gallery	London
Tate Gallery	London
Victoria and Albert Museum	London
Wallace Collection	London
Courtauld Institute	London

Greece

Acropolis Museum	Athens
National Museum of Antiquities	Athens
National Archaeo- logical Museum	Athens

Israel

Israel Museum at Jerusalem	Jerusalem

Italy

Uffizi Gallery	Florence
Pitti Palace	Florence
Academy Art Museum	Florence
Bargello	Florence
Accademia	Venice
Vatican	Rome
Palazzo Borghese	Rome
Palazzo Farnese	Rome
Museo Nazionale	Naples
Brera Gallery	Milan

Japan

Imperial Museum	Tokyo

Japan (continued)

Kyoto Museum	Kyoto
Nara Imperial Museum	Nara

Mexico

Museo Nacional de Arte Moderno	Mexico City
National Museum of Archaeology	Mexico City

Netherlands

Rijksmuseum	Amsterdam
Stedelijk	Amsterdam
Mauritshuis	The Hague

Portugal

National Museum	Lisbon
Museum of Ancient Art	Lisbon

Russia

The Hermitage	Leningrad
New Museum of Modern Art	Moscow

Scotland

National Gallery of Scotland	Edinburgh
Corporation Art Galleries	Edinburgh

Spain

Prado Museum	Madrid
Escorial	Madrid
Armeria	Madrid
El Greco Museum	Toledo

Sweden

National Museum of Sweden	Stockholm

Switzerland

Swiss National Museum	Zurich
Kunsthaus	Zurich
Kunstmuseum	Basel
Bern Museum of Art	Bern

Turkey

Turkish Museum of Antiquities	Istanbul
The New Museum	Istanbul

United States

Metropolitan Museum of Art	New York
Museum of Modern Art	New York
Whitney Museum of American Art	New York
Frick Collection	New York
Guggenheim Museum	New York
Brooklyn Museum	New York
Museum of Fine Arts	Boston
Gardner Museum	Boston
Fogg Museum of Art	Cambridge, MA
Yale Gallery of Fine Arts	New Haven, CT
Walters Art Gallery	Baltimore
National Gallery of Art	Washington, DC

Corcoran Gallery of Art	Washington, DC	City Art Museum	St. Louis
Phillips Gallery	Washington, DC	M. H. De Young Memorial Museum	San Francisco
Hirshhorn Gallery	Washington, DC	Museum of the Legion of Honor	San Francisco
Smithsonian Institution	Washington, DC	San Francisco Museum of Art	San Francisco
Philadelphia Museum of Art	Philadelphia	Los Angeles County Museum of Art	Los Angeles
Barnes Museum of Art	Philadelphia	Museum of Contemporary Art	Los Angeles
Pennsylvania Academy of Fine Art	Philadelphia	J. Paul Getty Museum	Los Angeles
Albright Art Gallery	Buffalo, NY	Skirball Museum	Los Angeles
Cleveland Museum of Art	Cleveland	Southwest Museum	Los Angeles
Art Institute of Chicago	Chicago	The Huntington Library and Botanical Gardens Art Gallery	San Marino, CA
Detroit Institute of Art	Detroit	Ringling Museum of Art	Sarasota, FL
Nelson Gallery of Art	Kansas City, MO		

Nabis: *See* modern art.

nail heads: Ever since the **Gothic** period, nail heads have been employed to attach leather or fabrics to the wood frames of upholstered furniture. Made of iron or brass, they are ornamental as well as functional. During the eighteenth century, nail heads were also used to create designs as decorations on cradles, chests, and screens.

National Trust for Historic Preservation: A private organization chartered by Congress in 1949 as a charitable, educational, nonprofit corporation to further the national policy of, and encourage public interest in, preserving districts, sites, buildings, structures, and objects important in America's history and culture.

nave: The central part of a church, running lengthwise from the narthex to the chancel, and flanked by aisles.

N.C.: Abbreviation for "no charge."

N.C.I.D.Q.: The National Council for Interior Design Qualification. This organization establishes standards for the qualification of interior designers.

needlepoint: An embroidery of woolen threads in close, usually diagonal, stitches on canvas or scrim. Used for pillows and as a covering in upholstery.

Nelson, George (1908–): Contemporary American furniture designer and architect. Nelson began his career as an architectural journalist and served as editor and consultant to *Architectural Forum* from 1935 to 1949. A 1945 article, in which he proposed using walls for storage, led to his appointment as director of the Herman Miller Furniture Co. He began the firm's association with **Charles Eames.** In addition to furniture and buildings, Nelson has designed interiors, exhibits, graphics, and business equipment, and is a well-known writer on design.

neoclassical style: A late-eighteenth-century European style of furniture design and decoration, characterized by the use of classical forms. This movement reflected a newly revived interest in Greek and Roman art and architecture, brought about by the archaeological discoveries unearthed at Pompeii and Herculaneum in the 1740s. The principal designers who created neoclassical furniture using architectural sources of design were British: **Adam, Hepplewhite,** and **Sheraton.** Interpretations in other countries led to the **Louis XVI, Empire, Directoire,** and **Italian** neoclassic styles. In America, neoclassical forms in architecture are exemplified by most State Capitols and numerous buildings in Washington, D.C.

neoimpressionism: *See* modern art.

neon lighting: Lighting in the form of semiflexible, hollow tubes of clear acrylic, inside of which are tiny bulbs that are either wired to light up all at once, or sequentially, to create a "chasing" effect. Sometimes referred to as *disco lighting,* it has brought new options to illuminating homes. Lighting designers view their work in neon lighting as a form of art.

Nervi, Pier (1891–1979): Italian avant-garde architect and engineer. His brilliant concrete roof structures made him famous. Some are cantilevered, others are vaults of diagonally intersecting concrete beams or trusses of precast concrete. He is also noted for his flying spiral concrete staircases.

nest of tables: A set of small tables graduated in size so that each one fits beneath another. They were introduced in the eighteenth century and originally used for serving refreshments.

netsuke: A small Japanese sculptured piece of ivory, wood, or porcelain, varying from one-half to three inches in height and width. The carvings are of mythological figures, flowers, animals, gods, and goddesses. Originating in the fifteenth century, netsuke pieces were first used as toggles. A cord was passed through a hole in the netsuke and slipped under and over the obi. A small medicine box, cosmetic box, purse, or knife was suspended from the cord. The netsuke prevented these objects from slipping. The very old ones, which are valuable collectors' pieces, have exquisite detail.

Neutra, Richard (1892–1970): Austrian-born architect. Emigrated to the United States in 1923 and became a disciple of Adolf Loos and Frank Lloyd Wright. His special talent was for insinuating a house into the landscape—linking it with nature, and using Wright's dramatic cantilevers.

Nevelson, Louise (1900–1988): Russian-born American sculptor and painter. Her archaeological studies in Mexico influenced her terra-cotta sculpture. She has also worked in wood.

newel: A post at the bottom or landing

of a flight of stairs that supports the hand-rail and **balusters.**

New York School: *See* modern art.

N.H.F.L.: National Home Fashions League. A league of executive women in the home furnishings industry. Founded in 1948.

niche: A small recess in an exterior or interior wall, intended to hold an urn, statue, or ornament.

nickel silver: *See* German silver.

Niemeyer, Oscar (1907–): Foremost Brazilian architect, born in Rio de Janeiro. A disciple of Le Corbusier, with whom he worked. He used concrete sculptural forms in curved lines to interpret modern architecture. Niemeyer was the chief architect for Brasilia, the capital of Brazil.

night table: Any table, small cabinet, or commode used beside a bed to hold a lamp, telephone, clock, ashtray, and personal articles.

Noguchi, Isamu (1904–): American-born sculptor and furniture designer who spent his childhood in Japan. His early glass-topped and walnut-based free-form cocktail tables are now considered museum classics, as are his lighting fixtures, which are made of paper, plastic, and bamboo.

noise absorption: The noise level within a room can be lowered by discontinuous construction of floors, walls, and ceilings. In an existing house, the attic floor and the space between the studs can be filled with sound-absorbing material.

nonbearing wall: A wall that divides a space, carries its own weight, but does not support a ceiling or roof.

nonglare glass: A nonreflecting glass used in picture framing. It darkens the artwork slightly.

nonobjective art: Painting or sculpture in which there is no trace of a recognizable object. Also referred to as *nonrepresentational art.*

nosing: The rounded edge that projects beyond the face of the riser of a stair tread.

Nottingham earthenware: English pottery made from the thirteenth to the late eighteenth centuries. (The last authenticated piece was made in 1799.) Usually brown, with a faint metallic luster. Often decorated with lines incised around the piece.

numdah: An Indian felt rug. Designs are embroidered or printed on the surface.

nurseries and children's rooms: When designing a nursery, the interior designer does not usually go "all out" unless the parents wish to impress relatives and friends, as the infant soon outgrows its surroundings, becomes a toddler, a preschool child, a preteenager, and then a teenager. Nurseries should be carefully designed with an eye to future growing needs.

A child's room is used for many purposes: sleeping, playing, eating, and entertaining. At first, furniture needs are minimal. Safety is the prime requisite for the infant.

Consider the following suggestions:

1. Use a closet to store the baby's bath.

2. Use a room that receives as much sunlight as possible.

3. Newborn infants react to color. Their favorites are the warm colors: bright crisp yellows, red, peach, and warm pinks.

4. The scale of furniture used should be appropriate for the child's age and size.

5. A nurse can use a daybed or convertible sofa bed. This saves space. As the infant grows, room must be made for a playpen. Plans must also be made for storage space for toys and playthings. Provide as much closet and drawer space as possible.

6. A plastic-top table can serve as a dining, work, or play table. It is natural for most growing children to be a bit careless in their treatment of furnishings. Therefore, it is wise to choose rugged materials and designs.

7. Remember that a child can be taught to appreciate and respect possessions and can be educated to be neat and tidy.

8. A young person's room should be decorated in a practical manner so that he or she will not have to be scolded constantly.

9. Do not use any breakable or heavy accessories or lamps that can be easily overturned.

10. Any carpeting used should be nonallergenic. If hard-surface flooring is to be used, cushioned vinyl is recommended.

11. Children enjoy using large floor cushions for additional seating.

12. Inexpensive curtains and bedspreads can be made out of bedsheets. They are available in plain and patterned drip-dry materials.

13. Blackout window shades may be ordered in the same fabric as the bedspread. Shades may also be appliquéd with a choice of decorative children's designs.

14. Narrow metal Venetian blinds are available in many colors and are a practical choice, as they are long lasting, easy to clean, and provide both temperature and light control.

15. Denim and corduroy are sturdy fabrics for a youngster's room.

16. Children enjoy eating and playing with friends in their room. So, to conserve space, instead of the conventional beds, consider using bunk or daybeds, which also serve as sofas.

17. Arrange furniture against the walls, leaving the center of the room free for play. A number of units are available, containing a built-in desk, bed, and wardrobe.

18. Shelves should be provided for the collection of souvenirs, toys, books, games, and the like. A child's room should be decorated according to his or her interests.

19. Equip the room with a bulletin board and chalkboard.

20. Illumination is an important factor in a child's room. There should be no glare or harsh reflections. Install a light dimmer. Also recommended is a light switch next to the bed, to work in unison with one at the entrance to the room. Provide bright but nonglare lighting for studying.

21. Use at least one full-length mirror on a door.

22. Carpeting printed with indoor games is a worthwhile indulgence.

23. Use washable murals, vinyls, and "fun" papers on walls and ceilings. Graphics can be hand painted. They are also available in the form of wallpapers. There are special patterns for doors, walls, and ceilings.

A child is never too young to respond to color and order. If a young person is exposed to good taste he or she will, without conscious thought or volition, grow up with a sense of beauty and refinement.

It is wise to consult the child when choosing the style and colors for his room. A young person will respect his own choices and usually will not abuse the furniture unduly.

There is no such thing as a perfectly designed and decorated house. The reason: there is no such thing as a perfect house.

Anonymous

oak: A coarse, pale yellow-brown **hardwood.** Used for furniture because of its durability rather than for its beauty. Adapts well to paneling and office and country furniture.

obelisk: A tall, four-sided, tapering shaft. Made of stone or marble when used as a public monument. Obelisks are also made to be used as objects of art, ranging in height from twelve to twenty-five inches.

objet d'art: An object valued for its artistry.

obscure glass: Translucent (not transparent) glass.

Obsidian: A lustrous black volcanic glass.

occasional table: A small, easily moved table for occasional or auxiliary use.

offices: In the past decade, great strides have been made in office design. The office environment is now engineered and viewed as a flexible tool that can change with future expansion or contraction through the use of open-plan design. Open-plan systems consist of a variety of panels, both acoustical and hard-surfaced, which are available in various heights. Component parts include shelves, tackboards, and a system of drawers. The open-plan office does not lock you in. These portable offices can be moved or changed as conditions dictate.

In the open plan, unwanted noise—conversation, the humming of machines, and the clatter of typewriters—must be engineered out through planned acoustical controls such as balanced acoustical screening, carpeting, and acoustical ceiling tiles.

Heating and air conditioning are more easily controlled in the open plan. It is no longer necessary to have separate zone controls for large numbers of individual offices. The single, open office space conserves energy, with resulting savings in money.

ogee: A molding having an S-shaped curve in profile. Introduced about 1350.

O'Gorman, Juan (1905–): Mexican modern painter and architect, particularly known for his anti-Fascist murals, many of which have been destroyed.

oil painting: A technique of painting that employs an oil base as the vehicle for its pigments. Linseed or nut oil are the bases most often used. Oil paintings were done on wood panels until the latter part of the fifteenth century, when canvas became the predominant support for easel paintings.

In early traditional painting, the support (canvas or wood) was primed in various hues—browns, pinks, and grays—then built up with glazes of color for shadows, lights, and local color. In the nineteenth century the technique known as *direct* painting developed, and the ground-color technique was eliminated. The impressionists and neo-impressionists introduced other methods of painting in oils: broken brush strokes, smooth brush strokes, globs of color, pointillism or dots of color, thick masses of paint, and palette-knife painting.

Cleaning and preserving oil paintings is an art and should only be done by an expert. Various chemicals and oils are used, including varnish solvents, alcohol, turpentine, castor oil, dammar varnish, balsam, powdered resin, beeswax, glue, acetone, benzine, and ether.

O'Keeffe, Georgia (1887–1986):   American painter. A pioneer of modernism, particularly known for her desert scenes and enlarged, close-up views of flowers, leaves, and other organic forms.

Olmstead, Frederick Law (1822–1903): American landscape architect who was one of the designers of Central Park in New York City.

op art: *See* modern art.

open account: An interior designer's account against which orders may be charged.

orangery: A seventeenth-century hothouse-greenhouse, two sides of which were formed of windows.

orders of architecture: Styles of ancient Greek and Roman architecture. The orders consist of three Greek modes—Doric, Ionic, and Corinthian—and five Roman modes—Tuscan, Doric, Ionic, Corinthian, and Composite. Each order is characterized by the type of column employed—in particular the ornamentation used and the relative proportion of the various parts. Classical columns have been used as applied ornaments on the fronts of cabinets, consoles, buffets, and other pieces of furniture since the **Renaissance.**

oriel window: *See* bay window.

Oriental furniture: Chinese furniture as we know it today has its roots in the fourteenth century, when the Western world first discovered Oriental styles. However, remarkable examples of bronze, pottery, religious objects, and statuettes of humans and animals were produced as far back as the fourth century. Tables, chairs, chests, and cabinets have been made by the Chinese since the seventh century. They invented wallpaper in the eighth century.

The ruling classes traditionally used elaborately carved lacquered furniture. The finest pieces were made from A.D. 1368 to 1643. From the seventeenth through the nineteenth centuries, Chinese motifs were adapted freely by the English and French. Thereafter, the Oriental influence spread throughout Europe. Latticework and pierced wood carving were used extensively.

Oriental furniture was made from a variety of woods, including rosewood, teak, sandalwood, bamboo, cypress, camphor, and cedar. Wood was often inlaid with such materials as pewter, mother-of-pearl, faience, brass, marble, copper, and ivory.

Furniture was finished in various colored lacquers or painted with decorative figures. Red and black were the predominant colors.

Oriental furniture has changed so little over the centuries that it is difficult to designate exact periods of style. In the table of periods reproduced at right, the two most important dynasties are Ming and Ching.

JAPANESE PERIOD	
Jomon	?–A.D. 100
Yayoi	A.D. 100–200
Haniwa	A.D. 200–537
Asuka	A.D. 538–645
Nara	A.D. 645–794
Heian	A.D. 794–1186
Kamakura	A.D. 1186–1393
Muromachi	A.D. 1393–1573
Momoyama	A.D. 1573–1615
Edo	A.D. 1615–1867
Meiji	A.D. 1867–1912
Taisho	A.D. 1912–1925

KOREA PERIOD	
Lo-Lang	108–57 B.C.
Koguryo	37 B.C.–A.D. 668
Paekche	18 B.C.–A.D. 663
Silla	57 B.C.–A.D. 663
Unified Silla	A.D. 668–935
Koryo	A.D. 918–1392
Yi	A.D. 1392–1910

THAILAND PERIOD	
Nancho Era	A.D. 650–1253
Mon People	A.D. 650–800
Cambodia	A.D. 800–1238
Sukhothai	A.D. 1238–1350
Ayudhya Era	A.D. 1350–1767
Bangkok Era	A.D. 1767–1932

CHINESE DYNASTY	
Hsia	2205–1766 B.C.
Shang	1766–1122 B.C.
Chou	1122–249 B.C.
Warring State	481–221 B.C.
Chin	221–206 B.C.

CHINESE DYNASTY (*continued*)

Han	206 B.C.–A.D. 220
Six Dynasty	A.D. 221–589
Sui	A.D. 581–618
Tang Dynasty	A.D. 618–906
Liae	A.D. 907–1211
Sung Dynasty	A.D. 960–1279
Yuan	A.D. 1280–1368

MING DYNASTY
REIGNING EMPERORS

Hung Wu	1368–1398
Chien Wên	1399–1402
Yung Lo	1403–1424
Hung Hsi	1425–1426
Hsüan Tê	1426–1435
Chêng T'ung	1436–1449
Ching T'ai	1450–1457
Tien Shun	1457–1464
Cheng Hua	1465–1487
Hung Chih	1488–1505
Chêng Tê	1506–1521
Chia Ching	1522–1566
Lung Ch'ing	1567–1572
Wan Li	1573–1619
T'ai Ch'ang	1620
Tien-Chi	1621–1627
Ch'ung Chêng	1628–1643

CHING DYNASTY
REIGNING EMPERORS

Shun Chih	1644–1661
K'ang Hsi	1662–1722
Yung Chêng	1723–1735
Ch'ien Lung	1736–1795
Chia Ching	1796–1820
Tao Kuang	1821–1850
Hsien Fong	1851–1861
Tung Chih	1862–1873
Kuang Hsu	1874–1908
Hsuan Tung	1909–1912

Oriental rugs and carpets: Traditional Oriental rugs are made of either wool, camel hair, goat hair, or silk. They are knotted entirely by hand by the native craftsmen in the countries of Asia and the islands of the Western Pacific. No two rugs are alike, just as no two works of art are alike. Rugs are considered representative of the national culture of the country in which they originate. Oriental rugs can be divided into six types:

Turkoman	Central Asia
Caucasian	Russia
Turkish	Anatolia
Persian	Iran
Chinese	China
Indian	Pakistan

Carpet weaving began about two thousand years ago in Persia, and around twelve hundred years ago in China. Carpets were originally used for warmth, as blankets or mattresses. Fine workmanship in carpet weaving was at its height in the sixteenth century.

Antique Oriental rugs are held in esteem for their pleasing designs, their unusual shades and tints of color, and their fine texture, luster, and quality of workmanship. Construction is of two types: a flat tapestrylike weave or a pile weave. Hand knots form the pile.

Chinese rugs tell a story through symbols and designs that are usually geometric, floral, or animal. Many patterns illustrate religious and philosophical beliefs. For example:

Dragon	God or emperor
Lion	Authority
Horse	Nobility
Part dragon, part deer	Animal of good omen
Crane or Stag	Long life
Two fish	Married happiness
Bats	Happiness, riches, long life
Butterfly	Happiness and love
Peach tree	Purity
Bamboo	Longevity
Ying-yang crescents:	Male and female
Carp	Perseverance
Conch shell	Victory
Pearl	Charm against holocausts
Phoenix	Bride
Vase	Peace
Two books	Learning
Peach blossom	Spring
Lotus	Summer
Chrysanthemum	Autumn
Narcissus	Winter

Until 1860, Chinese rugs were made of coarse-textured wool. After 1860, much finer textures appeared, as dictated by European demands.

The old handcraftsmen are dying off, and by the year 2000, hand production will probably be an art of the past. Machine-made Oriental reproductions are available and economical. Their artistic worth is comparable to that of reproductions of antique furniture.

ormolu: An alloy of copper and tin or zinc that resembles gold. It has been used to decorate furniture, moldings, and architectural ornaments since the seventeenth century.

Orozco, José Clemente (1883–1949): Preeminent Mexican muralist and lithographer.

orphism: *See* modern art.

Ørrefors: Swedish glass, developed in the latter part of the nineteenth century and still popular today. Often finely engraved.

orthographic projection: The projection of lines perpendicular to the plane of projection. Also, an **elevation** drawn by means of this method.

ottoman: A low, cushioned footstool, usually without exposed legs. Originally Turkish in style and draping.

outlet: A receptacle connected to a power supply and equipped with a socket for a plug.

overdoor: Designating a decorative treatment such as a painting, **bas-relief,** carving, or **pediment** attached to the wall above a door.

overhang: A projection of a roof or second story beyond the wall that carries it.

overmantel mirror: A mirror designed to hang above a fireplace. Its frame traditionally has the same design and carving as the surrounding paneling. It is often given added importance by the addition of a **trumeau** or candle-arms at either side.

oxbow front: The curved face of an eighteenth century chest or secretary, convex at either end and concave in the middle—the reverse of a **serpentine** curve.

There is more to color than meets the eye.

Anonymous

pad foot: The flattish end of a **cabriole leg,** similar to a club foot without the disk at the base. Found on English furniture of the **Queen Anne** period.

pagoda: A religious building of the Far East, particularly China, Japan, and India. Pagodas are generally pyramidal in shape, with ornamented roofs projecting from each side of their several stories. Pagodas were used as decorative motifs atop English and French cabinets during the eighteenth-century **chinoiserie** craze.

paint: The interior designer uses paint as a design element. Whether painting or lacquering walls in one solid color or graduating the tone, shade, and tint as he paints up the walls to the ceiling, he or she makes a definite color statement. In order to evaluate a paint job, a knowledge of paints and procedures is required. The best time to paint an interior is in the late spring or summer: the paint will dry quickly, and the windows can remain open to help eliminate any odor. The exterior, if wooden, should be painted after rainy, foggy, or inclement weather is over, because moisture is the major enemy of painted surfaces. Failures on exterior paint jobs are almost always due to moisture. This can be prevented by proper surface preparation. On interior surfaces, plaster cracks must be cut out and filled, and rough wood must be sanded. If walls or ceilings are stained by smoke, soot, or grease, they must be washed down. A sanded surface must be dusted or washed and allowed to dry before it is painted.

PRODUCT SELECTION

- *Exterior wood siding:* Latex house paint, oil house paint, redwood stain, latex stain, spar varnish
- *Exterior wood trim:* Oil house paint, redwood stain, latex stain, spar varnish
- *Interior walls:* Latex wall paint (quick-drying, durable)
- *Interior walls* of kitchens, baths, children's rooms, playrooms, service areas: Alkyd semigloss enamel, latex semigloss enamel, alkyd flat enamel (All have good hiding capabilities.)
- *Ceilings:* Latex wall paint
- *Children's Furniture:* Latex semigloss enamel

Both brushes and rollers are used on most paint jobs. Rollers save a great deal of time on flat interior surfaces.

Choosing a color from a chip can be misleading, as paint colors intensify with the size of the area. Incandescent lighting changes colors. Fluorescent lighting may or may not change a color, depending on the type of light tube used. For homes, warm white bulbs are recommended. For powder rooms, deluxe warm white will offer better color rendition and is flattering to the complexion. Incandescent light casts a yellow glow, and a painted surface will thus react as if yellow had been added to the paint color. Soft or bright light diminishes or increases, respectively, the intensity and value of colors. *See also* lighting; color.

The correct choice of the proper paint colors, tones, and values will make dim, dark, or bright areas more pleasant. The higher the reflectance factor of the paint used, the brighter the room will be. Brightness contrast must be kept to a minimum to eliminate glare. A room is rarely illuminated evenly—the difference in light levels depends on the placement of lamps or other sources of illumination. Thus, the walls receiving the most light will be bright; those with less illumination will be darker in color. On window walls, paint the remaining wall space in a light color to minimize glare between the windows and the walls flanking them.

A guide to mixing decorative colors follows. Remember that white should be used as a base for all of these mixtures:

PERCENTAGE OF LIGHT REFLECTED BY VARIOUS PAINT COLORS

white	85–90
pale gray	65–75
light tan	72–79
pale yellow	77–83
pale green	65–74
pale blue	58–68
red	25–35
brown	12–15
pale orange	72–78
ivory	75–81
medium gray	50–60
medium tan	50–60
medium yellow	65–70
medium green	52–58
medium blue	41–48
pink	66–76
turquoise	65–75
peach	60–65

Colonial Green: Deep green, deep blue, raw sienna.

Kelly Green: Chrome green medium, chrome green dark with a touch of lamp black.

Dusty Green: Ultramarine, yellow, and touches of crimson and umber.

Dusty Blue: Ultramarine, crimson, and a touch of umber.

Turquoise: Ultramarine, yellow, and a touch of red.

Emerald Green: Ultramarine, yellow, and a touch of crimson.

Chartreuse: Yellow, ultramarine, and a touch of red.

Rose: Crimson, yellow, and touches of ultramarine and umber.

Raspberry: Bright red, red-orange, and deep blue.

American Beauty Red: Bright red, burnt umber, and raw sienna.

Coral: Venetian red, ochre, yellow, orange, and sienna.

Venetian Red: Vermilion with touches of yellow and brown.

Dusty Yellow: Yellow with a touch of crimson and umber.

Beige: Touches of crimson, yellow, and umber.

Gold: Yellow with touches of crimson and umber.

Mauve: Crimson, ultramarine, and a touch of yellow.

Gray: Touches of ultramarine and umber.

The covering capacity of paint materials is as follows:

Enamel	525 to 600 square feet
Interior Flat Paint	500 to 575 square feet
Interior Gloss Paint	325 to 450 square feet
Latex Base Paint	250 to 350 square feet
Calcimine (Water Base)	250 to 350 square feet
Stain	400 to 500 square feet
Varnish	435 to 500 square feet

paisley: A soft woolen or other fabric woven or printed with a pattern of colorful, abstract, curved shapes derived from the palmette motif of Persian rugs.

palisander: The English transliteration of *palisander,* the French word for Brazilian rosewood, which is a flesh-pink, purplish, or rose-tone wood. It is very hard and dense. Native to Brazil, the West Indies, Honduras, and Rio de Janeiro, it is also known as *jacaranda.* First known to furniture makers in Europe during the **Renaissance,** it became very popular during the **Régence** period in France and the British Isles. Used for all types of furniture.

Palladio, Andrea (1518–1580): Influential Italian architect who designed palaces, villas, and churches in various parts of Italy but mainly in Vicenza. His designs revived fine Roman proportions, elegance, and simplicity of line. The term *Palladian* designates this style, which was first introduced in England in 1620 and brought Palladio lasting fame. His characteristic façade contained a templelike center section with a columned portico. A wing extended from either side. Windows were framed by superimposed **pilasters** or **columns.** Palladio's use of arches supported by columns has been much imitated. His buildings were given further importance by the use of sculpture as ornamentation. In 1570 he published his *Quattro libri dell' architettura*, a statement of his theories on architectural design. The work included measured drawings of Roman architecture as well as his own designs. Palladio's work strongly influenced both architecture and furniture design in England and America.

palmette: A classical, fan-shaped ornament; a representation of the palm leaf. Originating in ancient Egyptian art, it was adopted as a decorative motif by furniture makers as early as the Renaissance.

paneling: Wood boards glued or nailed to walls or studs. Sometimes held in place by an enclosed frame consisting of stiles (verticals) and rails (horizontals) that are grooved to receive a panel.

panetière: A **French Provincial** bread box or cupboard with open spindles topped by finials. The average size is about thirty-five inches wide by thirty-eight inches high. They are often carved with foliage motifs and are made to hang or be placed on a table.

paperweights: Glass paperweights made their first appearance in Murano, Italy in the year 1500. About that time, the Venetians discovered how to etch and engrave glass. In 1565 lead glass, flint glass, or crystal, as it is called today, was invented in England. Its basic components are lime or lead mixed with sand. Various colors are produced by introducing metallic oxides into the "batch" and by varying the temperature and the amount of lead used.

Paperweights became universally popular around 1845, with most masterpieces coming out of the French factories of **Baccarat,** Clichy, and St. Louis. The most outstanding weights were created by Baccarat.

During the latter part of the nineteenth century, paperweights were made in England. They did not compare with the French makes for brilliancy of color, lustrous softness, or quality. In America, from 1840 to 1885, some of the finest paperweights and glass doorknobs were manufactured by the **Sandwich** Company and the New England Glass Works. Other American factories that produced excellent paperweights were: Whitall, Tatum Company, Mount Washington Glass Company, Pairpoint Company, and the South Ferry Glass Works.

A glossary of glass paperweight terms follows:

Batch: A receptacle in which are placed all the raw materials used in making glass.

Blowpipe: A long, tubelike rod with a wooden mouthpiece that is used to inflate and blow glass.

Candy-type: A paperweight made of

odds and ends of leftover glass bits that are arranged in a hit-or-miss configuration.

Canes: Glass rods made with layers of different-colored glass.

Facets: Small, cut, flat surfaces made on the outside of a paperweight.

Latticinio: A trelliswork of interlacing bands of white opaque glass. *Filigree* is unflattened *latticinio.*

Millefiori: Rods of different colors fused together to resemble flowers.

Motifs found in glass paperweights include: landscapes, fruits, vegetables, flowers, butterflies, lizards, snakes, snow, leaves, sailboats, seals, arrows, *latticinio,* medallions, stars, filigree, *millefiori,* fish, birds, animals, cameos, and portraits. Many paperweights were faceted. Certain paperweights can be identified by signatures on the base. Baccarat is signed "B" and the date; Saint Louis is signed "SL" and often the date; Clichy is recognized by the letter "C," the full name Clichy, or by the "Clichy Rose" in one of the canes.

papier-mâché: A material made from paper pulp mixed with glue, oil, resin, chalk, fine sand, or a combination of the above. This substance can be molded into various shapes when moist, after which it is allowed to dry. It becomes hard enough to saw and take a high polish. Once used mainly for picture frames, it

has also been used to make snuffboxes, tables, fire screens, desk sets, and many other small pieces of furniture. These objects were often inlaid with mother-of-pearl.

parapet: A low, protective wall or railing along the edge of a roof or balcony that acts as a firebreak and prevents sudden drop-offs.

pargework: Stucco or plaster applied to a wall or ceiling, forming an ornamental design in relief.

parking areas: A well-designed parking facility will provide optimum space utilization. The following steps should be followed in laying out a parking lot:

1. Make an accurate outline drawing of the parking area, using a scale of twenty feet to one inch.

2. Show adjacent sidewalks, streets, and traffic directions on streets in the drawing.

3. Show the location of the nearest street intersection and fixed obstacles, such as poles, trees, etc., in the drawing.

4. Check for any special requirements for parking areas under local ordinances or by-laws.

par lamp: An incandescent lamp with a built-in reflecting surface. Available in spot or flood types.

parlor: The designation for a living room, until the turn of the century.

parquetry: Inlaid woodwork in geometric or other decorative patterns, and generally of different colors. Used principally on floors in the seventeenth century and on furniture in the early eighteenth century.

Parsons table: A square or rectangular table with heavy square legs. These tables are usually painted or covered in wallpaper or fabric, and finished with a clear plastic coating for protection of the wood, fabric, or paper. Named after the Parsons School of Interior Design in New York, where the design evolved in the 1950s.

partners' desk: A double desk that allows two people to work facing each other. Developed in England in the late eighteenth century.

Party Wall: A common wall between two buildings.

Pascin, Pincas (Julius) (1885–1930): Outstanding French painter, particularly known for his portrayals of women.

passementerie: Trimming for a garment of braid, lace, or metallic beads.

pastiche: A direct copy of the style and manner of another designer, often with satirical intent.

patchwork: The art of taking odd patches of fabric and sewing them together. This handicraft was known as early as the Middle Ages.

patina: A thin layer of corrosion, usually green or brown, that copper and copper alloys acquire through oxidation. *Patina* also refers to sheen, color, texture of furniture, produced by age and many waxings or polishings. It is one of the characteristics of well-cared-for antique furniture.

patio: An inner, roofless courtyard that is open to the sky.

pavilion: A light, ornamental building often used as a summerhouse or, in a park, as an entertainment center. Also, an annex, or one of a group of related buildings forming a complex.

peacock chair: A curved, high-back armchair made of rattan.

pedestal: An architectural support for a statue, candelabrum, or table. In classical architecture it consists of three divisions: the *base;* the *dado,* which forms the main body; and the *cornice,* or cap, at the top.

pediment: A low, triangular gable in the Greek or classic style, crowned with a

projecting **cornice** and used over a **portico.**
It is often ornamented with sculptures.
The term is also applied to a similar triangular structure over doors and windows. In furniture, pediments came into
use over cabinets in the latter part of the
sixteenth century. A widely used variant
was the broken pediment, in which the
lines stopped before they reached the
apex. A swan neck or scrolled pediment
consists of opposed S curves. There is
usually a **finial** placed on a **plinth** in the
center opening.

Pei, I.M. (1917–): Renowned Chinese-
American architect. He designed the new
East Wing of the National Gallery of Art
in Washington, D.C.

pelmet: A frame or cornice board surrounding a window on three sides. It is
usually covered with fabric.

Pembroke table: A **drop-leaf table** of
oblong shape with narrow leaves supported by hinged brackets. A drawer is
fitted into the apron. Introduced in England about 1755.

Pennsylvania Dutch furniture: Furniture made by eighteenth-century German,
Swiss, Swedish, and Dutch settlers in
southeastern Pennsylvania. The furniture
which included massive, architectonic,
heavily carved pieces and smaller,
brightly painted ones, was made of pine,
maple, walnut, or fruitwoods. The smaller
pieces featured such fanciful folk motifs
as fruit, hex signs, hearts, flowers, pea-
cocks, parrots, animals, people, tulips,
geometrical designs, and pomegranates.

Percier, Charles (1764–1838): French
architect appointed by Napoleon as the
government architect. He worked on the
palaces of the Louvre and the Tuileries.
He also helped design the Arc de
Triomphe and shares responsibility, along
with Pierre Fontaine, for the development
of the French **Empire** style.

pergola: A garden arbor formed of trelliswork supported on columns or posts
over which vines are trained.

period style: Furniture of a distinct style
or character that was produced during
a certain historical period or monarch's
reign, or by a particular school of design.
Styles in interior design change because
styles of living, politics, climatic influences, materials, morals, religion, and
economic conditions change. Styles also
change because of the influence of individuals, basic home-furnishing needs,
technological changes, and scientific
inventions.

The following is an outline of the major
periods and styles, arranged chronolog-
ically. Precise dating of period styles is
arbitrary because styles not only overlap,
they merge from one into another.

MAJOR PERIODS AND STYLES OF FURNITURE DESIGN

PERIOD	CHARACTERISTICS	COLORS	FABRICS	FURNITURE	WOOD
Antiquity					
Egyptian 4000 B.C.–A.D. 300	Obelisks Lotus columns	Salmon Pink Blue	Leather	X stools Folding chairs Tables	Sycamore Cedar

Grecian
1200 B.C.–A.D. 168
	Greek orders
	Classical motifs
	Marble columns
	Egyptian influence
		Red-violet
		Blue-violet
		Yellow-green
		Purple
		White
			Linen
			Tapestry
			Leather
			Wool
				Trestle tables
				Couches with
				  backs
				Oblong chests
				Large
				  armchairs
				Bronze tables
					Yew
					Ebony
					Cedar

Roman 753 B.C.–A.D. 455	Greek art forms Murals on stucco Mosaics	Blue Violet Terra-cotta Cream Black Scarlet Green	Linen Leather Silk Wool	Chairs Chests Cupboards Bedsteads	Unknown (painted furniture)
Dark and Middle Ages					
Byzantine 328–1453	Pseudo-Roman Ecclesiastical Mosaics	Gold Silver Purple	Unknown	Folding stools Chests	Unknown
Gothic 1100–1515	Linenfold carving Wrought iron Massiveness Stained glass	Dark red Green Gold Blue Gray	Velvet Tapestry	Chests Crude refectory tables Benches	Oak
Italian Renaissance					
1400–1600	Followed Roman design Gothic carving Massive Classic inspiration	Red Yellow Blue White Cream Turquoise	Silk Tapestry Embroidery	Canopied beds Chests Throne chairs	Walnut Oak Chestnut Pine

*Italian Baroque
and Rococo*
1560–1750
	Ornate
	Overscaled
	Theatrical
	Architectural
	Sculptural
		White
		Pink
		Peach
		Yellow
			Silk
			Velvet
			Tooled
			  leather
			Lace
				Tables
				Chairs
				Benches
				Headboards
				Cassones
				Low pedestals
				Credenzas
				Writing
				  cabinets
					Walnut

FURNITURE DESIGN (continued)

PERIOD	CHARACTERISTICS	COLORS	FABRICS	FURNITURE	WOOD
French Periods					
Renaissance 1515–1643	Massive Classic inspiration	White Gold Blue Green	Tapestry Silk Velvet Embroidery	Beds Consoles Sofas Commodes Bergères Chairs	Chestnut Walnut Oak
Louis XIV: Baroque 1643–1715 *Régence* 1715–1723	Majestic, elaborate Extravagant ornamentation Richly carved marquetry Comfortable uphol- stered furniture Parquet floors Mirrors	White Gold Green Blue Rose Silver Red	Tapestry Silk Brocade Velvet Satin Damask Embroidery Leather	Consoles Desks Bonnetières Huge beds Bookcases Commodes	Almond Holly Box Ebony Rosewood
Louis XV Rococo 1723–1774	Smaller-scaled furni- ture than Louis XIV Curved, delicate furniture Walls upholstered in silks Cabriole legs Inlay work	Pink Yellow Violet Blue Gray Ivory White Citron Light green	Damask Silk Taffeta Satin Moiré Toile de Jouy Brocade Needlework Tapestry	Consoles Commodes Side chairs Armchairs Elaborate desks Mirrors Sconces	Walnut Ebony
Louis XVI 1774–1793	Straight tapering legs Classic ideals Reduced scale No curves Classic proportions in- fluenced by excava- tions at Pompeii	Pastel White Gold Pale pink Gray Beige Peach	Tapestry Silk Brocade Velvet Damask Striped and lattice designs Toile de Jouy	Side chairs Consoles Cabinets Commodes Upholstered beds	Mahogany Oak Ebony Satinwood Tulipwood Rosewood
Directoire 1795–1804	Same curve in chair legs as in Greek chairs Columns Urns No ornateness Classic in feeling Overstuffed	White Blue Gray Maroon Gold Orange Black	Damask Chintz Toile Striped satin Velvet Needlework	Wing chairs Love seats Pedestal furniture	Ebony Cherry Mahogany Chestnut
Empire 1804–1830	Greek, Roman, and Egyptian forms Massive Elegant Bee motif Lavish in form, con- trolled in ornament	Red Brilliant green Yellow Gold Apricot Pink Cocoa	Satin Brocade Velvet Tapestry Leather Ticking	Sideboards Desks Beds Cabinets Ormolu mounts	Rosewood Mahogany Ebony Maple Elm

FURNITURE DESIGN (*continued*)

PERIOD	CHARACTERISTICS	COLORS	FABRICS	FURNITURE	WOOD
French Provincial Seventeenth century	Rural interpretations of prevailing Paris fashions and popular styles of wealthier class High-relief carving	Red Blue Green Yellow Brown Cream	Chintz Toile Gingham Plain or quilted fabrics Leather Embroidery Gros point Petit point	Simpler forms of Louis styles Chests Wardrobes Cupboards Armoires Rush-seated chairs Panetière developed	Walnut Cherry Oak Beech Elm Apple

English Periods

PERIOD	CHARACTERISTICS	COLORS	FABRICS	FURNITURE	WOOD
Tudor 1485–1558	Gothic forms Massive Strapwork Tudor arch Beam ceilings Gothic windows Linenfold carving	Red Green Blue Dark tones Henna Gold	Velvet Pongee Leather Damask Tapestry Crewelwork	Cupboards High-back chairs Tables of all sizes Library tables Low-relief carving Heavy wood-canopied beds	Oak Black walnut
Elizabethan 1558–1603	Massive bulbous table supports Italian Renaissance carving Gadrooning Strapwork Wrought iron	Yellow Red Blue Green Purple Dark tones	Linen Crewelwork Velvet Brocade Damask Chintz	Chests Cupboards Wardrobes Settles Wainscot chairs Slant-top desks	Oak Elm Pine Black walnut Chestnut
Jacobean 1603–1688	Universal term applied to the period of the reign of the Stuart kings in the seventeenth century.				

James I (1503–1625)
   Charles I (1625–1649)
   Commonwealth,
   Cromwellian,
   and *Protectorate*
   (1649–1660)
   Carolean (Charles II)
   (1660–1685)
   Restoration—James II
   (1685–1688)
	Sturdy
	Tudor Rose carving
	Wood-paneled walls
	Elizabethan-style characteristics
		Green
		Rose
		Brown
		Red
		Blue
		Yellow
		Gold
			Needlework
			Tapestry
			Leather
			Gros point
			Velvet
			Crewel
			Petit point
			Damask
			Chintz
			Brocade
			Indian patterns
				Welsh dressers
				Chairs with caning
				Spiral-turned legs
				Wing chair introduced
				Stool, benches
				Round tables introduced
				Gaming tables
				Wood firescreens
				Gate-leg tables
					Oak
					Walnut
					Holly
					Pine grained to imitate walnut
					Walnut left in natural waxed finish

FURNITURE DESIGN (*continued*)

PERIOD	CHARACTERISTICS	COLORS	FABRICS	FURNITURE	WOOD
William and Mary 1688–1702	Flemish influence Delicate lines French as well as Dutch influence Inverted trumpet, cup, or bell-shaped legs Ivory inlay	Rose Blue Red Gold Green Salmon	Velvet Brocade Chintz Damask Crewel Needlepoint Linen	Introduction of the highboy Cabinets Clocks Desks Dressing tables Lowboys Secretaries	Colored veneers Walnut
Queen Anne 1702–1714	Cabriole leg Pad or club foot Shell carving Dutch and Chinese influence Painted paneling Claw-and-ball foot Broken-pediment tops	Red Green Yellow Salmon Blue Black	Linen Gros point Embroidery Silk Needlepoint Crewelwork Chintz	Large over- stuffed wing chairs Kneehole desks Fiddle-shaped splat-back chairs Gate-leg, drop- leaf tables Secretaries Pie-crust tables	First use of mahogany Walnut Lacquer
Georgian Period	Embraces reigns of George I, George II, and George III, with the following outstanding designers.				
Thomas Chippendale 1718–1779	Influenced by Chinese, Gothic, Louis XV, and Queen Anne designs Broken pediments Superb wood carving Chinese fretwork Serpentine fronts Treillage Pagoda tops	Black Lacquer red Yellow Blue Green Gold Eggplant White	Brocade Velvet Damask Horsehair Linen Needlework Leather Tapestry Silk	Ladder-, splat-, and ribbon-back chairs with ball- and-claw feet Square legs on Chinese chairs Tier tables Canopied beds Galleries around tops of tables	Mahogany Cherry
The Adam Brothers 1728–1792	Straight lines influ- enced by Louis XVI and Roman remains at Pompeii Elegant simplicity Low-relief carvings Painted decorations Neoclassic	Pastels Beige Ivory White Gray Yellow	Satin Taffeta Toile Chintz Moiré Brocade Stripes	Shell-topped corner cabinets Dining room sideboard introduced	Satinwood Waxed Pine Tulipwood Harewood

FURNITURE DESIGN (*continued*)

PERIOD	CHARACTERISTICS	COLORS	FABRICS	FURNITURE	WOOD
George Hepplewhite ?–1786	Designs influenced by Louis XVI and Adam brothers Legs slender, tapered, reeded or fluted Painted designs	Pastels Pink Turquoise Gray Blue Yellow Green	Silk Brocade Taffeta Chintz Satin Velvet Horsehair Leather	Sideboards Card tables Pembroke tables Secretaries Bookcases Daybeds Chests of drawers Serpentine fronts Slender four-poster beds Heart- and shield-back chairs	Mahogany Satinwood Tulipwood Sycamore Rosewood
Thomas Sheraton 1751–1806	Slender round, tapered, reeded legs Inlay Fine carving and veneering Classic lines à la Louis XVI Broken pediment	Delicate Pink Gray Blue Yellow Green Violet	Brocade Silk Satin Taffeta Toile Chintz Damask	Shaving stands Sewing tables Knife cases Round or oval tables with banded, inlaid, or painted tops Square chair with broken top rail	Mahogany
English Regency 1810–1820	Empire characteristics Simple carvings Brass inlays Classical forms	Black Dark colors Deep reds Browns	Damask Chintz Toile Satin	Caned-seat chairs Clumsy copies of previous Georgian furniture	Mahogany Rosewood Lacquer
Greek Revival 1820–1860	This period marks the decline of English furniture Some bad Greek Revival designs Lavish use of Greek orders	Maroon Orange	Brocade Velvet	Cabinets with brass grilles	Ebony
Victorian Period (English) 1837–1901	Heavy, clumsy, overornamented Papier-mâché products A style of revivals, especially rococo Heavy carving Exaggerated curves	Red Blue Gray Puce Black White	Horsehair Plush Gay chintz Linen Damask Needlework Satin	Tufted and fringed chairs Framed upholstered furniture Étagères Marble-topped tables Thonet bentwood chair Morris chair	Black walnut Mahogany Maple Rosewood Oak Ebony Black lacquer Cherry

FURNITURE DESIGN (*continued*)

PERIOD	CHARACTERISTICS	COLORS	FABRICS	FURNITURE	WOOD
American Periods					
Early American or Colonial (1607–1789)	Functional and primitive Inspired by English styles Some Dutch and French influence Pennsylvania Dutch From 1740 to 1790 wealth increased, and furniture showed Queen Anne influence Hepplewhite, William and Mary, and Chippendale	Red Yellow Blue Green Cocoa Gray Ivory Black Tan	Linen Calico Horsehair Chintz Leather Crewel India prints Toile Tapestry Velour	Chests Cupboards Trestle tables Benches Slat- and wainscot-type chairs Cradles Gate-leg tables Highboys (Philadelphia style) Stenciled chairs Windsor chairs Rocking chairs	Maple Pine Oak Cherry Mahogany Walnut Cedar Birch Hickory Ash
Duncan Phyfe 1768–1854	Finest American cabinetmaker, influenced by Chippendale, Sheraton, Hepplewhite, Directoire, and Empire styles American classicism Motifs: lyre, concave legs, lion claws, arrows, swags, lion masks	Red Yellow Green Blue Turquoise	Damask Brocade Satin Velvet Taffeta Leather Chintz Linen Haircloth Toile de Jouy	Pedestal dining tables Cane backs on chairs Daybeds Other furniture followed prevailing styles Lyre used for chairbacks, sofa arms, and table supports Tester beds	Ebony Rosewood Mahogany
Federal Period 1790–1830	Influenced by styles of Adam, Hepplewhite, Sheraton, and Directoire Use of classical orders Furniture had feeling of heaviness and solidity	Red Blue Green Gold Black Orange	Satin Horsehair Taffeta Chintz Brocade Velvet	Serpentine-front sideboards Chest on chests Tambour desks China cabinets Hitchcock chairs	Maple Walnut Fruitwoods Mahogany Satinwood Rosewood
Victorian (American) 1840–1880	Eclecticism—a turning to many periods of the past for inspiration, particularly: Gothic, Regency, Empire, and Rococo	Red Green Black White Gold Lavender	Damask Leather Glass beads Plush Horsehair Needlework Bamboo	Belter chairs Turkish divans Built-in sofas Circular settees Bulky upholstered furniture What-nots Nests of tables Papier-mâché furniture Blackamoor statues Antimacassars	Golden oak Rosewood Black walnut

	FURNITURE DESIGN (*continued*)				
PERIOD	CHARACTERISTICS	COLORS	FABRICS	FURNITURE	WOOD
Eclecticism 1880–1901	The artistic selection of furniture from a variety of distinctive styles that harmonize and appear well integrated	White Biege Violet Orange Yellow Red Blue Green	Prints Velvets Leather Fur Chintz Satin Linen	Chosen from various period styles and designs	Mahogany Yew Teak Walnut Oak Rosewood Pine
Modern					
Contemporary 1901–Present	A symbolic art form of sinuous line	White Beige Tan Brown Red Orange Blue	Tapestries Rough textures Velvets Cottons Satins Leather Needlework	No specific styles but modernization of traditional furniture Simplification Modern innovation	Walnut Pine Ebony Rosewood Mahogany Fruitwoods
Art Nouveau 1890–1910	Interlacing lines Victorian style of decorations Symbolic vegetable forms used as motifs Elements of fantasy Stained glass Marquetry	Ivory Gold Blue Silver Copper Green Black Chartruese	Batik Japanese designs in prints All fabrics as in Contemporary	Natural forms as source of inspiration Spindly Sinuous lines Exotic inlay	Ash Fruitwoods Mahogany Oak Walnut Elm
Art Deco 1910–1935	Rectangular shapes Cubist inspired decoration Geometrical designs Cubist forms	Jade Green Black Primitive colors Eggshell Yellow	Glossy fabrics Egyptian motifs on prints Plastics Leather	Steel Aluminum Marble Glass Brass Chrome Linear design	Lacquered wood Shiny finishes Obscure woods Primavera Ebony

peristyle: A group of columns surrounding a building or courtyard.

perspective: Any of various techniques for rendering three-dimensional objects and depth relationships on a two-dimensional surface.

Isometric projection: A method of drawing a complete view of a room, looking down into it.

Two-point perspective: This is the most effective means of showing a room set-up. Two walls are visible, with the corner becoming the center of vision.

One-point perspective: A head-on view of a room and its contents, where lines and planes are considered to meet at infinity.

petit point: A form of needlepoint done on canvas, with very small stitches.

pewter: An alloy of tin with lead, antimony, or copper. Pewter was traditionally used for making tableware, pitchers, and bowls.

Philadelphia Chippendale: Notable for fine copies of Chippendale highboys, lowboys, and chairs by outstanding cabinetmakers of the mid-eighteenth century.

Phyfe, Duncan (1768–1854): America's most famous cabinetmaker and furniture designer of the early nineteenth century. Most of his furniture designs were adaptations of **Sheraton, Hepplewhite,** French **Empire,** and **Directoire** styles. His work was of the finest quality. His most frequently used design motifs were: lyres, plumes, saber legs with brass feet, lion masks, arrows, pillars, swags, acanthus, paw feet, pedestal supports for tables, and fine reeding. His finest work was produced between 1790 and 1817. After 1830 his furniture became overornamented and heavy, and the quality declined. Phyfe's favorite woods were mahogany and satinwood.

physical dimensions of furniture: Variations in body measurements will alter dimensions of this basic guide.

Chairs (desk or dining): Seat height for men: 17 inches. Seat height for women: 18 inches. Seat depth: 16 to 18 inches. Lower back needs support.

Sofas and lounge chairs: Seat height: 15 to 18 inches. Seat depth: 22 inches. Arm height: 7 to 8 inches above seat cushion. Overall height: 26 to 34 inches.

Cocktail tables: Height: 13 to 17 inches.

Dining tables: Height: 28½ inches. Width: 42 to 44 inches. Allow a minimum of 45 inches between edge of table and a wall. Allow 24 inches of space for each place setting.

Desks: Height: 29 inches.

Buffets: Height: 32 to 35 inches.

Love seats: Length: 54 to 60 inches.

Game groups: Allow 6½ feet by 6½ feet of floor space for the average game table and four chairs.

Clothes closets or cabinets: Minimum depth: 25 inches. Minimum height: 78 inches.

Small baby grand pianos: 5 feet, 3 inches long by 5 feet wide.

Bars: Height: 44 inches. Length: 42 inches, minimum. Working bar to underside of top of bar: 14½ inches clearance. Depth: 18 to 24 inches.

piano: When buying a piano, consider the following factors:

1. Tone Quality: Avoid harsh tone quality.

2. Tuning Stability: Will the piano tune well.

3. Touch: There should not be any variation in consistency of touch.

4. Workmanship: Watch for quality control and exacting craftsmanship.

5. Beauty and wood finish.

Picabia, Francis (1878–1953): French surrealist and cubist painter.

Picasso, Pablo (1881–1973): Spanish painter, sculptor, potter, ceramist, and graphic artist. Well known for his great skill in drawing, and regarded as the foremost cubist painter. Occasionally, his work yielded strongly to surrealism. His masterpiece is the twenty-five-foot mural *Guernica.*

pickled finish: A white, mottled glaze on light-colored wood that results when old paint and its **gesso** undercoat are cleaned from the wood.

piecrust table: A small, round, eighteenth-century table whose edges were carved or molded into a scalloped outline.

pier: A built-in or freestanding masonry support.

pier table: A small table designed to stand against a pier—the section of wall between two windows or doors. A tall mirror, called a *pier glass,* often hung above it. Originated in the seventeenth century and popular well into the nineteenth century.

pilaster: A rectangular or half-round column or pillar attached to the face of a wall or article of furniture as an ornamental motif.

pills: Small round threads that form on the surface of a fabric.

pine: A **softwood,** clear or knotty, that is easily worked and carved. It is off-white or pale yellow and is associated with Early American and country furniture. Knotty pine is used extensively for wall paneling. Though today the knots are considered decorative, in the past, they were often concealed by paint.

pineapple: A decorative architectural motif used as a finial, particularly on early nineteenth-century American bedposts.

piping: A tubular band of material containing a cord; used in trimming upholstery seams and edges.

Piranesi, Giovanni Battista (1720–1778): Italian **neoclassical style** architect, engineer, and engraver. He is best known for his imaginative engravings of reconstructed ancient Roman buildings and monuments. Piranesi wrote a number of books illustrated with engravings of furniture and decoration, which were quite influential in the development of eighteenth-century neoclassicism.

pitch: The angle of incline of a roof surface or of the length of a run of pipe. Also, a black tar substance used in roofing work.

plank: A length of lumber that exceeds 2 inches in thickness.

plants: Indoor gardening has come into its own as an integral part of interior decoration. From a design perspective, there are four categories of plants: floor plants, table plants, flowering plants, and nonflowering plants. A tall plant will frame a window. A row of plants can act as a divider between a living room and dining area or create an entry hall where none existed. Plants do well in bay windows, on window sills, or hanging from the ceiling in baskets. Plants will do better if the temperature is not above 78 degrees Fahrenheit.

In a room with a wall of glass, plants must be protected and shades or draperies closed part of the day. Plants will grow in a dark corner with the proper use of artificial light. The magic ratio is four watts of fluorescent daylight or cool white tubes to one watt of incandescent light, or two watts of incandescent light from a pink bulb. The other important ingredients of successful indoor gardening are watering and fertilizing. When watering, soak the plant until the soil is fully saturated. Then, about a week later, check the soil. If it is dry to the touch, add water slowly until the water seeps through the drainhole. Then stop. Never use ice water. The water must be lukewarm. In a pot without a drainhole, be careful not to overwater. (You will know that you have done so if the water puddles and is not absorbed by the soil for some time.) If the lower leaves of a plant begin to drop, the plant has been overwatered. Water is the means by which food is made available to the plant. Read directions carefully on water-soluble fertilizer and follow them; otherwise, you may overfeed and burn the roots.

Tablet plant food is satisfactory if you water the plant immediately. Once a month, wipe both sides of the leaves with a cloth dipped in warm water to remove accumulated dust.

plaque: Any thin, flat piece of metal, wood, porcelain, or other material used for ornamentation on a wall.

plaster: A surfacing material composed of lime or gypsum, sand, water, and sometimes hair or another fiber. It is applied wet and allowed to harden and dry.

plaster of Paris: A cement made by heating gypsum in a kiln and subsequently grinding it to a fine powder. When mixed with water, this powder hardens in a few minutes. It is used in making casts, molds, and sculpture.

plastic: A generic term for a group of complex organic compounds, produced by polymerization, which can be shaped when soft. Plastics are designated by numerous chemical and trademark names, including the following: vinyl, Lucite, nylon, Styrofoam, polyethylene, polypropylene, polyurethane, polyester, melamine, and acrylic.

plate: In wood-frame construction, a horizontal member that caps the exterior wall studs, and on which the roof rafters sit.

plateau: Any flat surface on a piece of furniture. Also, a large ornamental dish.

plate rail: A shelflike wooden molding along a wall, intended to hold ornamental plates.

playroom: *See* den.

plenum: A cavity or space above the ceiling construction and below the floor construction above, used for utility conduits.

plinth: The lower, slablike, projecting base of a column, doorway, or any trimmed opening. Also, the base or foundation supporting a piece of sculpture or cabinet furniture.

Plochere color system: A color system founded on the principles of Dr. W. Ostwald, who thought of color as a psychological sensation. The system consists of formulas for 1,248 colors.

plumb: Exactly vertical.

plush carpet: A dense, cut-pile carpet in which the end of each tuft merges into a common surface.

plywood: A building material consisting of several layers, or plies, of wood glued together so that the grain of one ply is perpendicular to that of the adjacent ply. This results in a material that is stronger and more flexible than solid wood.

pointillism: *See* modern art.

pole screen: *See* fire screen.

Pollock, Jackson (1912–1956): American abstract expressionist painter. Inventor of the "drip-and-spatter" mode of painting.

polychrome: Having many colors. Polychromed furniture is decorated with multicolored paints, or gilding over a **gesso** base.

pomander: A small box, made of a precious metal, used up to the seventeenth century for carrying sweet-smelling spices that were supposed to ward off infections.

Pompeii: An ancient Italian city that was buried, along with Herculaneum, by an eruption of nearby Mount Vesuvius in A.D. 79. Much of the city has been excavated, and the discoveries influenced the development of **neoclassic** furniture and interiors.

Ponti, Gio (1891–1979): Italian architect, furniture designer, and industrial designer. Founder of the world's leading architectural magazine, *Domus.* Ponti's designs can be seen as a bridge between prewar middle-class traditional aesthetics and the modern movement. His best-known architectural work is the Pirelli Tower in Milan (1955–1958). He also designed the very popular Chiavari chair (1949), now known as the Superleggera chair.

pontil mark: The mark left on the bottom of blown glass where it was attached to the iron rod (*pontil*) that is used in handling the molten glass as it is worked.

pop art: *See* modern art.

porcelain: A hard, vitreous, translucent, nonporous ceramic ware. True porcelain is made of kaolin or china clay and was first discovered in China about A.D. 800. True porcelain is also called *hard-paste porcelain. Soft-paste porcelain* is made by adding powdered glass to the kaolin clay and firing at a lower temperature. In England, bone ash was added to the hard-paste porcelain clay. The Europeans discovered the secret of making porcelain in 1707.

Meissen was the site of the first hard-paste porcelain made in Europe.

The terms *china* and *porcelain* are synonymous. Unglazed porcelain is called *bisque* or *biscuit.*

porphyry: Rock containing conspicuous crystals embedded in a fine-grained igneous ground.

porringer: A lidded, handled, silver or pewter cereal bowl, also used for hot drinks made of wine; also called a *caudle cup.*

porte-cochère: A covered entrance or driveway designed to provide shelter for those getting in and out of vehicles.

portico: A porch or walkway with a **pediment**-type roof supported on columns.

Portman, John (1924 –): American architect specializing in hotels. Known for his use of the atrium.

post-and-beam: Referring to a system of architectural construction based on vertical supports and horizontal beams (as opposed to vaults or arches).

postimpressionism: *See* modern art.

pottery: Stoneware, earthenware, ceramics, or any objects modeled out of clay and fired in a kiln. It is opaque, never translucent.

poudreuse: A small **dressing table** of the eighteenth century, popular in France and England, whose top unfolded. The central section of the top was hinged at the back and had a mirror on its underside, which was exposed when the top was opened.

pouf: A round, upholstered **ottoman** introduced in France in the middle of the nineteenth century, and popular in Europe and America throughout the 1800s.

powder room: A functional room that should contain every convenience a guest might require, even aspirin, antacid tablets, and Band-Aids. The room may be gay and colorful with unusual decorative effects, since as a rule it is for temporary use.

Lighting may be in the form of a crystal fixture or any illumination that is not too bright but flattering to the complexion, such as deluxe warm-white fluorescent tubes. Details such as an unusual carved mirror, a highly stylized wallpaper, or a marble-topped counter can make the smallest and dullest powder room a delight. Antique accessories add elegance. It is wise to avoid clutter.

pre-Columbian: Designates arts and artifacts of native Indian cultures of Mexico and Central and South America created before the discovery of the New World by Columbus.

pressed glass: Glass pressed in a patterned cast-iron mold. This method originated in the United States about 1825 and radically changed the glass industry. One of the first to use this method was the Sandwich Glass Company.

prestressed concrete: Reinforced concrete in which the reinforcing steel is replaced by wire cables. These, in turn, can be tensioned before or after the concrete is cast, thus ensuring compression of the concrete.

pretrimmed wallpaper: Wallpaper in which **selvage** is trimmed at the factory.

prie-dieu: A small, low prayer stand with a ledge for kneeling. Developed in the late seventeenth century.

primary colors: The pigment colors red, yellow, and blue, which cannot be produced by any combination of colors. The combination of any two primary colors is known as a *secondary* color. The combination of any secondary color with a primary color is called a *tertiary* color.

primavera: A light-colored **hardwood** with a striped grain, used in cabinetwork; often called *white mahogany*.

prime coat: The initial or underlayment coat of paint, which seals the pores of a surface.

primitive: An artist who is self-taught and belongs to no school or tradition in painting. Good primitive works have a freshness and simplicity of form.

Prince of Wales plumes: A decorative motif of three ostrich feathers tied together at their shafts (the heraldic blazon of the Prince of Wales). Found frequently on **Sheraton** and **Hepplewhite** furniture

print: A design or picture transferred from an engraved plate, block, or other medium.

proxemics: The study of how people respond and react to the physical space between them. Proxemics can be broken down into four categories: intimate, personal, social, and public. Anthropologists and psychologists have found that the approximate distance maintained between people who are intimate is 24 inches. People who are close to each other but not intimate ("personal") favor a distance of about 48 inches. In "social" situations, people prefer a distance of about 84 inches. The distance maintained in public places is about 12 feet or more.

psychology of color: The power and influence of color on the emotions is most vividly illustrated in hospitals.

A controlled color environment has been proven to speed patient recovery. Color effects are not absolute, however, but depend on a number of factors. To wit:

1. The type of illness: mental or physical.
2. Age: Is the patient an infant, juvenile, adult, or elderly person?
3. The medical treatment used.
4. The environment.

5. Condition: Is the patient ambulatory?

Retirement homes, rest homes, hospitals, sanitaria, convalescent homes, nurseries, kindergarten schools—all must be planned to eliminate monotonous environments of any sort. Depending on the patient and illness, color must be used for very specific purposes. Some rooms should excite, others relax the patient.

Warm colors such as yellow, peach, or pink tend to be moderately exciting. Cool colors like blue, green, or turquoise tend to be relaxing. Blue is an actual emotional sedative. Doctors' reception rooms should be done in cool colors. This will help calm the nervous patient.

Physiotherapy rooms should be done in cool colors as well.

Pediatric areas ought to have many brilliant colors so that patients never feel the stress of sensory deprivation.

Ceilings in hospital rooms should never be painted white. It is too monotonous and becomes depressing.

Decorate orthopedic wards in warm colors to project the feeling of energy and drive.

Hospital rooms done in two complementary colors, such as two walls painted turquoise, and the other two walls peach, have been found to be beneficial, reassuring, and restful to the average patient in a rest or convalescent home.

A violent mental patient might recover sooner if he or she is placed in a blue room without sharp color contrasts but with textural interest. If a patterned paper is used, it must be innocuous—one that will not disturb the patient. In other words, the pattern must not have sharp color contrasts.

Color can also be used to control temperature. Dark colors absorb heat. Light colors throw off heat. The best reflecting color is white, the best absorbing color, black. In plants where refrigeration creates cool temperatures, warm colors such as pale cocoa, pale rose, peach, and dusty orange can be used. Conversely, in plants where heat is a problem, use cool colors: blue, turquoise, or green.

Color can also be used effectively in the workplace. Accident rates can be greatly lowered, fatigue can be diminished, and eyestrain and nervous tension alleviated by the correct use of color formulas.

To make time move more swiftly in factories, use cool colors for all routine, boring, and monotonous tasks.

To make time move slowly in restaurants and bars, use warm colors. In coffee shops, for a quick turnover, use cool colors and bright lights.

In factories and warehouses, heavy objects or crates can be made to look lighter by painting them in light, cool colors. Objects look smaller and shorter under cool lighting and colors; larger and longer under warm lighting and colors.

Purple and chartreuse should not be used for walls, ceilings, or floors in specialty or department stores: these colors repel buyers. If chartreuse is used in a restaurant, its reflection makes food look unappetizing, and diners can be overcome with nausea.

Tunnel effects in long halls and corridors can be eliminated by painting one wall the color of your choice and the opposite wall a darker, grayed shade of the same color. If doors in a long hall are each painted a different color, the tunnel effect will be alleviated.

Research has shown that when yellow is used in study rooms, students' grades have risen noticeably.

The most unpopular colors are purple, taupe, and chartreuse.

In direct-mail advertising, warm-colored envelopes and letterheads receive a greater response than black-and-white stationery.

The most legible color combinations, arranged according to relative visibility, are:

1. Black on yellow
2. Red on white
3. Green on white
4. Yellow on black
5. Blue on white
6. Black on white
7. Orange on black
8. Red on green

pulls: Cabinet handles.

pull-up chair: A small, lightweight chair, usually without arms; also referred to as an *occasional chair.*

purchase order: A numbered, printed form used to verify a purchase and giving all details of the purchase.

purlin: A horizontal timber between rafter and joist.

purple heart: *See* amaranth.

pylon: A gateway to an Egyptian temple in the form of a pair of truncated pyramids or obelisks.

quartering: Sawing a log into four quarters in order to produce symmetrically arranged grain.

quarter round: A wood molding in the shape of a quarter circle.

quatrefoil: An ornament composed of four lobes, leaves, petals, or flowers. Commonly used on **Gothic** furniture.

Queen Anne style: Furniture designed in England from 1702 to 1750, during the reigns of Queen Anne, George I, and George II. (Queen Anne reigned from 1702 to 1714.) Furniture of the period is characterized by use of curvilinear lines, the **cabriole leg,** and the **pad foot.** The wood most commonly employed was figured walnut veneer. During the latter part of the period, mahogany was introduced. Ornamental motifs include the carved shell and the acanthus leaf. Architecture was characterized by red-brick construction, hipped roofs, and the modification of classical architectural forms.

queen's ware: The name given by Josiah **Wedgwood** to his cream-colored earthenware, introduced around 1762.

quilt: A coverlet or bedspread made of two layers of fabric with down, cotton, wool, or another filling between them, stitched together (quilted) in an ornamental pattern.

quilting: The effect attained by attaching a backing material to a fabric, sandwiching cotton or a synthetic fabric in between, then giving the decorative fabric a design by stitching the two together in lines or patterns. Quilting is used in the making of bedspreads and in upholstering materials.

quoin: An exterior angle of a wall; also, a stone that forms such an angle.

*The many make the household,
But only one the home.*

James Russell Lowell
(1819–1891)

rabbet: A slot or groove cut in the edge of a board in such a way that the raised edge of another piece of wood can be fitted into it to form a joint.

rafter: A sloping timber or beam extending from the eaves of a building to the ridge of a roof and serving to support the roof.

rake: The angle of inclination or slant from the perpendicular on furniture legs.

ramp: An inclined flat surface joining two different levels.

ram's head: A decorative motif used on furniture and buildings. A favorite of the **Adam** brothers.

ranch house: A low, long, one-story house, first popular in the western United States.

rapid-start fluorescent lamp: A fluorescent lamp designed to operate on a ballast circuit, which provides a low-voltage winding for preheating the cathodes. This eliminates the need for a starting switch or the application of relatively high voltage to the lamp. All high-output and 1500 milliampere lamps are rapid start. A rapid-start lamp and circuit must be used if fluorescent lamps are to be dimmed or flashed without reducing lamp life.

rattan: The slender, tough, vinelike stems of several climbing Asian palm trees, used for caning and to weave wicker furniture.

Ravenscroft, George (1618–1681): British glassmaker. The developer of **flint glass.**

reading chair: A leather-covered chair with an adjustable wooden rest for reading and writing, used in the early eighteenth century. Not to be confused with a **cockfight chair.** The reader places his back to the front of the chair (i.e., faces the back of the chair) and rests his arms on the top yoke. Usually made of walnut or mahogany.

realism—representational: A type of artwork in which the artist or sculptor faithfully reproduces the physical appearance of a person or scene in nature.

Récamier, Madame Jeanne (1777–1849): A French social leader of the late eighteenth and early nineteenth centuries, for whom a graceful, backless **chaise longue** was named. The chaise has curved ends, one higher than the other.

récamier: An **Empire-Directoire** backless **daybed** or **chaise longue** having ends of unequal height. Named after the renowned Parisian social and literary figure, Madame Jeanne Récamier.

receding color: A cool color, such as green, blue, turquoise, or blue-violet, which gives the illusion of being farther away from the viewer than it actually is.

redwood: A **softwood** grown almost exclusively in northern California. Used in construction, for paneling, and for outdoor furniture, as it is very resistant to decay.

reed: The slender stalk of tall grasses. Used as a form of molding attached to door frames.

Reed and Barton: Twentieth-century American silversmiths specializing in flatware.

reeding: Ornamental carving consisting of half-round convex moldings placed side by side. Similar to **fluting,** but convex rather than concave.

refectory table: A late-sixteenth-century dining table, very long and narrow. The table was designed with four or more ponderous turned legs, which were joined by heavy stretchers placed close to the bottom of the legs.

Régence style: Transitional French style covering eight years, from the end of the reign of Louis XIV in 1715, when a regent was appointed for Louis XV, until 1723. The style is a combination of **Louis XIV** and **Louis XV** styles. Chinese designs and the shell motif made their appearance.

Regency style: A transitional English style that developed in the years 1811–1820, when George, Prince of Wales, acted as regent for his father, King George III. The style is a form of exaggerated Greek and Roman Revival. Cabinetmakers used classical forms—Chinese, Egyptian, and Gothic motifs. The style continued until about 1838 and was characterized by its eclectic qualities. Ornamentation consisted of the lion's mask, lyre, swan, honeysuckle, cornucopia, sphinx, pagoda, and fretwork. Rosewood and mahogany were widely used.

regionalism: A style of painting practiced by a group of American artists in the 1930s and early 1940s, which concentrated on the realistic depiction of rural subject matter, particularly scenes from the Midwest and South. Prominent regionalists included: Edward Hopper, Thomas Hart Benton, Charles Burchfield, John Steuart Curry, and Grant Wood.

reinforced concrete: Poured concrete containing steel rods, which are placed in the forms before the concrete is poured, thus increasing its tensile strength.

relief: The projection of a sculptured figure or design from the ground or plane on which it is formed.

remodeling: Not all houses are worth remodeling. A list should be made of all changes and improvements desired. An architect should then be called in to draw preliminary plans. The plans should be sent out to two or three contractors for firm bids or estimates for the complete package. It is then time to evaluate whether adding space, revising the floor plan, or giving the house a complete face-lift is worth the cost.

It is unwise to remodel a house and leave obsolete electrical wiring, plumbing, heating equipment, cracked walls, or out-of-date bathrooms and kitchens. Rehabilitating the entire house can be more costly than building a completely new house.

Renaissance: A rebirth of ancient Roman standards, motifs, and classical cultural influences that made its appearance in Italy during the latter part of the four-teenth century. From Italy, the movement spread to France, Spain, and England. It brought the medieval world into the modern world. In terms of design, the period is characterized by the revival and adaptation of classical orders, motifs, and forms. Furniture was marked by simplicity of line and carving, with a definite architectural feeling. **Pilasters, cornices,** and **pediments** were applied to furniture as decoration. The outstanding architect of the period was the Florentine Filippo Brunelleschi, and the most important schools of painting were the Florentine and Venetian. This revival in the arts, architecture, and literature ended in the sixteenth century.

rendering: A black-and-white or color representation of a proposed design, faithfully reproduced. Also referred to as a *delineation.*

repeat: In fabric or wallpaper, the distance from the center of one pattern to the center of another.

replica: An accurate copy of a piece of fine old furniture. Technically, a replica is a copy manufactured during the time when the original was made. If manufactured later, it is called a *reproduction.*

repoussé: In metal working, the technique of forming a pattern in relief.

reproduction: *See* replica.

Restoration furniture: Furniture produced in England during the restoration of the monarchy of Charles II (1660–1688). This period is also referred to as *Carolean, late Stuart,* and *late Jacobean.* It marks the start of the age of walnut. Furniture was highly carved, with scrolls and spiral turnings. *See also* period styles.

retainers and deposits: It is customary practice for a designer to request and obtain a *retainer* before starting a job. Others charge a flat consultation fee for the initial visit. If the client makes a substantial purchase, it is credited to his or her account. A *deposit* is required from the client before beginning a job, and additional monies are generally due during specified phases of the job, with the balance being due upon completion.

return: That part of a surface at right angles to the face or front. On draperies, the fabric from the front of the drapery to the wall.

reveal: That part of a jamb of an opening or recess that is visible from the face of the wall back to the frame.

Revere, Paul (1735–1818): Boston silversmith, copperplate engraver, bell-caster, and participant in the Boston Tea Party. Revere's silver craftsmanship and designs marked with the name "Revere" are highly prized today.

ribbon-back chair: An eighteenth-century mahogany chair with a back splat carved to simulate the folds of knotted ribbons and bows. Ornamented in **rococo** style.

rinceau: An eighteenth-century French ornamental motif consisting of connected series of spiraling foliage stems, either carved, inlaid, or painted.

riser: The vertical face of a stair step.

Rivera, Diego (1886–1957): Mexican muralist, renowned for his frescoes in Mexico City. One of Latin America's foremost artists.

Rivers, Larry (1923–): American artist and sculptor. Among the first generation of pop artists.

Rockingham porcelain: A factory founded in Yorkshire about 1742 that produced brown and white earthenware decorated with purple-brown glazes.

rocklath: Perforated gypsum board used as a base for plastering.

rococo style: A style of decoration developed in France in the mid-eighteenth century. It is characterized primarily by elaborate and profuse ornamentation based on natural forms, including foliage, rock work, shell work, and C scrolls. Furniture and designs were asymmetrically arranged. *See also* period styles.

roll-top desk: A desk fitted with a flexible cylindrical hood or *tambour*, which, when pulled down, forms a lid for the working space. This form was introduced by **Hepplewhite**.

Romanesque style: The style of European ecclesiastical architecture in the eleventh and twelfth centuries. Based on the use of the round arch, the vault, and interior bays. In England, this style was referred to as "Norman." There was little furniture making during this era. Romanesque style was followed by the **Gothic** style.

Roman order: *See* Composite order.

romanticists: Late-eighteenth century and early-nineteenth-century painters who revolted against **neoclassicism** and **realism.** Their paintings brought into play imaginative environments that encourage the viewer to escape from the realities of daily life to romantic, visionary, fanciful places.

room divider: A divider is used to separate open areas and thus multiply their uses, providing, for example, dining, play, or music areas. Storage space can be arranged on the divider itself. A divider can be a traversed drapery, a folding screen, a bamboo blind, vertical louvers, or a cabinet that can serve as a bar or buffet on one side and a music center or general living area on the other.

rosette: A circular motif, carved, inlaid, or painted, enclosing a formation more or less resembling a rose.

rose window: A circular window decorated with a symmetrical pattern of roselike tracery or **mullions** arranged like the spokes of a wheel.

rosewood: A fine, black-streaked reddish **hardwood** used in making furniture.

Rothko, Mark (1903–1970): American abstract, expressionist painter.

rotunda: A circular building or room, usually domed. The Pantheon is an example of a rotunda.

Rouault, Georges (1871–1958): French expressionist painter, engraver, lithographer, and etcher.

Rouen faience: Tin-glazed **earthenware** made in Rouen, France in the fourteenth century.

Rousseau, Henri (1844–1910): French primitive painter.

Royal Copenhagen: A hard-paste Danish porcelain that first appeared in 1770.

Royal Worcester: *See* Worcester china.

ruffle: A pleated, gathered, or shirred band of fabric.

rush seating: A woven chair seat made of rushes, reeds, or any of various grasslike plants with hollow stems. Plaited rush has been used since medieval times. It was originally used for covering floors and making baskets.

rustic furniture: Garden furniture of wood, aluminum, cast iron, or cement, with carved framework. Tree branches are one of many design motifs used.

Saarinen, Eero (1910–1961): American architect and furniture designer born in Finland. He studied sculpture in Paris, and the sculptor's touch is very noticeable in his work. Saarinen's unique roofline shapes are one of his trademarks: the warped roof on three supports, the steeply pointed roof, the shell-domed roof, the outward-swinging arched roof, and the down-curving roof ridge with outward-leaning concrete supports. Among his best-known architectural projects are the TWA terminal at Kennedy airport, New York (1956–1962), and Dulles airport, Washington, D.C. (1958–1962). His furniture designs, characterized by organic shapes and experimental use of materials and technology, include the Womb chair (1946) and the Pedestal group (1957).

saber leg: A rearword-curving front leg on a chair or sofa, similar to the curve on a saber or sword. Typical of the **Regency** style.

saddle seat: A wooden seat usually found on **Windsor chairs** and stools. The wood is cut away in a sloping manner from a central ridge, leaving a concave indentation on either side.

salt glaze: A thin, hard glaze used on stoneware, formed by throwing salt into the kiln during the firing.

salver: A flat, circular silver tray mounted on low, spreading feet. The border is molded, plain, pierced, or scrolled.

sampler: A piece of needlework with an embroidered design. It can be framed and hung as a picture or used as a cover for pillows. Dates back to the seventeenth century.

Sandwich glass: Blown, molded, or pressed glass produced by the Boston and Sandwich Glass Company between 1825 and 1886.

Saruk carpet: A sturdily constructed Persian carpet with a closely knotted, deep pile.

sash: The frame of a window, in which the panes are set.

satinwood: A smooth, light-colored hardwood from southern Asia, used in fine furniture since the early eighteenth century.

Satsuma ware: Japanese pottery, yellow to brown in color, with a hard, crackled glaze. Originally made in the sixteenth century in Satsuma, Japan.

satyr: A decorative motif representing a mythological creature, part man, part goat, usually with horns on his head and the feet and tail of a goat. Used on furniture since about 1730.

sauna: A Finnish steam bath. Steam is created by running water over hot rocks.

Savery, William (1721–1787): A Philadelphia cabinetmaker, regarded as one of the outstanding proponents of the **Chippendale** style. *See also* Philadelphia Chippendale.

Savonarola chair: Nineteenth-century name for an Italian **Renaissance** X-shaped folding chair named after the Italian monk. It consisted of six or more serpentine, interlaced X-shaped frames. The wooden back was ornamented with carving and inlay work.

Savonnerie carpet: A knotted-pile carpet made in France in the Turkish manner with French designs. Under Napoleon, the Savonnerie factory was consolidated with the **Gobelin** works in 1825.

scagliola: A composition imitation of marble consisting of ground plaster of Paris mixed with glue, lime, and hardening solutions.

scale: The size of a piece of furniture relative to that of other pieces of furniture or to the dimensions of the room in which it is placed.

scales and dimensions: The following schedule of calibrations is accepted by all architects:

$\frac{1}{4}$ inch	1 foot
$\frac{3}{8}$ inch	1 foot
$\frac{1}{2}$ inch	1 foot
$1\frac{1}{2}$ inches	1 foot
3 inches	1 foot

For plans and elevations: $\frac{1}{8}$ inch = 1 foot or $\frac{1}{4}$ inch = 1 foot

For sections and details: $\frac{3}{8}$ inch = 1 foot or $\frac{1}{2}$ inch = 1 foot

For large-scale sections: 1 inch = 1 foot

For large-scale details: $1\frac{1}{2}$ inches = 1 foot or 3 inches = 1 foot

scarf joint: A joint in which two timbers or other structural members are fitted together with long end laps of various forms and held in place with bolts, straps, or plates.

schematic: Pertaining to a diagram, plan, arrangement, or drawing.

school of Paris: An international group of painters and sculptors who gathered in and around Paris in the late nineteenth and early twentieth centuries. Their art was a potpourri of postimpressionism, Fauvism, and cubism. When World War I began, the movement gradually receded, then vanished.

sconce: An ornamental wall bracket consisting of a back plate and branches or arms for holding candles or electric lights.

scratch coat: The first coat of plaster a wall surface receives.

screed: A thin layer of mortar used on concrete as a bed to receive floor tiles.

screen: A decorative partition, fixed or moveable, made with anywhere from two to twelve hinged or folding panels. It serves to conceal, protect, shield, shelter, or divide an area. Screens are covered in paper, fabrics, leather, or are lacquered. Many are of solid, pierced, or carved wood or metal. Japanese screens usually consist of six panels.

scribe: To mark a material by scratching a line with a straight, pointed instrument, a *scriber*, to show where it is to be cut.

scrimshaw: Hand-carved objects of ivory, bone, or shell, decorated with intricate carvings or designs.

sculpture: The art of cutting, carving, hewing, modeling or chiseling in stone, marble, wood, clay, wax or plaster to create the human figure or animals, in three dimensions. Sculpture also covers the designing and execution of medals and bas-reliefs, the carving or engraving of gems.

secondary color: *See* primary color.

secretary: A slant-front desk with a cabinet or bookcase attached atop it, and drawers below. It evolved from the *escritoire* and reached its peak of popularity in England and America in the eighteenth century.

section: A cut-away view of a building, room, or piece of furniture.

sectional furniture: Upholstered pieces composed of several independent sections that can be arranged in various combinations.

selvage: A specially woven edge of a fabric, which prevents the fabric from raveling. Wallpaper also comes with a blank selvage edge.

semainier: A tall, narrow, seven-drawer

chest first made in France during the reign of Louis XV. The name derives from the French *semaine* ("week"), as the seven drawers could hold clothing and linens for each day of the week.

serigraph: A print made by the silk-screen process.

serpentine: Composed of a convex center flanked by concave curves on either side. It is the opposite of an **oxbow.** A serpentine front was a common feature on **rococo** case pieces.

Sert, José Luis (1902–): Spanish-American architect.

servante: A French serving table of the **Empire** or **Directoire** period.

settee: A light-scaled, seventeenth-century forerunner of today's **love seat.** It is often framed, with an upholstered back, seat, and arms.

settle: A long, all-wood **settee,** often with a chest boxed-in beneath the seat. It invariably had a high, paneled or carved back and was massively constructed. One variety had a hinged back that flipped down so that the settle became a table. Settles were first introduced during the **Gothic** period. They were generally made of oak in Europe, pine in America.

Sèvres ware: French soft-paste porcelain first made in 1740. It is decorated with figures, gilding, and festoons of flowers.

sewing table: A work table fitted with a drawer and often a cloth bag to hold a current sewing project.

sgraffito (graffito): A form of decoration on pottery or enamel, formed by scratching through a surface with a pointed tool, exposing an undercoat of a different color or material.

Shahn, Ben (1898–1969): American socially conscious painter and muralist, born in Russia.

Shaker furniture: The Shakers were an American religious sect active in the eastern United States in the early nineteenth century. They observed a doctrine of celibacy, a form of communalism, and community living. Their furniture designs were unadorned, simple, functional, sturdy, well designed, and well made. They worked chiefly in pine but also used maple and the fruitwoods. They were called *Shakers* because of the dancing movements that constituted a part of their religious ritual.

Shearer, Thomas (active, late 1700s): English cabinetmaker and designer in the **neoclassical** style. He published a book of engraved plates on furniture in 1788,

The Cabinet-Maker's London Book of Prices, later reissued as *Designs for Household Furniture*. **Hepplewhite** and **Sheraton** were influenced by Shearer's designs.

sheathing: A layer of boards, plywood panels, or other materials, applied to the outer studs, joists, and rafters of a frame building to strengthen the structure and provide a base for weatherproof cladding. Also, the act of applying such a layer.

Sheetrock: Plasterboard of gypsum between paper.

Sheffield plate: The earliest substitute for wrought silver. It is composed of fine sheets of silver fused over copper. The name is derived from the city of Sheffield, England, where it was first manufactured.

shell: An eighteenth-century carved motif found on mirror frames, chests, sideboards, headboards, and other furniture forms.

shellac: An alcohol-soluble resin used in making varnish and in the finishing of wood furniture.

Sheraton, Thomas (1751–1806): Important English cabinetmaker and designer. He published a number of influential books: *The Cabinet-Maker and Upholsterer's Drawing Book, The Cabinet Dictionary*, and *The Cabinet-Maker, Upholsterer, and General Artist's Encyclopedia*.

His designs were noted for their excellent proportions, refined lines, and elegant and graceful forms. He favored delicate, painted furniture. His favorite woods were mahogany, satinwood, and rosewood. Sheraton was influenced by **Robert Adam** and the **Directoire** and **Louis XVI** styles. Some characteristics of his work are the straight tapered leg and motifs that included the lyre and urns. *See also* period styles.

shield-back chair: A typical **Hepplewhite** chair with an open back in the form of a shield, filled with a variety of openwork designs (e.g., swags, ribbons, and Prince of Wales plumes).

shim: A thin, wedge-shaped piece of wood used to fill a gap and level a piece of furniture or an appliance.

shingle: A fabricated piece of wood, slate, or composite materials, applied in overlapping layers over the exterior **sheathing** of a house, providing either a wall finish or a roof finish.

shiplap: An overlapping joint, as a **rabbet,** between two boards joined edge to edge.

shoji: A Japanese screen or sliding panel used as a door or window. The frame was traditionally filled with fretwork or rice paper; today, a variety of translucent materials are used.

sideboard: An English **neoclassical style** furniture form; a table fitted with drawers or shelves, intended to be placed against a dining-room wall and used to serve food and drink.

side chair: A dining room chair without arms.

side table: A seventeenth-century rectangular dining-room table, often with a marble top, that was used as a server. The side table was long, narrow, and often flanked by two pedestals carrying urns. When suspended by brackets instead of legs, it is called a **console table.**

siding: Exterior wood covering for a building.

silk-screening: A printing process for fabrics and wallpapers in which a stenciled design is imposed on a screen of silk that is tightly stretched on a frame. A different screen is used for each color. Blank areas are covered with an impermeable substance, and ink is forced through the cloth onto the printing surface.

sill: A heavy horizontal timber or line of masonry supporting a house wall. Also,

a horizontal piece forming the bottom frame of a door or window.

silver: Silverware was first used in seventeenth-century France and England, but there is silver in England that survives from the sixteenth century, and every piece bears its own documented evidence of age and origin. **Hallmarks** are stamped on objects to attest to their authenticity and date of origin. Each symbol of an English hallmark means something different. One tells what the silver content is, another where the piece was made, third where the piece was tested, and a fourth in what year it was made.

Sterling silver is top-quality silverware that is composed of more than 90 percent pure silver or 925 parts silver and 75 parts copper.

German silver is an alloy used for imitating silver articles and came into use in 1847. One of the formulas contained three parts nickel to eight parts copper and one part zinc.

During the Medieval period, plate was decorated. It was common to insert semiprecious stones and/or overlay the silver with a layer of mercurial gilding. Silver thus treated was known as *silver-gilt*. Gilding was used until the sixteenth century. During the late eighteenth century, machines for stamping and etching replaced hand labor, which led to mass production.

sisal: A fiber of great tensile strength,

used in making rope and cordage and in upholstery.

size, sizing: A gelatinous sealer used to prepare a wall for wallpaper. Also used to stiffen fabrics.

sketch: A simple, rough drawing giving the essential features without the details.

skirt: A strip of fabric extending from the bottom of an upholstered piece of furniture to the floor, thereby concealing the furniture legs. *See also* apron.

skylight: A framed window inserted in a roof or ceiling. A skylight can distribute five times as much daylight inside a house as a sidewall window of the same size.

slab: A concrete floor between beams or walls.

slat-back chair: A seventeenth-century English chair whose back consists of spaced horizontal slats or rails. Similar to the **ladderback chair,** but the slats of the former are carved and shaped, while those of the latter are thin and often pierced.

sleeper: A wood strip set in a concrete floor slab to provide a nailing-strip surface for the finished flooring.

Sleepy Hollow chair: An open-arm upholstered chair with a high back, which is a continuation of the seat. Both the seat and the back are usually tufted.

sleigh bed: A nineteenth-century American version of the **Empire** bed. It had a high, scrolled headboard and a similar but lower footboard, thus resembling a horse-drawn sleigh.

slimline fluorescent lamp: An instant-start **fluorescent lamp** with a **ballast** circuit that supplies relatively high voltage to start the lamp. Most slimline lamps have a single pin base, requiring only one connection to each end of the lamp.

slip: Clay thinned to the consistency of cream.

slipcover: A removable, fitted fabric cover for a chair or sofa.

slipper chair: A small, upholstered, short-legged chair. Popular in America in the eighteenth and nineteenth centuries.

slip seat: A thin, upholstered or caned seat that fits into the framework of a chair. Developed in the eighteenth century, it is still in wide use today. Also known as a *drop-in seat.*

Sloan, John (1871–1951): American genre painter.

snakewood: *See* zebrawood.

social realism: An art movement started in 1930 by such prominent American artists as **Soyer, Gropper, Shahn, Evergood,** and **Grosz.** Their aim was to use art as a vehicle for messages of social protest.

sofa: An all-upholstered sitting piece that accommodates three or more people; if it holds less than three, it is called a **love seat.**

sofa table or library table: A late-eighteenth-century oblong table with drop-end leaves, which stood in front of a sofa. Today it is used behind a sofa. It is generally the length of the sofa (seven or eight feet), and as a rule does not have drop leaves. The width of the table varies from sixteen to twenty-two inches, and the height is even with the top of the sofa—usually twenty-seven to twenty-nine inches.

soffit: The underside of a structural component such as a ceiling, cornice, arch, staircase, or roof overhang.

soft-paste porcelain: Porcelain that is both softer than true or hard-paste porcelain, and thus requires less intense heat to fuse it.

softwood: The wood of a coniferous, or cone-bearing tree, such as a pine, hemlock, or spruce. Rarely used for furniture, which is generally constructed of **hardwood.**

Soutine, Chaim (1894–1943): Lithuanian-born French expressionist painter. A gifted portraitist.

Soyer, the brothers Moses, Raphael, and Isaac: American painters and lithographers. Moses Soyer (1899–   ) is considered the most important of the three brothers. His paintings of urban scenes, dancers, and models hang in the Metropolitan Museum of Art, the Museum of Modern Art, and other major American museums. Both he and his twin brother Raphael Soyer (1899–   ) were born in Russia. Raphael is best known as a painter of urban genre scenes. He studied with Guy Pène Du Bois. Isaac Soyer (1907–   ) is both a painter and a print maker. His subdued paintings reveal deep sympathy with the poor of New York's Lower East Side.

space planning: The organization of interior space from a functional and psychological point of view.

Spackle: A trademark for a plastic paste or a powder mixed with water, used to cover cracks and joints in plaster before painting or papering.

spandrel: The area that lies between two adjacent arches. Also, the area below or above a window in exterior **curtain-wall** assembly.

Spanish furniture: Spain was susceptible to many foreign design influences: Visigoth, Roman, Syrian, Gothic, Moorish, and Flemish. From the eighth to the sixteenth centuries, Spain was ruled by the Moors, who left their Islamic influence on design. In general, Spanish furniture throughout the centuries was massive, ornate, heavy, and crude, with some characteristics analogous to those of other countries in similar periods, especially the Italian and French **Renaissance** designs. Spanish furniture lacks variety, but it does have a certain crude, charming simplicity. Tables, canopied beds, and chests were introduced as early as the fifteenth century. After the Moorish period, a Spanish **baroque** style was instituted, with furniture extravagantly decorated with filigree and ironwork.

During the sixteenth century, ornate carving, spiral-turned legs, and painted finishes were in widespread use. Silver was introduced as inlay work in tables and cabinets. Chairs were high-backed, upholstered in tapestry, velvet, or leather, and trimmed with fringe. Chair supports were in the form of the spiral-turned leg or the "Spanish foot," which has grooved and vertical ribs terminating in a backward-turned scroll. The English adopted this foot in the late sixteenth century. Spanish furniture of the seventeenth century was of Italian inspiration. There was much carving and bad construction, which was concealed by heavy coats of paint. Ironwork and iron and brass nail heads were used extensively as decoration. In addition, wrought-iron furniture was made into tables, chairs, and beds. Large floor cushions of velvet were often used as seats.

The *vargueño*, a secretary-type cabinet with a fall-front, appeared. The cabinet enclosed drawers, and the whole was mounted on simple trestles or turned legs braced by wrought iron. Made in the early part of the seventeenth century, it is one of Spain's singular contributions to furniture design.

The French influence came into play in the eighteenth century. Furniture decreased in size and bulk; carving was simplified but still remained crude and exaggerated.

Toward the end of the eighteenth century, comfortable upholstered furniture was brought into general use. Spanish furniture makers united French, English, and Venetian designs into a melange of overdecorated styles. Furniture was painted, lacquered, and gilded. During the nineteenth and twentieth centuries, various European styles exercised a degree of influence, including the **Empire**, and **Victorian** styles.

In the eighteenth and nineteenth centuries, a typical Spanish interior consisted of white plaster walls with a **dado**, floors, or even walls of tile, and dark, beamed ceilings. The house was built around a patio. The windows facing the street were small, and the **reveals** were fitted with decorative wrought ironwork.

The interior walls were hung with tapestries over the rough plaster or cork walls. Cork was also used to make small pieces of furniture. Popular woods were chestnut and walnut. Upholstered furniture was finished with heavy fringe, braid, or decorative nail heads. The colors of fabrics and paints were raw and brilliant. Upholstered materials were leather—plain, painted, or tooled—tapestry, red velvet, and, in the sixteenth century, embroidered silks and brocades.

Benches, chairs, and stools were the most commonly used articles of furniture. The seats were of rush, leather, or velvet. Tables had wooden tops and splayed legs supported by iron braces. Painted four-poster beds were prevalent. Bedspreads had the name of the bride and wedding date woven into the fabric. Most rooms had the ubiquitous chest that was used to store everything of value: clothes, linens, silver, even tools. Chests were usually covered with leather or velvet and decorated with iron plates and brass-headed nails in decorative patterns.

Floors were usually left bare or covered with braided leather or wool throw rugs.

Today, Spain has leading architects and interior designers. However, authentic antique Spanish furniture is quite difficult to find in the United States.

spar varnish: An extremely durable **varnish,** resistant to sun, salt, and water.

spatter-dash: A method of painting floors. A solid ground color. Then, a whiskbroom is dipped in the first color to be applied (spattered), and the wrist is given a quick jolt with the other hand. Successive coats of different colors are spattered *without* waiting for each coat to dry thoroughly.

spindle-back chair: An eighteenth-century chair with a back composed of two rows of vertical uprights or *spindles*, with horizontal rails.

spinet: A small harpsichord with a single keyboard.

spinning wheel: A primitive spinning machine fitted with a single spindle, used for spinning raw wool, cotton, or flax into thread or yarn. Used until the nineteenth century.

splat: The flat, central, vertical member of a wooden chairback, often an important ornamental element.

splay: An oblique slope across the full width of a surface. Sloping jambs are found on doors and windows. Can also refer to the surface of a leg or foot of furniture that flares or spreads outwards.

spline: A long, thin, flexible strip of wood, metal, or hard rubber used in drawing curves. Also, a wooden or metal strip or **splat.**

Spode, Josiah (1754–1827): British potter who founded a factory in 1770 in Staffordshire. Spode produced both earthenware and porcelain. In the early years the most popular pieces were in the Chinese style. He also made **Jasper ware** and black-printed wares of good quality. About 1805 he invented bone china, a **hard-paste** china that is durable and transparent.

spool furniture: Furniture with spool turnings for legs, stretchers, and arms. This style first appeared in Cromwellian England. In nineteenth-century America, after the introduction of the machine lathe, spool furniture appeared in many forms, such as bed frames, mirror frames, and table legs.

spoon-back chair: A chair with a high back shaped to fit the human spine. Developed in the eighteenth century.

Staffordshire: A county of west-central England that was the center of English pottery making in the eighteenth century. Both fine china and clay pottery were manufactured in Staffordshire, including the works of **Isaiah Wedgwood, Thomas Minton,** and **Josiah Spode.**

stained glass: There has been a renaissance in the use of stained glass in the latter half of the twentieth century. No longer is its appeal strictly ecclesiastical. It is now used as an integral architectural element and as a decorative device.

Its historic origin is obscure, though it is believed that stained glass was first made about 1000 B.C. Chemicals and metallic oxides are used to obtain a range of colors. Accidental colors or irregularities occurring in the manufacture are considered an asset.

staircase: A staircase can be an important decorative feature. Stairs should be carpeted for safety and to muffle sound. If there is a space beneath a staircase, plants in boxes with concealed lighting, or a statue, are practical solutions. In a corner, a bust or plant on a pedestal is suitable.

The walls of the stairwell can be papered or muraled as in the lower hall. If the wall going up the stairs is painted and looks sterile, hang a group of pictures, masks, trophies, or small carved figures on brackets to dress it up. If there is a large window on the middle landing it can be draped, shuttered, or treated with glass shelves, which can be used to display a collection of colored glass, porcelains, or plants. The color scheme takes its cue from the wallpaper or floor covering, and should blend or contrast with the adjacent rooms.

statuary bronze: A dark finish usually given to bronze statues, created by the application of acid.

steel engraving: The process of **engraving** on a steel (rather than a copper) plate.

More impressions can be taken from a steel than from a copper plate.

steel furniture: During the late eighteenth and nineteenth centuries in France, steel mantels, folding chairs, tables, desks, and beds became popular, especially in the **Directoire** style. A Russian weapons company, the Tula Ironworks, produced steel furniture and accessories in small quantities in the eighteenth century, as did England.

Stella, Frank (1936–): American abstract expressionist painter.

stenciling: A technique of applying color with a brush through openings cut in heavy waterproof paper or other material. Used in the decoration of furniture, **tole,** textiles, and borders for hardwood floors. In colonial times, stencils were used as substitutes for wallpapers and rugs, which were scarce. Itinerant stencilers often moved into the house they were decorating until the job was finished.

stereophonic sound: Sound reproduction that achieves a "dimensional" effect through the use of two or four sound tracks. Recorded through microphones so placed as to provide separation of sounds, and heard simultaneously through two speakers.

sterling: *See* silver.

Steuben glass: Brilliant, iridescent art glass made at the Steuben Glass Works in Corning, New York. Numerous distinguished artists and sculptors have designed works for Steuben.

stile: A vertical member of a door, window, panel, or chest. Also, one of the two vertical rear supports of a chair.

still life: A painting portraying inanimate objects such as fruit, bottles, flowers, or books, arranged in an organized artistic manner.

Stone, Edward Durell (1902–): Successful American architect who did much work abroad and became well known for his characteristic non-load-bearing, pierced-screen exterior walls. Example: U.S. Embassy at New Delhi.

stone china: An inexpensive English china resembling **ironware.**

stool: A seat for one person, consisting of a horizontal surface with legs, without arms or back.

stretcher: A crosspiece connecting the legs of chairs or tables, designed in H or X configurations.

strike-off: A sample of a special color or design for paper or fabric, run off before actual production.

stringer: A long, horizontal piece of timber used to support either side of a stairway.

stucco: An exterior coating or finish for masonry or frame walls, usually composed of cement, sand, and hydrated lime, mixed with water and laid on wet. Color may be introduced into the mix. It is also used as a **fresco** base.

stud: (1) a large, decorative nail head; and (2) the vertical two-by-four-inch wooden members that are used to frame a structure. They are almost always spaced sixteen inches on center.

subflooring: A rough wooden floor, laid on joists, which serves as a base for the finished floor. Used as a platform during construction; also provides additional resistance to lateral stress.

Sullivan, Louis Henri (1856–1924): American architect. He was of great importance in the evolution and construction of modern skyscrapers. Sullivan broke free from old concepts, believing that a building should faithfully express the functions for which it was built. His was truly *American architecture*. One of his pupils was **Frank Lloyd Wright.**

surcharge: A charge added to the purchase price when an interior designer buys less than the minimum required quantity.

surrealism: *See* modern art.

swag: A festoon of ribbons, fruits, and flowers representing drapery. Used in decorative carvings and paintings during the seventeenth and eighteenth centuries, usually above a mantelpiece. In the late eighteenth century swags began to be made of fabric and were hung above windows as a finish for the tops of draperies.

Swansea: A British pottery, founded about 1764, that produced both earthenware and porcelain. In the early days, coarse red wares were manufactured. Later they produced porcelain similar to **Staffordshire.**

swatch: A small cutting of fabric, carpet, or wallpaper.

swell front: *See* bow front.

sycamore: An American **hardwood,** yellow with a maple grain. It was used extensively by the English for marquetry work in the late seventeenth century. In the eighteenth century it was often dyed gray and given the name of *harewood*. Still used as a veneer, in panels, and in inlay work.

T

You can't appreciate home 'til you've left it.

O. Henry (1862–1910)

tallboy: A double **chest of drawers** or a **chest-on-chest** of the early eighteenth century. The top tier is composed of two narrow drawers, with six wide ones below. First made in mahogany then gradually supplanted by walnut. In America it is called a **highboy.**

tall-case clock: *See* grandfather clock.

Tamayo, Rufino (1899–): Mexican muralist and easel painter who has worked in many styles.

tambour front: A flexible sliding door composed of narrow strips of wood glued side by side on a canvas backing and fitted to a cabinet or writing desk. When the space is open, the tambours slide into a groove and disappear inside the cabinet. Perhaps the best-known use of a tambour front is in the **roll-top desk.**

Tanguy, Yves (1900–1955): French-American surrealist painter.

tapestry: A heavy fabric in which a multicolored design is woven across the warp. It is a bobbin-made ribbed fabric, alike on both sides. The technique has been in use since the early Egyptian period. European history has been recorded in tapestries for more than a thousand years.

task lighting: Light used to illuminate visually demanding activities such as reading, sewing, or drafting. For task lighting, the fixture should be placed as close to the observer's head as possible. The light should accent the task as well as gently illuminate the rest of the room. Too much contrast tires the eyes.

tatami: A thick Japanese woven straw mat, usually three by six feet, used as a standard unit of measurement in rooms.

tea caddy: A box designed to hold tea. Caddies were made in the eighteenth century, from various materials: wood (primarily mahogany, satinwood, and rosewood), porcelain, tortoiseshell, pewter, and silver. Tea caddies were invariably provided with locks and interior partitions lined with lead or fitted with canisters.

teak: A strong, Oriental hardwood, medium brown in color, and resistant to moisture. It is widely used for furniture, especially in Scandinavia and the Orient. It is also employed in shipbuilding.

teenagers' rooms: If left to her own devices, not every young girl will opt for a sweet pink-and-white bedroom. Many prefer bold, clashing colors, huge graphics, offbeat furniture, and more than one patterned fabric.

The usual basics—a desk, a daybed that also serves as a sofa, a bookcase, shelves for records and hi-fi equipment, and a comfortable lounging chair—are de rigueur.

With the exception of darker colors, woods and textured fabrics, nautical, cowboy, and other such themes, the same basics apply to a boy's room. Teenagers' rooms should be furnished with durable, rugged materials that will withstand rough usage and still be easy to maintain.

Provision must be made for housing hobbies.

tempera: A painting medium composed of powdered colors held in solution by either egg yolk and white or only the yolk. It is water soluble and is usually painted on a ground of chalk, plaster, or gesso.

template: A pattern or gauge, used as a guide for drawing or cutting material.

tented ceiling: A decorative effect achieved by draping the ceiling and walls of a room with fabric, thus creating the illusion of being in a tent. Though very effective, tented ceilings are not practical. They must be installed by a professional tent-company drapery installer.

tenon: A projection formed on the end of a timber that is made to be fitted and inserted into a corresponding hole or **mortise.**

terrace: A raised, level promenade of wood, paving, or grass alongside a building.

terra-cotta: A hard, semifired, unglazed clay material. It is used for making cornices, statuettes, relief plaques, and a variety of architectural ornaments. When covered with a clear glaze it is called **faience** and has been in use since the sixteenth century. Common brick and clay flowerpots are examples of terra cotta. Color will vary according to the firing.

terrazzo: A flooring material composed of marble or other stone chips set in cement and polished when dry.

tertiary color: *See* primary color.

tessera: One of the small pieces used in a mosaic work. The plural is *tesserae*.

tester: A canopy suspended from a ceiling or attached to a four-poster bed. Made of fabric or wood.

tête-à-tête: A small, eighteenth-century French settee for two, the ends of which curved forward, so that the people sitting in it almost faced each other.

textiles: Fifteen centuries before Christ, humans interlaced threads at right angles and discovered weaving. Fabrics have been used since then for wall coverings, upholstery, draperies, and decorative adornment. Today, the interior designer or consumer may choose fabrics that are woven, felted, braided, or knitted. They may select from a wide range of textures, colors, designs, and fibers—natural or manmade. The value of any textile is a function of the use to which it will be put, the properties it must possess—such as tensile strength, draping quality, colorfastness, wrinkle resistance, sunlight resistance, abrasion resistance, and dyeability—and a variety of other qualities. There are three fundamental weaves (all others are variations): 1) the *plain weave*, also known as bedford cord, poplin, rep, tapestry, homespun, or taffeta; 2) the *twill-weave*, a diagonal gabardine, denim, or herringbone design; 3) the *satin weave*, which has luster. The following is a concise list of textile fibers, fabrics, their properties, and comparative qualities.

Aubusson: Handwoven tapestry weave. Tapestry works in the French city of Aubusson date from the late fifteenth century.

Batik: A fabric in which the pattern is made by applying wax in a resist technique.

Batiste: A fine, sheer, lightweight fabric made of various fibers. Frequently embroidered or printed.

Brocade: A patterned fabric made with a raised embroidered design woven into it. The ground can be of silk, satin, or velvet.

Brocatelle: A fabric similar to *brocade* but with the design woven in high relief so that the pattern stands out noticeably.

Buckram: A stiffened, plain-weave, sized, coarse cotton, used for reinforcing headings and valances of draperies.

Burlap: A coarse fabric made of jute, flax, or hemp.

Calico: A plain-weave cotton, usually printed with small, bright-colored patterns.

Casement cloth: All loosely woven, semisheer, lightweight, plain, or insignificant-patterned drapery fabrics.

Chenille: A soft fabric woven with a fluffy yarn that produces a protruding, soft, deep pile.

Corduroy: Customarily a heavy cotton fabric having ridges or velvety cords in the pile. Also made in cotton combined with manmade fibers.

Cotton: The most versatile of all fibers, despite inroads of the synthetics. It blends well with other fibers and can be permanently creased.

Damask: A flat-patterned fabric that combines a taffeta weave against a background of satin weave. Originally made only from silk, now made of linen, cotton, or synthetic fibers as well.

Denim: A coarse, twilled cotton. Very serviceable.

Faille: A type of *rep,* with a flat, ribbed effect.

Felt: An unwoven fabric whose fibers are matted and compressed by heat and moisture.

Flax: The only fiber that can legally be used in the manufacture of pure linen. Stronger than cotton but has poor wrinkle resistance.

Fortuny print: A hand-blocked print on cotton. Made in Venice, Italy. Color overlays give a textured effect.

Frieze: A coarse, shaggy woolen fabric with uncut loops. Twill construction. Very durable. Also called *frisé.*

Gingham: A yarn-dyed, plain-weave, cotton fabric with a striped or checkered pattern.

Glass fiber: A fabric manufactured from molten glass and containing remarkable properties of high tensile strength and resistance to mildew, heat, sunlight, and moisture. Used for draperies but does not hang or drape well.

Hair cloth: A popular nineteenth-century fabric made of horsehair or a mohair/horsehair mixture. It can also be made of cotton and linen.

Homespun: Coarse, loosely woven fabric made of bulky yarns.

Jacquard: A figured weave produced by a Jacquard loom. The loom has an endless belt of perforated cards that translate the desired design, color, and pattern into a tapestry, brocade, or damask.

Jute: A strong, glossy fiber obtained from either of two Asian plants.

Linen: See Flax.

Marquisette: A transparent fabric of tightly twisted yarns of silk, rayon, cotton, or nylon. Used for curtains, clothing, and mosquito nets.

Matelasse: A fabric having a raised pattern as if quilted. Characteristically a heavy-weight, double-weave cloth.

Mohair: A fabric woven from the hair of the Angora goat. Wrinkle resistant. Often combined with cotton, wool, or linen for many types of twill and pile fabrics.

Moiré: A watered or wavy effect, usually on *taffeta* or *faille.*

Muslin: A plain-weave cotton cloth of medium weight.

Ninon: A sheer, crisp, plain-weave fabric of silk, rayon, or nylon used for curtains.

Organdy: A stiff, sheer, plain-weave material made of tightly spun cotton.

Paisley: A soft wool fabric with an elaborate, colorful pattern of abstract, swirled shapes.

Percale: A fine, lightweight, closely woven cotton cloth, sometimes printed. Used for draperies and bed linens.

Plissé: A puckered fabric made from cotton or synthetic fibers treated with a caustic soda.

Plush: A closely woven cut-pile fabric of silk, rayon, cotton, or other materials, with a deeper pile than velvet.

Rep: A plain-woven fabric of various materials with narrow ribs running lengthwise.

Sailcloth: A heavy, plain-weave cotton, linen, or jute material originally used for sails. Also called *canvas* or *duck.*

Sateen: A satin-weave fabric of mercerized cotton yarns. The amount of sheen can be regulated.

Satin: A fabric with a glossy face and a dull back. Made of cotton, silk, or synthetics.

Silk: A fine, soft, glossy fiber extruded by the silkworm in the spinning of its cocoon. It is a strong fabric with good wrinkle resistance and can be dyed in brilliant colors.

Suede cloth: A fabric made to resemble suede. Can be either woven or knitted. It has a very short nap.

Taffeta: A fine, crisp, lightweight, closely woven, lustrous fabric. Made of silk, cotton, rayon, wool, or acetate.

Tapestry: A complex, single-weave, yarn-dyed fabric, woven with multicolored yarns on a Jacquard loom.

Ticking: Closely woven cotton or linen fabric in a herringbone or twill weave. Used to make ticks.

Toile de Jouy: A cotton or linen woven fabric, plain or twill, produced in the eighteenth and early nineteenth centuries in France. Pastoral or mythological scenes were usually printed in one color on a beige ground.

Tweed: A coarse, loosely woven woolen fabric in a twill or herringbone weave, characterized by two or more colors. Originally an all-wool homespun made in Scotland.

Velour: A napped, velvetlike fabric generally woven in a satin or plain weave.

Velvet: A fabric with a soft, thick pile. Velvets are woven double, face to face, and cut apart while still on the loom. Background may be twill or satin weave.

Voile: A plain-weave, sheer, transparent fabric made with highly twisted yarn. It can be made in any fiber.

Wool: The naturally highly crimped fiber from sheep, lambs, or Angora goats. It is universally known for its resilience, strength, and ease of maintenance.

MANMADE FIBER GLOSSARY

Generic Name	Best-Known Trade Names
Acetate	Celanese, Avisco
Acrylic	Orlon, Acrilan, Creslan
Glass	Fiberglass
Metallic	Lame, Lurex
Modacrylic	Dynel, Verel
Nylon	Antron, Caprolan, Vectra, Cumuloft, Enkatron
Olefin	Herculon, Vectra
Polyester	Dacron, Fortrel, Kodel, Vectra, Mylar
Rayon	Bemberg, Fortisan, Avisco, Nupron
Spandex	Lycra

Thomas, Seth (1785–1859): American clock manufacturer.

Thonet, Michael (1796–1871): German-born Austrian furniture designer and manufacturer who invented the **bentwood** process.

threshold: A marble, metal, or wood member that lies beneath a door. Also called a *doorsill.*

tie-dye: A resist technique in which parts of a plain fabric are bunched up and tied and then dipped in various dyes, resulting in a mottled or streaked effect.

Tiffany glass: Stained or iridescent glass made by Louis Comfort Tiffany (1848–1933), American **art nouveau** glass designer, artist, and interior decorator. He revived stained glass as an art form and made lamps, shades, windows, vases, and jewelry. Tiffany arranged for the coordination of his glass designs, colors, and patterns with textile and tile manufacturers.

tilt-top table: A pedestal table with a hinged top that can be tilted vertically when the table is not in use, to save space. Developed in the eighteenth century.

toenail: To secure boards with obliquely driven nails, thereby creating a greater bond than would be obtained by driving at right angles.

toggle switch: A switch in which a projecting lever employing a toggle joint and a spring is used to open and close an electric circuit.

tole: Painted and decorated tinware. Used in America since the eighteenth century. Popular in the form of accessories such as boxes, trays, and lamps.

T & G: *See* tongue-and-groove joint.

tongue-and-groove joint: A rabbeted joint in which a projecting member (*tongue*) of one board fits into a corresponding rabbet (*groove*) of another board.

torchère: A floor lamp giving **indirect light.** Also, a tall ornamental stand for a candlestick, used in the eighteenth century.

Townsend, Job (1732–1809): American furniture maker. He and his partner, John Goddard, are credited with developing blockfront cabinet furniture. They also made furniture in the **Queen Anne** and **Empire** styles.

transept: Either of two lateral arms of a cruciform church.

transfer printing: A method of printing patterns on pottery from a thin paper engraving, which is transferred to the pottery from the paper.

transom: A hinged window over a door or another window.

trapunto: A high-relief quilting method. The high, raised pattern is achieved by outlining the design with running stiches and inserting thick filler between the fabric and its backing.

travertine: A beige-colored, marblelike limestone. It polishes well. Used in place of marble.

tread: The horizontal upper surface of a step in a staircase.

trefoil: A **Gothic** three-lobed motif inscribed within a circle.

treillage: *See* lattice.

trestle table: A long, narrow, dining table supported by stout truss end supports joined by a single stretcher, usually of metal. Originating in medieval times, the form was popular through the seventeenth century and has experienced a revival in recent years.

tripod table: A small table with a center pillar support with three spreading legs. The top is often decorated with a **gallery.** First manufactured in the early eighteenth century.

triptych: A three-paneled altarpiece on hinges, depicting a religious story in painting.

trivet: A three-legged metal stand used for holding a pot or kettle. It was traditionally used near a fireplace for keeping food warm.

trompe l'oeil: French for "fool the eye," a type of painting that appears three dimensional and very realistic. First used on walls in Rome around 100 B.C., to make a room or church look larger and more impressive.

trumeau: A mirror surmounted by a painting, both enclosed and surrounded by an elaborately carved, gilded, and painted frame.

trundle or truckle bed: A low bed on wheels, designed to roll under a larger bed when not in use. Developed in the late Middle Ages and popular until the mid-**Georgian** period.

tub chair: *See* barrel chair.

Tudor rose: A conventional, five-petaled, carved rose motif, created in 1486 as the heraldic emblem of the Tudor dynasty. Used as a decorative motif on English carved oak furniture of the sixteenth and seventeenth centuries.

Tudor style: *See* period styles.

tufted carpet: Carpet formed by leaving enough nap to be cut off or left as loops.

tufting: An upholstering technique in which folds or *tufts* are set by gathering in the fabric by means of a button that is pulled through the upholstery at designated spacing.

Turkish rug: A type of Oriental rug made during the fourteenth and fifteenth centuries in Asia Minor, characterized by warm colors and angular designs. These fine-quality rugs were also used as wall hangings, prayer rugs, and tablecloths.

turnery: The process of shaping a piece of wood by applying a cutting tool to the rotating or turning wood. The machine that turns the wood is called a **lathe.**

Tuscan order: One of the Greek **orders of architecture.** It is similar to Roman **Doric** but with unfluted columns and no decoration other than moldings.

There's nothing half so pleasant
As coming home again.

Margaret E. Sangster
(1838–1912)

ultramodern: Futuristic; suggestive of a period beyond the contemporary.

ultraviolet (black) light: Light rays of extremely short wavelength. UV light is used to inspect works of art to ascertain if they are forgeries, and to detect repairs, replacements, and fake signatures in bronzes, paintings, porcelains, and old marbles.

umbrella stand: A large, vaselike container made of brass, porcelain, wood, or leather. First used in English entry halls about 1844.

underframing: The arrangement of supports for chairs, tables, cabinets, and desks. It is usually indicative of the period style.

underglaze: Painting, colors, decoration, or designs applied to porcelain or pottery before the glaze is put on.

underpainting: In fine art, the first coat of paint in a **gesso** background on which subsequent glazes and coats of paint are applied.

undressed timber: Timber that has been sawn but not sanded or smoothed.

upholsterer: A craftsman who makes furniture in which stuffing, springs, cotton, down, and other materials are attached to a wooden framework, the whole covered in leather or textiles. In the early part of the fifteenth century he was referred to as an *upholder*, later as an *upholdster*, finally *upholsterer*.

upholstery: The craft and skill of stuffing and covering the wood frame of a sofa, chair, or any padded seating unit. The coverings consist of textiles or leather. The seat stuffings consist of down, springs, horsehair, cotton, manmade fibers, or foam rubber. Upholstered furniture was first made about 1560.

upright: The outside vertical post or member of a chair back.

urban renewal: The replanning of existing blighted city centers to bring them up to date, thereby improving the aesthetic climate, deterring crime, and clearing up traffic congestion.

Urbino: A city in central Italy that was generally regarded as the major center for the production of highly glazed Italian ceramics from the fifteenth well into the seventeenth century.

urn: A large decorative vase in various forms and shapes, made of stone or clay and used as a container for plants and shrubbery in a garden. It is also used as a finial for the façades of buildings and as a carving motif. Of **classical** derivation.

Utrillo, Maurice (1883–1955): French impressionist who painted street scenes of Paris from postcards. He was the son of the artist **Suzanne Valadon.**

*If mankind's sense of duty
was as strong as birds',
what ideal homes we'd have.*

Anonymous

Valadon, Suzanne (1865–1938): French model and painter who began her Parisian stay as a wrestler and then became a model for Renoir, Puvis de Chavannes, and others. In 1888 she had a son, **Maurice Utrillo.** Valadon exhibited with the Impressionists, and then the Symbolists. In the twenties her style was tempered by the Fauves.

valance: A border of fabric used as a heading over draperies to achieve a finished look, and to conceal drapery hardware. The valance, made of fabric, is pleated or shirred. It can also be attached to the bottom of sofas, chairs, to tester beds, and to the lower part of a two-piece bedspread, in which case it is called a **skirt.** First used in the sixteenth century.

van de Velde, Henri (1863–1957): Belgian architect and designer. A prominent figure in the **art nouveau** movement, he was strongly influenced by both **William Morris** and Charles Rennie Mackintosh.

vargueño: A richly decorated Spanish cabinet-desk with a drop lid. Developed in the sixteenth century. *See also* Spanish furniture.

varnish: A wood-finishing preparation made of resinous substances dissolved in linseed oil. It imparts a glossy, transparent coating.

vault: An arched structure forming a ceiling or roof.

veneer: A thin layer of decorative wood or other material that is bonded to a less expensive material for decorative effect. Richly figured woods can thus be used at reduced cost. The strength of the wood is also increased. The use of veneer goes back to ancient Egypt.

Venetian glass: Thinly blown soda glass developed in about the fifteenth century. Ice or crackled glass and white glass threads were embedded in clear glass.

Venetian painted furniture: A charming eighteenth-century style of rich individuality. The furniture was developed from the **rococo** by the Venetians. It was highly ornamental, with graceful curving lines and fancifully painted exotic birds and flowers.

verdigris: A green or greenish-blue coating of copper sulfate or copper chloride that forms over time on brass, bronze, of copper that is exposed to air or salt water.

vermeil: Gilded metal—usually silver or bronze—used for decorative accessories. The gilding takes on a vermilion or rosy tone.

Vernis Martin: A brilliant lacquer furniture finish that imitates Chinese lacquer but is less durable. The technique is attributed to the French Martin brothers.

vestibule: A small entrance hall or room either to a building or to a room within a building. Also, a passage between two doors facing each other as in cars in a train.

Victorian period: The years in which the British monarch, Queen Victoria, reigned (1837–1901). The Victorian period is divided into three eras:

Early Victorian	1837–1850
Mid-Victorian	1850–1880
Late Victorian	1880–1901

The term "Victorian furniture" does not designate a true period style but many styles of English and American furniture made from 1837 to 1901. The cabinet-makers of the era adapted Louis XIV, Louis XVI, Rococo, Empire, Gothic, Italian and French Renaissance, Sheraton, Queen Anne, Adam, Elizabethan, Jacobean, Morris, Belter, Hitchcock, and Eastlake designs. Very late in the century, art nouveau and Japanese themes were briefly popular.

Furniture was of exaggerated scale and curvature. In the early part of this era, carving was simple, but it soon became heavy and ornate, with coarse fruit and flower carvings. Sofa and chair frames were made of rosewood or mahogany. Satin, damask, plush, or black haircloth were popular fabrics used to cover the overly stuffed upholstered furniture. Tufted, upholstered furniture was to be seen everywhere. Much Victorian furniture is regarded as tasteless and without much artistic merit, although the framed oval-shaped-back chairs and sofas were graceful and delicately carved. Marble tops for tables were common. Footstools in needlepoint, and fancy étagères were commonplace during the Victorian years. Papier-mâché was formed into tables, chests, and chairs.

video vocabulary: Video jargon has invaded the field of the interior designer, now that the designer uses a great deal of hi-fi and video equipment in decorating.

A.E.F.: Automatic Edit Function.

audio dubbing: Substituting or adding sound to tape.

decibel: Measure of sound.

definition: Sharpness of a television picture.

digital clock/timer: A device that tells time and allows you to preset a VCR to record in your absence.

freeze frame: A device that stops the tape, permitting you to examine the image on the screen.

glitch: Picture distortion.

hardware: Equipment.

L.E.D.: Light-emitting Diode.

pause control: A device that allows you to stop the tape. Useful for skipping commercials while recording from television.

resolution: Capability of the unit to project clear detail.

software: Program material.

video cassette: A reel of video tape.

video disc: Video from a round disc.

Vienna furniture: *See* bentwood furniture.

Villanueva, Carlos Raul (1900–): British-born architect, Villanueva, more than any other individual architect, is responsible for the development of modern architecture in Venezuela and most of South America.

vinyl: Any resin formed by polymerization of compounds containing the vinyl group (CH_2CH) or plastics made from such resins. The first commercial vinyl-coated fabric was introduced after World War II. The basis of all vinyl-coated fabric is a polyvinyl chloride film, backed by knit or woven fabric or a nonwoven **polyester** material. Knits and nonwoven backings are generally used in upholstery fabric; woven backings in wallcovering material.

Vinyl-coated fabric is easy to maintain. However, like any other upholstery fabric, its ongoing maintenance is important to the durability and beauty of the fabric.

When major spotting and staining problems arise, it is important to take immediate action. The instructions listed are intended as general guidelines; be sure to see specific manufacturer's directions.

CLEANING DIRECTIONS FOR VINYL-COATED FABRIC

The everyday variety of dirt washes off. Most dirt whisks off quickly with soap and water. Apply warm, soapy water to a large area and soak it for a minute or so. Rub briskly with a soft cloth or soft brush. For stubborn dirt, resoak, then brush again. Tough dirt stains may require using small quantities of cleaning powder—but never on wood or metal parts, as it scratches. Rinse and polish with a soft cloth.

Vinyl upholstery fabric, like other fabrics, may be irreparably damaged when staining substances come into contact with fabric for any length of time.

Nail polish or polish remover must be wiped up immediately or blotted with a soft cloth or the fabric will be permanently damaged.

Chewing gum should be scraped off gently, then the vinyl should be cleaned with a soft cloth dampened with naphtha or kerosene. Ice cubes can also be applied until the gum becomes brittle and flakes off.

Ball-point ink has the best chance of being removed if rubbed immediately with a damp cloth, using water or rubbing alcohol.

Tar, asphalt, and creosote will all stain vinyl. Remove quickly with a soft cloth, then clean with a white cloth dampened with kerosene or naphtha.

WAXING AND REFINISHING VINYL-COATED FABRIC

Any hard wax will improve the wearability and cleanability of vinyl.

Caution should be exercised in using flammable solvents. Keep cleaning materials from contact with soft fabrics or wooden areas of furniture, as damage may result.

There are now numerous products manufactured specifically for the care of vinyl-coated fabrics.

vitreous: A silicate glass-fired on metal, resulting in a material with glasslike quality. Commonly used in the manufacture of bathroom fixtures.

vitrine: A cabinet with a glass door and sometimes glass sides, used for display of decorative objects or china. Also known as a *curio cabinet.*

Vlaminck, Maurice de (1876–1958): French impressionist and Fauvist painter, noted for his landscapes.

volute: A spiral scroll used to ornament column capitals in the Ionic, Corinthian, and Composite orders of classical architecture.

Vuillard, Jean Edouard (1868–1940): French impressionist painter, noted for still-life and flower paintings.

No house should ever be on any hill or on anything. It should be of the hill, belonging to it, so hill and house could live together— each the happier for the other.

Frank Lloyd Wright
(1867–1959)

wainscot: A wooden lining of an interior wall, usually paneled. Also, the lower three feet of an interior wall when finished differently from the rest of the wall.

wainscot chair: An armchair of the sixteenth and seventeenth centuries. Made of oak, with carved panels attached to a simple, foresquare frame.

wall bracket: A wall shelf serving as a support for a vase, statuette, or any object of art.

wall coverings: The Chinese invented wallpaper about 600 B.C. Wallpaper first appeared in England and France in the late sixteenth century. Shortly thereafter, other European countries began to develop and use it. Wallpapers came into general use in Europe in the late seventeenth century. About that time, French designers began making wallpaper copies of tapestries and silks as an inexpensive substitute for these costly materials. By 1750 handpainted papers were replaced by printing from woodblocks. By the eighteenth century, England had become the principal manufacturer of wallpapers. Flocked papers were introduced in France in 1650. These decorative papers are made with finely powdered wool or silk (*flock*) applied over designs that have been stenciled with an adhesive or varnish. After drying, the flock is blown or brushed from the untreated surface, leaving a velvet effect on the design.

Wallpapers should enhance and coordinate with the furniture style featured in a room. Wallpapers can create a mood, a personality, a feeling of warmth. They can conceal architectural and structural flaws. A vertical striped paper can create the illusion of greater height. A scenic wallpaper or mural will endow a room with a vista and visually enlarge it. A long, narrow room can be widened by covering the short walls with a strong pattern in a warm color, and papering the long walls with a plain, cool-colored, textured paper. A small-scale pattern in a light color will enlarge a small room. Bold patterns and dark or warm colors will help create intimacy in a large room. Choose a quiet pattern if the draperies or upholstery have bold designs. If carpeting is patterned, apply a fairly quiet paper that repeats the carpet's dominant color.

Borders and bases in wallpaper are available at a low cost and can be as decorative and effective as expensive wood moldings. American wallpaper was first manufactured in Philadelphia in 1756. It was sold by upholsterers, stationers, and undertakers. Up to that time, most houses had whitewashed plaster walls. In 1884 the first color printing machine was imported from England for a Philadelphia factory. The year 1857 marked the end of hand-blocked papers as mechanization took over. The oldest American firm still operating today is A. L. Diament and Co., established in 1885.

In the 1920s, the method of paper printing changed from wood rollers to silk-screening. By 1930 wallpapers were being mass-produced by the rotogravure process. Today paper printing is being done more and more by computer. Paintings by old masters can be reproduced and printed by computers on cork, tapestry, jute, velvet, paper, or canvas. Paintings can be reproduced as large as fourteen by twenty feet and hung like tapestries or murals.

Before wallpaper is hung, the walls must be smooth, clean, and sealed with a coat of shellac or vinyl.

A practical choice for hallways, reception areas, offices, or any room where there is constant traffic is long-lasting vinyl. It is ideal for kitchens, bathrooms, and children's playrooms.

Vinyls are available in a beautiful array of colors and patterns and are easy to maintain—all that is necessary to keep them looking bright and clean is soap and water. Vinyl wallcovering resists fading and keeps its first-day brightness for years.

Here are some tips for estimating how much wallpaper you need: A standard single roll of paper covers thirty-six square feet of surface, regardless of the width of the paper. Measure the length and width of the room, and the ceiling height. Then check the chart on the following page. Subtract one roll for every two average-size windows or any other openings in the room. Allow 10 percent for waste.

Vinyl wallcoverings are estimated by the yard. Vinyls vary from forty-eight to fifty-four inches in width.

A number of Euro (European) and British wallpapers are available in the United States. There is no simple way to convert Euro rolls to American rolls. The Euro rolls, in both width and length, vary according to the manufacturer. The British roll is often 12 yards long, 21 inches wide, and contains 7 square yards. The French or Euro roll is generally 9 yards long, 18 inches wide, and contains approximately $40\frac{1}{2}$ square feet. It is important that the exact rollage be obtained from the wallpaper hanger.

CALCULATING WALLPAPER ROLLAGE

ROOM SIZE	Ceiling Height				CEILING
	8 FT.*	9 FT.*	10 FT.*	11 FT.*	
6 × 10	8	8	11	11	3
8 × 10	9	10	11	12	3
10 × 10	10	11	13	14	4
10 × 12	11	12	14	15	4
10 × 14	12	14	15	16	5
12 × 12	12	14	15	16	5
12 × 14	13	15	16	18	6
12 × 16	14	16	17	19	6
12 × 18	15	17	19	20	7
12 × 20	16	18	20	22	8
14 × 14	14	16	17	19	7
14 × 16	15	17	19	20	7
14 × 18	16	18	20	22	8
14 × 20	17	19	21	23	9
14 × 22	18	20	22	24	10
16 × 16	16	18	20	22	8
16 × 18	17	19	21	23	9
16 × 20	18	20	22	24	10
16 × 22	19	21	23	26	11
16 × 24	20	22	25	27	12
18 × 18	18	20	22	24	11
18 × 20	19	21	23	26	12
18 × 22	20	22	25	27	12
18 × 24	21	23	26	28	14

* Single Rolls

walls: They are a major factor to consider when decorating a room. Walls should make a definite decorative statement. Interior walls can be finished in a variety of materials. Among the foremost are: plaster, brick, acoustical tile, steel, glass, wood, and stone. They may be painted, papered, mirrored, paneled, carpeted, or covered with shingles, burlap, grass cloth, treillage, tapestry, or plastic laminates.

walnut: A dark brown hardwood. Since the early sixteenth century, walnut has been a leading furniture wood because of its warm golden brown color and the fact that it works easily and responds well to most types of finishing treatments.

211

There are six major species: African, English, Australian, French, East Indian, and American.

wardrobe: A large cabinet for hanging clothes, developed in Europe in the sixteenth and seventeenth centuries. It was also referred to as a *clothespress, cupboard,* or *garderobe.*

Warhol, Andy (1929–1987): American painter. Best known as a pop artist, he produced many series of mechanically silk-screened portraits, soup cans, and other everyday objects.

warp: A set of yarns placed lengthwise in the loom, crossed by and interlaced with the *weft* or *woof,* and forming the lengthwise threads in a woven fabric.

wash: A thin layer of paint used in the watercolor method.

wash stand: An eighteenth- and nineteenth-century piece of bedroom furniture for holding a basin, ewer, and soap dish.

Waterford glass: Irish glass manufactured since 1730. This glass is ideal for cutting in deep relief.

webbing: Narrow strips of a strong fabric that are interlaced and fastened to the base of an upholstered piece of furniture, and upon which the spring units are fastened.

Weber, Max (1881–1961): American painter and sculptor. His finest paintings have Jewish religious themes.

Wedgwood, Josiah (1730–1795): The most renowned English potter. He established his factory in 1759. Wedgwood is famous for the delicately designed neoclassical figures that are applied in cameolike relief before firing. Also noted for cream-colored ware, agate ware, and black basaltes.

Welsh dresser: An English furniture form that first appeared in the late seventeenth century. The upper half is an open-shelved oak cabinet. The lower half consists of drawers and compartments.

welt: A fabric-covered cord sewn into the seams of upholstery for decorative purposes, to add additional interest and to give the article a finished appearance.

what-not: *See* étagère.

wheel-back chair: A British **Windsor chair** with a pierced central **splat** ornamented with the image of a spoked wheel.

White, Stanford (1853–1906): American architect. Partner in the firm of **McKim, Mead & White.**

wicker: Small woven twigs or flexible strips of wood, used in weaving baskets and certain articles of furniture.

Willard, Simon (1753–1848): American clockmaker who invented the **banjo clock.**

William and Mary style: *See* period styles.

Wilton: A type of carpet woven on a **Jacquard** loom to produce a pattern and multilevel textures. Manufactured since the time of Queen Elizabeth I.

windows: There are five types of windows:

1. Double-Hung Windows: These open vertically from the bottom or the top, or from both. Traditional in spirit.

2. Casement Windows: These windows swing open like doors. Screens are mounted inside, and the window is operated by a crank.

3. Awning Windows: These contemporary-type windows are hinged so that they open outward from the bottom.

4. Fixed Windows: These windows are permanently fixed so that they cannot be opened for ventilation.

5. Sliding Glass Doors: A dramatic way to bring the outdoors inside a house.

window seat: A built-in seat in a recess or bay of a window. It normally has a loose cushion seat.

Windsor chair: A wooden chair popular in England and America since the early part of the eighteenth century. It typically had a high, spoked back with slender turned spindles set into it, and a wooden saddle seat. The legs were invariably splayed and connected by a crossbar. The back of the Windsor chair was designed in a variety of ways, including: fan-back, hoop-back, comb-back, wheel-back, loop-back, and central splat-back.

wine, wine racks, wine cellars: Wine-making dates back several thousand years B.C. Many people today find collecting wines quite interesting. Collectors of wine, or wine hobbyists, whether interior designers or their clients, usually begin with a few bottles stored in their kitchens. Before graduating to a collector of status, there are four important conditions that must be met in storing wine: *light, temperature, motion,* and *air.*

Light: Sunlight and fluorescent lights are enemies that can make red wines mature too quickly, become cloudy, and change flavor. All wines should be stored in a dark place.

Temperature: The ideal temperature for long-term storage is a constant 55 degrees Fahrenheit, for it permits slow maturation. Temperatures of 50 to 70 degrees are tolerable if the fluctuation is not sudden or frequent. Wines must not be stored close to hot water pipes, furnaces, or any obvious hot spots.

Motion and vibration: Both are harmful to wine. Avoid locations near any major appliances run by motors. Keep wine away from heavy traffic areas.

Air: Wine should be stored on its side or with the bottle neck tilted downward to keep the cork wet and expanded, so that no air can enter the bottle. Once it does, the wine soon spoils and turns to vinegar.

All fortified wines containing more than 14 percent alcohol may be stored in an upright position. Included in this category are sherry, port, dessert wines, and liqueurs. Any wine containing 20 percent or more alcohol will keep indefinitely after uncorking.

Very few homes have actual wine cellars per se. A small wine cellar or convenience storage at home need not be complicated or pretentious. The location can be a cabinet, closet, cupboard, or shelf. Cabinets in a garage, fitted with storage racks, will do if the wall does not face south or west. If the house has a basement, then a true wine cellar with optimum environment is at hand.

The most economical construction for wine-storage bins is the "X" method, attained by dividing a cabinet or box with two crossed boards. The cabinet should be eighteen inches deep. There is a large variety of ready-made wooden and metal racks available in wine and hardware stores. The simplest "wine cellar" is the case the wine comes in. Remove the top and turn the box on its side. Place on the floor of a cool, dark closet. Refrig-

erated wine vaults are available as free-standing units. They provide a constant temperature range and protection from light.

wine cooler: A watertight container originally made of mahogany, bronze, copper, silver, pewter, or marble, that came into use in England around 1730. The coolers were lined with lead, to contain ice or cold water. They averaged twenty-four inches in height and often had taps to drain off the water.

wing chair: A high-backed upholstered armchair with upholstered panels or *wings*. Also known as a *grandfather chair*.

Winthrop desk: A slant-top, drop-front writing desk designed in the **Chippendale** style.

Wolfe, Elsie de (1865–1950): American actress and international social leader who married Sir Charles Mendl in 1926 and became Lady Mendl. She was the first American woman to call herself an interior decorator. Lady Mendl had natural good taste, a daring spirit, and a creative imagination. Her favorite style was **Louis XVI.** She liked to cover formal furniture in chintzes and have draperies made to match, and thus came to be known as "'the chintz lady." Her rooms sparkled with glass and a profusion of mirrors. Her second choice in materials for sofas and chairs was fur. She also used fur throw rugs. White upholstery and white-painted walls were also her signatures.

woodcut: A wooden block engraved with a picture or pattern. Also, a print made from this block. Woodcuts are often used in printing wallpapers and fabrics.

wood stain: A dye or pigment used for coloring unfinished wood. Types of wood stains include:

1. Penetrating oil stain
2. Water stain
3. Alcohol stain
4. Wax stain
5. Chemical stain
6. Varnish stain

For light colors bleaching of the wood is necessary. These are referred to as blond, bleached, or pickled finishes.

woof: The threads that run crosswise in a woven fabric, at right angles to the **warp** threads.

Worcester china: English **soft-paste** porcelain containing very little clay. Made in England since 1751. Also called *Royal Worcester* and *Worcester porcelain.*

workplane: The plane to which work is usually done and at which the illumination is specified and measured. This varies with the type of work, but for most tasks it is a horizontal plane 30 inches above the floor.

Wren, Sir Christopher (1632–1723): Noted British architect who planned the rebuilding of London after the Great Fire. Sir Christopher also built St. Paul's Cathedral and a number of buildings at Oxford and Cambridge Colleges.

Wright, Frank Lloyd (1867–1959): Considered America's greatest architect. A poet-engineer, he initiated many styles during his lifetime and was never repetitive. He was opposed to classic architecture, preferring low, horizontal, earth-tied *prairie* houses with wide, spreading eaves reaching into space. Exterior ornamentation was extremely simple. The interiors of these houses had open plans, with terraces merging with the gardens. He innovated the picture window, the carport, and the split-level house. Wright went through many design phases, but he never lost his benevolent attitude toward nature and organic architecture.

His talent went beyond residential design. He created a vast variety of public buildings: the Imperial Hotel in Tokyo, which withstood the 1923 earthquake when most of Tokyo was destroyed; the Johnson Wax Tower, with walls of brick and glass tubes, in Racine, Wisconsin; and his last work, the Guggenheim Museum, which demonstrated his genius in basic geometrical forms.

wrought iron: Iron that contains approximately .02 percent carbon. It is tough and hard to break yet soft enough to be rolled or hammered into shape when hot. It differs from *cast iron*, which is brittle.

Wyeth, Andrew Newell (1917–   ): American painter known for his work in tempera and watercolor. A microscopically detailed realist.

The beauty of the house is order;
The blessing of the house is
contentment.

Anonymous

X-frame chair: A chair in which two supports are arranged to form the letter X. Two or more sets of these supports are joined by the seat and/or by stretchers or a bolt. This form was first found in ancient Egypt and Rome. When revived in the seventeenth century, it had a double X frame in front and back, with upholstered back, seat, and arms. It was usually covered in velvet and trimmed with heavy fringe.

X-stretcher: A **stretcher,** generally used to join chair legs in the form of the letter X. Also called a *cross stretcher.*

Yamasaki, Minoru (1912–): Distinguished American architect renowned for his use of thin shell concrete groin vaults and spectacular roof designs.

yankee screwdriver: A long screwdriver with a threaded shaft that causes the screw to turn quickly when the handle is pushed all the way down.

yard-of-ale: An English drinking glass 36 to 40 inches high, with a flared mouth and tapering to a bulb foot. First produced in the late seventeenth century.

yarn: A group of natural or manmade fibers twisted together to form a continuous strand which is used in weaving and knitting.

yarn-dyeing: The process of vat-dyeing yarn before it is used for weaving.

yeseria: Delicately carved decorative plasterwork, extensively employed as a frieze on walls and around windows and doors during the Spanish **Renaissance.**

yew: A close-grained, pale red **softwood.** It takes a high polish. The wood is not available in large sizes, so it is used chiefly for inlay and veneered effects.

yoke-back chair: Early eighteenth-century chair in which a crossbar in the form of two S curves is used for the top rail.

Yorkshire chair: A **Jacobean** oak chair with two carved and arched back panels. It is also called a *Derbyshire chair.*

zebrawood: A colorful **hardwood** from Africa, often called *snakewood*. It is heavy, straight-grained, light brown, irregularly striped, and figured. Used mostly for inlays and bandings, for it is difficult to work. Zebrawood reacts satisfactorily to finishes.

zig-zag ruler: A folding ruler made of six-inch long pieces of wood or metal pivoted together at each end.

zones of color vision: Division of color acuity and vision according to the following characteristics.

1. Marginal zone: No colors seen.
2. Intermediate zone: Only yellows and blues are seen.
3. Central zone: Full color vision.

zoning: The designation of an area in a city for a particular type of building, enterprise, or activity.

Zucchi, Antonio (1726–1795): Well-known Venetian artist who was employed by Robert Adam to paint ceilings and decorative wall designs.

In 1781 he married artist **Angelica Kauffmann,** with whom he worked.

zwischengoldglas: An eighteenth-century technique of laminating a layer of gold between two transparent glass surfaces. This technique was used in decorating walls, picture frames, and table tops.

BIBLIOGRAPHY

Aronson, Joseph. *The Encyclopedia of Furniture*. New York: Crown Publishers, 1965.

Austin, Richard, L. *Designing the Interior Landscape*. New York: Van Nostrand Reinhold, 1985.

Birren, Faber. *Light, Color, and Environment*. New York: Van Nostrand Reinhold, 1982.

Connoisseur magazine. *Encyclopedia of Antiques*. 3 volumes. New York: Hawthorne Books, 1954–57.

Cowan, Thomas. *Living Details*. New York: Whitney Library of Design, 1986.

Danby, Miles. *Grammar of Architectural Design*. London: Oxford University Press, 1963.

Editors of Better Homes and Gardens. *Good Decorating and Home Improvement*. 18 volumes. New York: Greystone Press (Meredith Corp.), 1970.

Entwisle, E. A. *A Literary History of Wallpaper*. London: Batsford Ltd., 1960.

Faulkner, Sarah, and Faulkner, Ray. *Inside Today's Home*. New York: Holt, Rinehart & Winston, 1975.

Getz, Lowell. *Business Management in the Smaller Design Firm*. Newton, MA: Practice Management Associates, 1986.

Gilliat, Mary. *Decorating*. New York: Pantheon Books, 1977.

Helsel, Margery. *The Interior Designer's Drapery Sketchfile*. New York: Whitney Library of Design, 1977.

Hill, Ann, ed. *A Visual Dictionary of Art*. New York: New York Graphic Society, 1974.

Hinckley, F. Lewis. *Historic Cabinet Woods*. New York: Crown, 1960.

Jackman, Dianne, and Dixon, Martin. *The Guide to Textiles for Interior Designers*. Winnipeg, Canada: Peguis Publishers, 1983.

Kleeman, Walter B., Jr. *The Challenge of Interior Design*. New York: Van Nostrand Reinhold, 1983.

Lang, Donna, and Robertson, Lucretia. *Decorating with Fabric*. New York: Clarkson N. Potter, 1986.

Murphy, Dennis Grant. *The Materials of Interior Design*. Burbank, CA: Stratford House, 1978.

Nassau, Kurt. *The Physics and Chemistry of Color*. New York: John Wiley & Sons, 1983.

Nuckolls, James L. *Interior Lighting*. New York: John Wiley & Sons, 1983.

Panero, Julius, and Zelnik, Martin. *Human Dimension and Interior Space*. New York: Whitney Library of Design, 1980.

Papanek, Victor. *Design for Human Scale*. New York: Van Nostrand Reinhold, 1983.

Pehnt, Wolfgang. *Encyclopedia of Modern Architecture*. New York: Harry N. Abrams, 1964.

Robinson, Jeremy, and Cymes, Sue, eds. *The House and Home Book of Interior Design*. New York: McGraw-Hill, 1979.

Scharff, Robert. *The Complete Book of Home Remodeling*. New York: McGraw-Hill, 1975.

Sutton, Ann. *Color and Weave Design*. Asheville, NC: Lark, 1984.

Szenasy, Susan S. *The Home*. New York: Macmillan, 1985.

Victoria and Albert Museum. *English Furniture Designs of the Eighteenth Century*. London: Victoria and Albert Museum, 1960.

Whiton, Sherrill. *Elements of Interior Design and Decoration*. New York: J.B. Lippincott, 1970.

Wilson, Forrest. *Graphic Guide to Interior Design*. New York: Van Nostrand Reinhold, 1977.